Friends and Relations

By the same author

THE NORTHREPPS GRANDCHILDREN
THE LAST OF THE ECCENTRICS
SPAM TOMORROW
OUR SQUARE
BEWARE OF THE CHILDREN
DAUGHTERS OF DIVINITY
THE FLO AFFAIR
SCRAMBLED EGG FOR CHRISTMAS

For children

VANLOAD TO VENICE
NINE TIMES NEVER
THE YORKS IN LONDON
CLOVER COVERDALE
CAMP FIRE COOK-BOOK
and ten books for Brownies

Friends and Relations

Three centuries of Quaker Families

Verily Anderson

Braiswick

ISBN 1-898030-83-9 Casebound
ISBN 1-898030-84-7 paperback

Previously published by Hodder and Stoughton
in 1980 ISBN 0 340 22214 X

British Cataloguing in Publication Data available

Printed by Lightning Source

Braiswick
111 High Road East
Felixstowe, Suffolk IP11 9PS

Contents

Illustrations

Between pages 160 and 161

Great Ellingham Hall, Norfolk
The House of John Gurney, Charing Cross, Norwich
'The Weaver's Friend'
Bartlett Gurney
Joseph Gurney
Hannah Middleton
Ury
The House in Cheapside, London
'Sam' Hoare (b. 1751)
'Sam' Hoare (b. 1807)
Lucy Barclay of Ury
Mary Anne Galton
'Johnny-for-short' Gurney
'Kitty' Bell
Earlham Hall
Rachel Barclay with two children
New Mills, Norwich
Hudson of Keswick
'Mag' Barclay
Hanbury and Buxton's brewery, Brick Lane, London

Maps

Family Trees

The family trees in the following pages refer only to those persons mentioned in the text.

Acknowledgements

Since this book records the early history of the Society of Friends, I must first thank God for the many friends (with both a small and a large F) who have given generously of their time to help in my researches.

In the spirit of George Fox, the Founder of the Society, I have omitted all honourable prefixes and academic distinctions but, by listing my benefactors in alphabetical order for convenience, have departed from his preference for 'placing them haphazard to avoid promoting vanity in those whose initials come early in the alphabet.'

As in the text of the book, family nick-names have been used where known. Since several of those whom I most want to thank, have contributed in more ways than one, I am leaving each benefactor to recognize his own cog or cogs in the alphabetically arranged auxiliary wheel which follows.

But of all whom I would mention, the late Dick Gurney stands alone. For it was he who, as sportsman, lay-Reader, banker and financial advisor to many charities, has most faithfully fulfilled and carried forward the virtues and qualities of those who have formed the substance of this book. It was a sad coincidence that, like our mutual great great grandfather, Joseph John Gurney who was also a banker, preacher and philanthropist, Dick should also have died after a fall from his horse in the same familiar Norfolk territory; and so I pay this posthumous tribute for all the help and encouragement he gave me in recording our family's share in a period of most significant social and religious reform, of which Dick was the ever faithful guardian.

9

Thank you also
Emma Anderson, Alex Allerhand, Nesta Barclay, David Bradby, Desmond Buxton, Rachel Buxton, Alan Carter, Philip Dowson, Pat Dykes, Doris Eddington, Ann Gurney, Betty Gurney, Caroline Gurney, Joe Gurney, John Gurney, Pauline Hardwick, Tony Hardwick, Elsie Herron, Jean Kennedy, Edward Milligan, Paul Paget, June Rose, Jane Thistlethwaite, Malcolm Thomas, David Waterfield.
And all other deserving thanks for
Advice, Bearing with answering my endless questions, Correcting my spelling, Directing me to bookshelves, Giving me access to their house, papers and pictures, Giving me permission to reproduce extracts and pictures, Preparing desks for me in libraries, Recording and indexing, Typing and everlastingly re-typing my illegible drafts.

My thanks, also, to the Castle Museum, Norfolk for their permission to use three paintings, *Edward and Priscilla Wakefield, with Mrs. Wakefield's sister Katherine Bell* by John Hamilton Mortimer (Katherine Bell shown only); *New Mills: Men Wading* by John Crome; and *Earlham Hall, South Front, Norwich* by Richenda Cunningham.

BUXTON FAMILY TREE

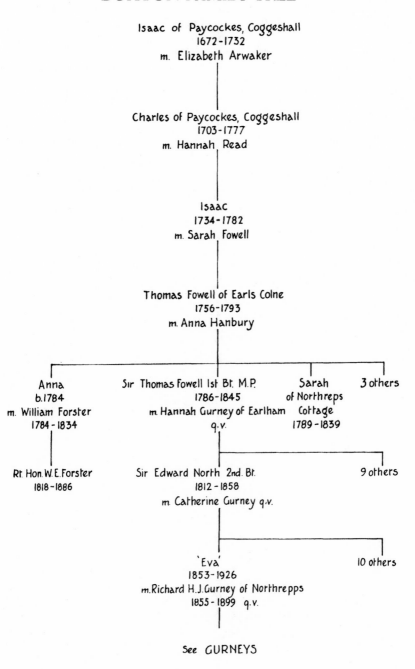

Isaac of Paycockes, Coggeshall
1672-1732
m. Elizabeth Arwaker

Charles of Paycockes, Coggeshall
1703-1777
m. Hannah Read

Isaac
1734-1782
m. Sarah Fowell

Thomas Fowell of Earls Colne
1756-1793
m. Anna Hanbury

Anna
b.1784
m. William Forster
1784-1834

Sir Thomas Fowell 1st Bt. M.P.
1786-1845
m. Hannah Gurney of Earlham
q.v.

Sarah
of Northreps
Cottage
1789-1839

3 others

Rt. Hon. W. E. Forster
1818-1886

Sir Edward North 2nd. Bt.
1812-1858
m. Catherine Gurney q.v.

9 others

'Eva'
1853-1926
m. Richard H. J. Gurney of Northrepps
1855-1899 q.v.

10 others

See GURNEYS

GURNEY FAMILY TREE

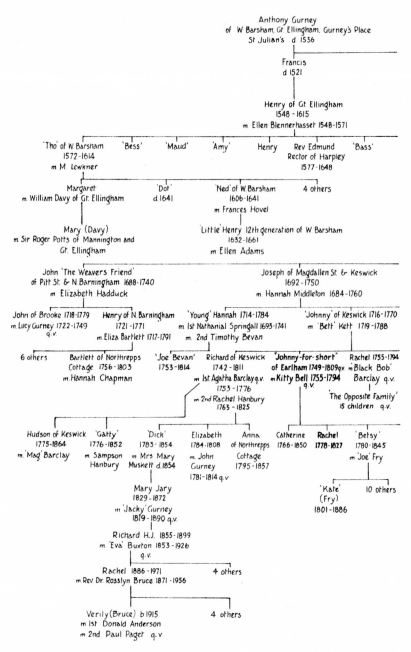

Anthony Gurney
of W. Barsham, Gt. Ellingham, Gurney's Place
St Julian's d 1556

Francis
d 1521

Henry of Gt. Ellingham
1548 - 1615
m Ellen Blennerhasset 1548-1571

'Tho' of W. Barsham   'Bess'   'Maud'   'Amy'   Henry   Rev Edmund   'Bass'
1572-1614   Rector of Harpley
m M. Lewkner   1577-1648

Margaret   'Dot'   'Ned' of W.Barsham   4 others
m William Davy of Gt. Ellingham d.1641   1606-1641
                                                  m Frances Hovel

Mary (Davy)   'Little' Henry 12th generation of W. Barsham
m Sir Roger Potts of Mannington and   1632-1661
Gt. Ellingham   m Ellen Adams

John 'The Weavers Friend'   Joseph of Magdallen St. & Keswick
of Pitt St. & N.Barningham 1688-1740   1692-1750
m Elizabeth Hadduck   m. Hannah Middleton 1684-1760

John of Brooke 1718-1779   Henry of N Barningham   'Young' Hannah 1714-1784   'Johnny' of Keswick 1716-1770
m.Lucy Gurney 1722-1749   1721-1771   m 1st Nathanial Springall 1693-1741   m 'Bett' Kett 1719-1788
q.v.   m.Eliza Bartlett 1717-1791   m. 2nd Timothy Bevan

6 others   Bartlett of Northrepps   'Joe' Bevan'   Richard of Keswick   'Johnny-for-short'   Rachel 1755-1794
           Cottage 1756-1803   1753-1814   1742-1811   of Earlham 1749-1809qv. m'Black Bob'
           m.Hannah Chapman   m 1st Agatha Barclayq.v. m Kitty Bell 1755-1794   Barclay q.v.
                                                    1753 - 1776   q.v.
                                                    m 2nd Rachel Hanbury   'The Opposite Family'
                                                    1763 - 1825   15 children q.v.

Hudson of Keswick   'Gatty'   'Dick'   Elizabeth   Anna   Catherine   Rachel   'Betsy'
1775-1864   1776-1852 1783- 1854   1784-1808   of Northrepps 1766-1850   1778-1827 1780-1845
m. 'Mag' Barclay   m. Sampson m Mrs Mary   m. John   Cottage   m 'Joe' Fry
                    Hanbury   Muskett d.1854 Gurney   1795-1857
                                             1781-1814 q.v

                               Mary Jary   'Kate'   10 others
                               1829-1872   (Fry)
                               m 'Jacky' Gurney   1801-1886
                               1819 - 1890 q.v.

                               Richard H.J. 1855-1899
                               m 'Eva' Buxton 1853-1926
                               q.v.

                               Rachel 1886 -1971   4 others
                               m Rev Dr. Rosslyn Bruce 1871 -1956

                               Verily (Bruce) b 1915   4 others
                               m 1st Donald Anderson
                               m 2nd Paul Paget q.v.

GURNEY FAMILY TREE

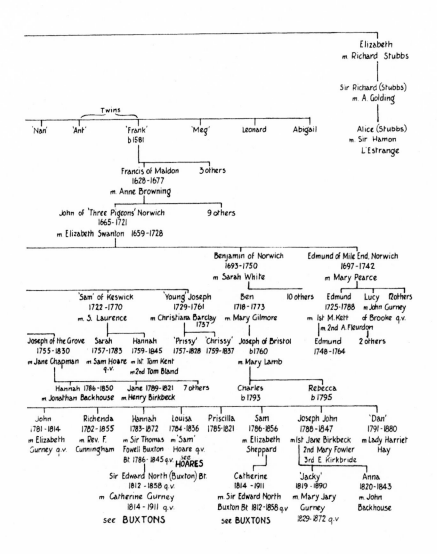

Elizabeth
m. Richard Stubbs

Sir Richard (Stubbs)
m. A. Golding

Twins

'Nan'   'Ant'   'Frank'   'Meg'   Leonard   Abigail

Alice (Stubbs)
m. Sir Hamon
L'Estrange

'Frank'
b.1581

Francis of Maldon   3 others
1628-1677
m. Anne Browning

John of 'Three Pigeons' Norwich   9 others
1665-1721
m. Elizabeth Swanton 1659-1728

Benjamin of Norwich   Edmund of Mile End, Norwich
1693-1750   1697-1742
m. Sarah White   m. Mary Pearce

'Sam' of Keswick   'Young' Joseph   Ben   10 others   Edmund   Lucy   12 others
1722-1770   1729-1761   1718-1773   1725-1788   m. John Gurney
m. S. Laurence   m. Christiana Barclay   m. Mary Gilmore   m. 1st M. Kett   of Brooke q.v.
1757   m. 2nd A. Fleurdon

Joseph of the Grove   Sarah   Hannah   'Prissy'   'Chrissy'   Joseph of Bristol   Edmund   2 others
1755-1830   1757-1783   1759-1845   1757-1828   1759-1837   b.1760   1748-1764
m. Jane Chapman   m. Sam Hoare   m. 1st. Tom Kent   m. Mary Lamb
q.v.   m.2nd Tom Bland

Hannah 1786-1850   Jane 1789-1821   7 others   Charles   Rebecca
m. Jonathan Backhouse   m. Henry Birkbeck   b 1793   b 1795

John   Richenda   Hannah   Louisa   Priscilla   Sam   Joseph John   'Dan'
1781-1814   1782-1855   1783-1872   1784-1836   1785-1821   1786-1856   1788-1847   1791-1880
m. Elizabeth   m. Rev. F.   m. Sir Thomas   m. 'Sam'   m. Elizabeth   m.1st Jane Birkbeck   m. Lady Harriet
Gurney q.v.   Cunningham   Fowell Buxton   Hoare q.v.   Sheppard   2nd Mary Fowler   Hay
Bt. 1786-1845 q.v.   see   3rd E. Kirkbride
HOARES

Sir Edward North (Buxton) Bt.   Catherine   'Jacky'   Anna
1812-1858 q.v.   1814-1911   1819-1890   1820-1843
m Catherine Gurney   m. Sir Edward North   m. Mary Jary   m. John
1814-1911 q.v.   Buxton Bt. 1812-1858 q.v   Gurney   Backhouse
see BUXTONS   see BUXTONS   1829-1872 q.v

13

BARCLAY FAMILY TREE

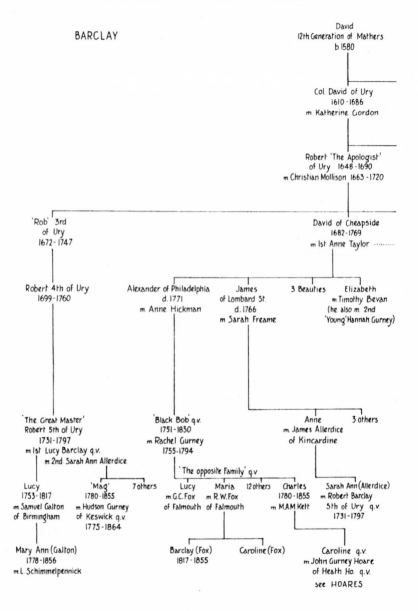

BARCLAY

David
12th Generation of Mathers
b.1580

Col. David of Ury
1610-1686
m. Katherine Gordon

Robert 'The Apologist'
of Ury 1648-1690
m. Christian Mollison 1663-1720

'Rob' 3rd
of Ury
1672-1747

David of Cheapside
1682-1769
m. 1st Anne Taylor ....

Robert 4th of Ury
1699-1760

Alexander of Philadelphia
d.1771
m. Anne Hickman

James
of Lombard St.
d.1766
m. Sarah Freame

3 Beauties

Elizabeth
m. Timothy Bevan
(he also m. 2nd
'Young' Hannah Gurney)

'The Great Master'
Robert 5th of Ury
1731-1797
m. 1st Lucy Barclay q.v.
m. 2nd Sarah Ann Allerdice

'Black Bob' q.v.
1751-1830
m. Rachel Gurney
1755-1794

Anne
m. James Allerdice
of Kincardine

3 others

Lucy
1753-1817
m. Samuel Galton
of Birmingham

'Mag'
1780-1855
m. Hudson Gurney
of Keswick q.v.
1775-1864

7 others

'The opposite Family' q.v.

Lucy
m. G.C. Fox
of Falmouth

Maria
m. R.W. Fox
of Falmouth

12 others

Charles
1780-1855
m. M.A.M. Kett

Sarah Ann (Allerdice)
m. Robert Barclay
5th of Ury q.v.
1731-1797

Mary Ann (Galton)
1778-1856
m. L. Schimmelpennick

Barclay (Fox)
1817-1855

Caroline (Fox)

Caroline q.v.
m. John Gurney Hoare
of Heath Ho. q.v.

see HOARES

14

BARCLAY FAMILY TREE

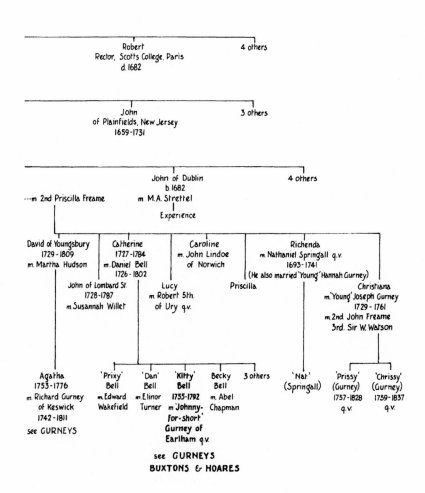

Robert
Rector, Scotts College, Paris
d. 1682

4 others

John
of Plainfields, New Jersey
1659-1731

3 others

John of Dublin
b. 1682
m. M.A. Strettel

4 others

····m 2nd Priscilla Freame

Experience

David of Youngsbury
1729 - 1809
m. Martha Hudson

Catherine
1727-1784
m. Daniel Bell
1726 - 1802

Caroline
m. John Lindoe
of Norwich

Richenda
m. Nathaniel Springall q.v.
1693-1741
(He also married 'Young' Hannah Gurney)

John of Lombard St.
1728-1787
m. Susannah Willet

Lucy
m. Robert 5th.
of Ury q.v.

Priscilla

Christiana
m. 'Young' Joseph Gurney
1729 - 1761
m. 2nd. John Freame
3rd. Sir W. Watson

Agatha
1753-1776
m. Richard Gurney
of Keswick
1742 - 1811
see GURNEYS

'Prixy'
Bell
m. Edward
Wakefield

'Dan'
Bell
m. Elinor
Turner

'Kitty'
Bell
1755-1792
m 'Johnny-
for-short'
Gurney of
Earlham q.v.

Becky
Bell
m. Abel
Chapman

3 others

'Nat'
(Springall)

'Prissy'
(Gurney)
1757-1828
q.v.

'Chrissy'
(Gurney)
1759-1837
q.v.

see GURNEYS
BUXTONS & HOARES

15

HOARE FAMILY TREE

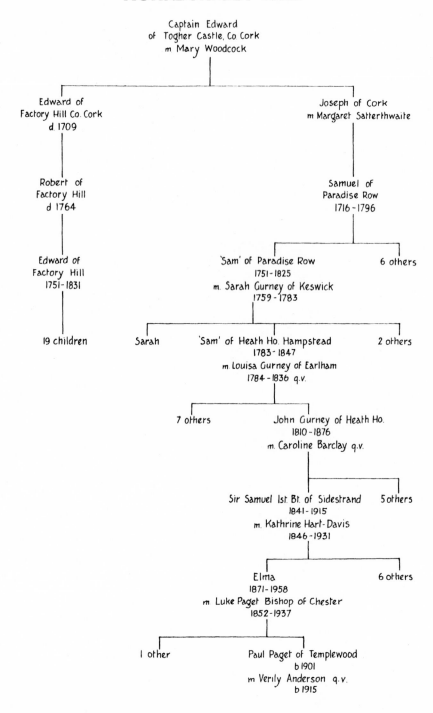

Captain Edward
of Togher Castle, Co Cork
m Mary Woodcock

Edward of
Factory Hill Co. Cork
d 1709

Joseph of Cork
m Margaret Satterthwaite

Robert of
Factory Hill
d 1764

Samuel of
Paradise Row
1716 - 1796

Edward of
Factory Hill
1751 - 1831

'Sam' of Paradise Row
1751 - 1825
m. Sarah Gurney of Keswick
1759 - 1783

6 others

19 children

Sarah

'Sam' of Heath Ho. Hampstead
1783 - 1847
m Louisa Gurney of Earlham
1784 - 1836 q.v.

2 others

7 others

John Gurney of Heath Ho.
1810 - 1876
m. Caroline Barclay q.v.

Sir Samuel 1st. Bt. of Sidestrand
1841 - 1915
m. Kathrine Hart-Davis
1846 - 1931

5 others

Elma
1871 - 1958
m. Luke Paget Bishop of Chester
1852 - 1937

6 others

1 other

Paul Paget of Templewood
b 1901
m Verily Anderson q.v.
b 1915

Foreword

Deciphering old letters and even holding them, turning the brittle, dehydrated pages of old journals, peering into faded iron-moulded engravings taken from paintings long ago disintegrated or destroyed – from these come the sensations that prompt new discoveries about their previous owners, as surely as when a bloodhound is given a missing person's glove. Variations throw themselves up to be investigated and confuted or confirmed as fact. Even in a family well documented with early memberships of the Society of Friends, supplying accurate registrations of births, marriages, deaths and removals from one place to another, it can take half a lifetime to untangle the intertwining of branches clearly enough to see the tree as a whole.

Much of this collation depends upon the work of previous enthusiasts who have sometimes recorded their findings in marble-backed exercise books and sometimes on the flyleaves of their Bibles; occasionally, in times of money-no-object, they have had them privately printed and bound in gold-embossed calf with gilt-edged pages. Then there are the contributions of the professional authors. Libraries, museums and public record offices, and particularly the Religious Society of Friends' library, must constantly be consulted for comparison with home findings.

Some people play card games for the excitement of finding matching pairs, despite the disappointment when again and again they fail to turn up. Some collect antiques on the same lines. Others collect dead ancestors. No attempt is made here to describe the whole conglomeration of closely intermarried cousins and uncles and aunts whose identities have been exhumed. But among the earlier members of the Society of Friends, 'mockingly called Quakers', were two men whose grandchildren were to be the first to unite in marriage the families of Gurney and Barclay, and whose great-grandchildren were to do so with even greater force. After that, the mass union of collaterals among the Gurneys, Barclays, Hanburys, Hoares and, later, Birkbecks and Buxtons, knew no bounds.

Their descendants rank today in tens of thousands, despite intermarriage, owing to the Quaker practice, that became a family habit, of marrying within the comparatively small sect. They were my ancestors and my husband's and quite probably yours.

The maximum number of great-great-grandparents per person is thirty-two. My mother had only fourteen. So frequent was the intermarriage of first and second cousins, and so determined must their genes have been, that she was descended from the same pair five times over (as am I). My husband is directly descended from this same pair through three other lines, leading to attic-loads of diaries inspired by the same Quaker tendency towards introspection.

Light falls then most clearly on this viviparous couple, John Gurney and Catherine Bell, who married in 1775 and eleven of whose children grew to memorable maturity, including Elizabeth (later Fry), the celebrated prison reformer. Both John and Catherine's great-grandfathers were themselves imprisoned for their faith, in the time of the founder of the Society, George Fox.

However, it is when the first signs of dissent are noticed in the Gurney family, a century before Quakerism was launched, that this account of it begins. John and Catherine Gurney of Earlham were fourth-generation Quakers, supporting the Society by regular attendance at its meeting-houses, and following many, but by no means all, of its tenets.

To Quakers, oaths and war were absolutely unlawful, and the use of weapons, even in self-defence, was contrary to Christian teaching. For the same reason it was insisted that women were entitled to equal rights with men in all matters, and that liberty of preaching should be common to all and not restricted to men specially ordained.

No actual rules were ever drawn up in the Society of Friends. There were merely points that evolved from the minutes of meetings, with recommendations for use in these individual meetings. Expulsion from the Society could be expected for offences committed against those tenets, particularly in respect of impurity, infidelity and dishonesty in business. Re-entry was exceedingly difficult. The body never accepted any creed or employed any liturgy; it rejected the sacraments and refused to acknowledge an ordained ministry. Teaching was that there was a direct revelation of the spirit of God to each individual, and that light comes to all, heathen or Christian.

By the fifth generation, many of this vastly intermingled family were beginning to abandon the long silences in Quaker meeting-houses in favour of Church of England services, but they continued to go to the great annual Quaker gatherings and to attend their noisy family tea-parties. They rejected the system of house-to-house visiting in order to 'caution' each other, but continued to turn up unexpectedly in each other's homes. They tolerated clergymen and lawyers, but continued to read the Bible aloud themselves at home and to conduct their own defences in court. They dismissed Fox's exhortation 'to keep out of the powers of the earth' and themselves became politicians. They modified their prejudices against the theatre, music and dancing, but continued their writing, preaching, teaching and tending the sick, eventually producing actors, composers, ballet dancers and television directors as well as the authors, archbishops and principals of academic and medical establishments that would have been more likely to emerge from their old style of plain living. They gave up their *thees* and *thous*, but stuck to their foreign languages and travel abroad (largely on behalf of their banking and brewing, which they never gave up). They let their enthusiasm for female preachers die down, but allowed them to keep their marital joint bank accounts. They cast off their black hats and drab suits of one colour, but continued to ignore changes of fashion. Above all they gave up their pacifism to become soldiers and sailors and airmen, but retained their fondness for the field sports that had once had to replace football, an activity regarded by Friends as being as much a form of combat as wrestling or fencing.

This then may show how the influence of George Fox continued to live on in a family whose genes must have been steeped in rebellious but loving tenacity and yet, like his own, been curiously lit with a vision of spiritual progress.

Chapter One

Henry
1548–1616

On Henry Gournay's cheerful creed hung the hopes of many of his successors. He was a compulsive rhymester and composed his own epitaph long before he needed it:

> So here doth rest the corpse of clay
> Of Henry Gournay squire,
> Until at joyful judgement day
> To soul he shall retire;
> And then through God's free special grace,
> By Christ shall both ascend,
> Unto the most delightsome place,
> And joys it never end,
> By Blennerhasset so his wife,
> He 13 children gat,
> Seven sons and daughters five in life,
> At once upon him sat.

In a tall, thick volume Henry made notes, copied out old muniments, deeds, rent-rolls and letters. He jotted down passing observations, kept accounts, worked out pedigrees, and expressed his thoughts more often than not in verse. His commonplace book[1] reveals that he was a magistrate, that he kept his property in good repair, that he loved his children, cared for his horses, and feared his fiercely Protestant wife's quick tongue.

[1] *The Commonplace Book or Register of Henry Gurnay* 1, Bodleian Library, Oxford, among the Tanner MSS, 175, catalogued as 'account of courts held and leases at Ellingham, Hingham and Irstede, in the county of Norfolk . . .'

The marvel of first holding this heavily-bound book in the Bodleian Library, where it had lain for 150 years, and recognising passages from a family transcription from it, can hardly be imagined. These were Henry's own unaltered notes in his often minute and so not very clear handwriting. Sometimes he wrote sideways down the margins of the pages. Here were his own lively asterisks and other decorative divisions between subjects, as well as merely inadvertent doodles. It was as though I were shaking Henry's very hand.

He was born on January 21st, 1548 at West Barsham Hall, then a moated manor house eight miles south of Wells-next-the-Sea, to which port it was still possible to convey 'hye or necessary fuell by the boate' along the River Stiffkey, now reduced to a trickle where once it flowed adequately through Walsingham. He was the last of his line to be born a Roman Catholic. His godmother was Lady Catherine Howard, a member of the most influential of the unswervingly Roman Catholic families in the kingdom, to this day. Her father, the Earl of Surrey, the poet, was cruelly executed, and so was her brother, the 4th Duke of Norfolk. The even more bloodthirsty retaliations pictured in *Foxe's Book of Martyrs*,[2] coincided with the natural but early death of Henry's own father, and the boy turned thankfully to the new moderate Protestantism prescribed by civil law.

Henry was ten years old when Queen Elizabeth I came to the throne. Already he had been lord of a handful of manors for nearly three years. Accounts show that his five sisters and a younger brother were educated out of the legacy left directly to him by his grandfather, on whose death he had been made a ward of court. The system was that the first bidder to apply to manage a dead man's inheritance while his heir was still a minor was entitled to 'buy' the wardship for a reasonable sum which he could considerably enhance while his control lasted. Henry's estate suffered the not unusual losses resulting from this system.

[2] *Foxe's Book of Martyrs* was first published in Latin and revised and published in English in 1563. For many years it was used practically as a companion-volume to the Bible in English churches and households.

There is no reference to his own education, though his grasp of mathematics suggests he must have had some instruction on the subject. He may have gone to Cambridge, but it is unlikely, for he admits that he was 'very meanly learn'd' and that 'in Latin verse I have no skill at all, nor any rules in English had I read.' However, he knew enough Latin to make his court reports in it, to copy out ancient court and rent rolls in it, and to translate Latin proverbs into homely English rhymes suitable for firing off at wayward children and family servants. Though not on a par with the great poets of his day – Spenser, Marlow, Sidney, de Vere or Shakespeare – he was able to express himself clearly in a rhythm almost Chaucerian in its simplicity. His subjects ranged from Euclid to 'the use of straw or broom, fir, flag, sedge, turf or brake in lieu of firewood', which latter alternatives to firewood are still being considered as novelties by today's conservationists. This was at a time when 92 out of 146 leading gentry of another remote county (Northumberland in the 1560s) were unable to sign their names.

As for libraries, only a dozen or so members of the upper classes are known to have owned more than 100 books in the sixteenth century. Bess of Hardwick had six, whereas Henry listed ownership of over seventy well-known books by distinguished authors, noting to whom he had lent volumes and whether he had 'receyued' them 'agayne'. Controversial divinity and history were his favourite subjects. Roger Ascham's *Schoolmaster* was among his books, and the Norwich physician, John Caius (or Key), after whom Caius College, Cambridge, was named, was one of his authors. Pamphleteers Green and Nash were other Norfolk writers of his choice. He acquired, when they were first published, two volumes of Holinshed's *Chronicle*, which he consulted so often that he later noted the necessity of having 'Hollingsett his Cron ij vol' rebound.

Henry took a sociable interest in the twenty-four families, besides his own, which were listed by his contemporary, Sir Henry Spelman, as having 'existed for many generations on the same property, as compared with the holders of monastic land'. Some of these lands had been given to the monasteries by earlier

Gournays, including gifts to Walsingham Priory, barely a league from Henry's birthplace, West Barsham.

He was as friendly with the new aristocracy as with the old, but he had no ambition to compete with either. Not for him soliciting at Court for position and monopolies that brought fame, fortune or disaster. He was content to rest on the laurels of a long line of fighting, scrambling, elevated and occasionally debased ancestors claiming descent from Hugh and his son Gerard, who brought the name of Gournay to England from the fortress they held and the abbey they founded in Le Brai at the town of Gournay, which name meant 'muddy place'. The 'de Gournays' settled in Norfolk at Yarmouth beside the same kind of marshy country as they had learnt to defend in Normandy. They built and maintained religious houses into which they sometimes entered as monks or retired in old age. There followed among others a run of crusaders, one of the regicides of Edward II, and an aunt of Ann Boleyn. Henry copied out an account of these and other more honourable courtiers and worthy persons of whom Sir Henry Spelman approved, together with the sources from which the account could be authenticated. Henry Gournay's intention was to reduce the number to one manageable box of documents concerning the manors of West Barsham, Great Ellingham, Attleborough, Irestead, Hingham, Hardingham and Harpley. He was of the eighth generation to own West Barsham and fourteenth to own Harpley. Henry refers to a bunch of letters that 'lie at the bottom of the eleventh box', all addressed to different generations. One, to his 'right-trusted and well-loved Tho. Gurnaye' is from the son of Edward IV, Richard, Duke of York, written not long before he was killed at the Battle of Wakefield in 1460. Another of the same decade – to 'my right well-beloved Will. Gurnay esquire, written at my castle of Hedingham the 16th day of December' – is from John de Vere, 13th Earl of Oxford. A letter to Henry's great-great-great-grandfather from Thomas, Earl of Surrey, who was slain at the Battle of Bosworth in 1485, suggests that some kind of banking may have begun in the Gurney family long before Gurney's Bank was officially opened at the end of the eighteenth century. A letter begins

'Right intyre beloved cosynne', and continues to butter him up
before mentioning the 'non-payment of such money as he owed
to Will. Gurnaye squire, longeing for it to be otherwise', and
asking for 'paciens' and ending 'your loving cosyn, Tho. Surrey'.
– the sort of letter about an overdraft which any customer would
write to his bank manager if he were his cousin.

Henry himself, in one of his longer poems, shows a marked
interest in economy, with an exceptional understanding of the
exchange of gold. He observes that the price of everything 'be
three or four times to that it was', but that everything *appeared* to
be much cheaper, owing to the excesses in this increasingly
wealthy country of

> . . . jewels, chains and plate
> Wherein we do fivefold at least
> Our ancestors exceed
> Which should not be if that the realm
> Of money stood at need.

Figures fascinated him. A coded poem hides the name of fourteen
Norfolk gentlemen with £1,000 a year to spend. A few reappear
in Spelman's list.

Henry was a tremendous Norfolk enthusiast, claiming in verse
that, of all English shires, Norfolk yielded the most pleasure and
produce – in fact, except for salt, it was not only self-supporting
but also had much to spare. Since half of the Norfolk circumference was seaboard, the county had fish in plenty, with
mariners and ships to be sent to sea for merchandise. About every
forty years the north-west was drowned by the rage of the sea
which, Henry points out, was no worse than the swift floods in
the hilly shires, which swept away their bridges. Thanks to
Norfolk's flat arable land with its pastures, meadows and woods,
heath and fens, lakes and meres (well stocked with birds and
beasts), labour was less strenuous than in most places. On the
low ground, hay and a great quantity of cheap good fuel were
carried, not by horse and cart, but by boat.

Most of Henry's recorded income was derived not from rents,
for tenants chiefly paid these in days of labour, but as with other

Norfolk landowners, from wool. For centuries Norfolk had been virtually one great sheep-run. Sheep grazed in the meadows and commons, on the cliffs and heaths, and the sound of their bleating mingled with the songs of larks. Sheep being moved from one grazing to another were the chief users of the roads and lanes. For generations East Anglia had not only been sustained by, but at times made immensely rich by the wool from their backs. The long, coarse wool, strands of which can be seen in the pattern of the cloth woven at Worstead, came from west Norfolk, where Henry's main properties lay. 'Oats, hemp, fat ox and cows also flowered in the west,' Henry writes. 'Barley, peas and wheat flowered in the east.' The short wool used for felting came from the south-east, where Henry also grazed sheep, and thus he would be able to supply both markets with the wool that made Norwich the third most important city in the country. After a depression in Tudor times, trade was revived by the fresh wave of immigrants from the Low Countries fleeing from Spanish persecution. They brought new ideas and skills which were far more important than new machines. They knew how to make delicate light-weight materials that, for the next two centuries, sold all over the world as the 'New Drapery'.

Henry was already 'well versed in his prospects' when he was free to manage his own estates. When he came of age in 1569 and took over his Leet Court at Great Ellingham Hall, the first thing he did was to build a new pound in the village, as the possession of stray animals was a manorial right of some importance. The strays had to be proclaimed in church and in the two nearest market-places and, if they had not been claimed in a year and a day, they became Henry's. Every Lord of the Manor, however petty, had his own little parliament in his Leet Court, in which his steward presided and a jury of tenants presented grievances and anything that had to be recorded. Great Ellingham was not particularly petty, but it was in an extreme state of dilapidation. Henry's grandfather, Anthony Gournay, had come by Ellingham Magna through his first wife, a co-heiress of the ancient Mortimer family, who were notoriously neglectful landlords. Through his second wife he had come by the much better cared-for Bury Hall only a quarter of a mile away, from whose relative comfort he could supervise the rebuilding of Great Ellingham Hall. Old Anthony had found that the house had not been maintained 'by the space of about one hundred and twenty yeres and was overgrowne with bushes and trees'; which dated its last maintenance back into the early 1400s. 'The Great Hall was being used as a kitchen and larder' (a not unusual arrangement in medieval farmhouses), with hams and herbs hanging from the rafters and cooking done on an open fire. The rest of the house had been invaded by the farm beasts, with cows splashing through the moat to be milked in what was supposed to be the solar. Henry's grandfather had started clearing and rebuilding, chiefly using old timber from nearby Scoulton Hall, which he had pulled down to prevent an avaricious co-heir from forcing him into accepting an 'unadvised price' for it. He used most of the best timber from Scoulton for spars for the hall, and gave or sold the rest to repair the chancel of the church at Hingham, his most important manor.

Within four years of beginning the work old Anthony's wife had died and Bury Hall was withdrawn by her family. Soon afterwards, Anthony died himself.

When young Henry returned to the restoration twelve years later, he began by cutting down timber in the 'hawe' or home enclosure 'for to build across the moat a massive barn' whose arched roof-timbers spread out like the trees from which they had so recently been made. Henry was concerned to conserve all possible timber for building. Even short willow and hazel rods were valuable, to be daubed with mud or clay, to form panels between intermediate timbers. The timber skeleton of the barn was framed up on the ground and 'reared', with appropriate celebrations, in a semi-prefabricated state. The barn was later to serve as the banqueting hall for many wedding breakfasts, deliberately planned for the season when the stored crops had been exhausted and the barn cleared to receive the new harvest.

As the barn went up, Henry surrounded it with smaller buildings on the farm side of the moat. He built a new mill house and homes for the all-important shepherds. He cut down two more trees in the 'hawe' to make a new bridge across the moat. He records finding 'the little house on the other side of the moate then used for the chifist gest chamber wherein Sr. Christ. Heidon and his lady did often lye'. This Heydon was the son of Anthony Gournay's first cousin, Sir Christopher Heydon 'the great housekeeper', who built Baconsthorpe, and his wife Temperance. They were still a couple famous enough in Norfolk to inspire wonder in young Henry. Although the palace of Baconsthorpe, near Sheringham, was abandoned before it was finished, Sir Christopher's hospitality was such as to make his earlier days as a guest of Henry's grandfather worth recording. Henry now turned this 'gest chamber' into a stable.

For the house itself, he used more mature timber, brought from nearby Hingham Gournay's, another of his properties. Henry's grandfather, Anthony Gournay, had been a flamboyant man, and had planned and begun rebuilding accordingly. Henry was always by nature more modest, and according to his records of changes made and materials used, rearranged the rooms in a comfortable but less ostentatious manner.

On Trinity Sunday 1571, Henry Gournay married Ellen Blennerhasset. They were both twenty-three. The Blennerhassets were a forceful and unusual family of Irish extraction with strong puritanical leanings. 'Blaundrehasset were a name to start a hare,' neighbour Paston had written a century before, and certainly the simple Norfolk rustics were startled by their long black puritan cloaks and unchurchman-like ways, which they could only associate with the devil. 'Old Hasset', they said, could frequently be seen soaring over the rooftops in his coach driven by a headless coachman and drawn by four headless horses. This was a great favourite local ghost story, and was applied also to Anne Boleyn and her father, each in a separate flying coach. Soon the Blennerhassets left the country for Norwich, where they took over from a Calthorpe cousin of Henry's the lease of a Norwich house on one side of the river, together with a ruined tower, once the town dungeon, which they used as an overflow for surplus guests. Here the stories began again, of dead bodies rolling about the floor, and mysterious sealed doors. The unghostly-looking house, in a walled and wooded garden, with a courtyard in front and a flight of stone steps up to the door, can be seen in Taylor's picture map of early Norwich. With Cow Tower still standing today as a guide, it is possible to find a few remaining courses of napped flint in the high old wall that had once been the garden wall of Hasset House, at the corner of what are now Barrack Street and Gurney Road.

Great Ellingham Hall was still unfinished, and West Barsham was let to Henry's brother-in-law, Thomas Golding. Henry's other houses were also let to relations, and so the bridal couple began their married life with the Blennerhassets in Norwich, where their first son was born. A page in Henry's commonplace book opens with '1572. Inprim Tho. their first sonne was borne on Saterdaye at afternone betwene foure and fyve of ye clock.' On other pages Henry records the restoration work began on Great Ellingham Manor, which he was determined to make into his own family home.

Great Ellingham lies just off the main London to Norwich road, two miles north-west of Attleborough. When 'Tho.' was two and his baby sister, Bess, a year old, Henry and Ellen moved into Great Ellingham Hall, where Henry continued to change his grandfather's rooms round to fit in with his expanding family. He notes how he 'translated' the kitchen with its oven into the parlour, 'making a bay window instead of the other', and supporting its lofty ceiling by a central wooden pillar. He built a new kitchen with a 'sink house', he modernised the larder and the 'entrie dierie', but left its little Tudor door untouched. This led out into a yard, enclosed by the brew-house (which he now tiled), the malting-house and a new wash-house. He made the 'lead pompe' out of the ground 'well and all' to serve the wash-house and kitchen. In his grandfather's great entrance hall, with its huge fireplace and grate, he fashioned a staircase whose broad treads, flanked by stout bannisters, led in easy flights up to the bed-chambers and then on, just as ornately, to the rooms he made in the attic storey for his growing family.

This attractive E-shaped Elizabethan house was sketched in 1856, when it was described as having 'a large entrance hall and a huge fireplace and grate with the original oak staircase leading to many dark rooms in the attic storey now blocked up. Outside the moat, the barn, of fine oak timber was thatched and still in perfect preservation.' In 1979 I had the unforgettably exciting experience of recognising Great Ellingham Hall from this sketch, and crossing the bridge over the moat in a dazzlingly dramatic thunderstorm. 'Outside the moat', the framework of the barn, first reared in the year of Henry's coming of age, remained complete, though the thatched roof and much of the original wattle and daub has been replaced. The house itself must be much as it was in Henry's day. It was certainly awe-inspiring to follow his footsteps up his oak staircase, using his original grip handrail supported by its carved posts, and on up into the now-disused attics. The present owner, Mr. Hardwick, acceded to my request to see the cellars. The freak thunderstorm had caused the moat to overflow into the undercroft with over a foot of water. It was only a faint glimmer from a torch that saved us from splashing on through it into Henry's great well, the rim of whose cobble and brick walls we could dimly discern below the flood-water. In Henry's day his large household would have drawn too heavily on both wells to permit either to overflow.

He filled in the details of the births of all his thirteen children as they arrived, almost annually, with the names of their godparents, their astrological signs, and the phases of the moon. When the record was complete, he sums up the family:

> Thomas, Henry, Edmund and Bassingborne
> Antony, ffraunces and Leonard for name
> Have those said sons and were in order borne
> As here before you see I set the same
> Like order now for daughter do I frame,
> Bess, Maude, Amy, Nan, Meg and Abegaile,
> Maud at seventeen and Meg at yeares age did quaile.

Poor little Meg more failed than quailed, for her father writes later in prose 'When the moon was 7 days owled and Meg was about 5 quarters of a year owlde she dyed after a fortnight's sickness, being at her death very fatt and a very fayre corse more amiable and beautiful then than while she lived.' Henry felt deeply about baby Meg, and long afterwards was remembering how he buried her beside his favourite brother ('he in good and seasoned oak of inch-thick') in Great Ellingham church, with her fat little feet within two yards of 'a chapel or pew'.

If Thomas was the hope of the family, Edmund was the brain. Bassingborne was called after his godfather, Bassingborne Gawdy, who had bought his grandfather's town house by the river in Norwich. Anthony and Francis were twins, 'ffraunces was born within less than a quartr of an houre of his brother, mine aunt Stubb, gossip.' This 'gossip', or godparent, was Elizabeth, born a West Barsham Gournay and married to Sir Richard Stubbs. The children's godparents were mostly relations, many of them with children of their own with whom the Henry Gournays played, did lessons, learnt to dance, and rode and hunted.

There was no shortage of ponies, thanks to the law whereby stray animals could be claimed by the lord of the manor after they had been proclaimed in church and two market towns a year and a day after being found. Henry writes that 'of the strays taken at Great Ellingham, none of them or very few were taken in court through my folly in not remembering them.' Most of them were taken by the inhabitants, according to his yearly books. However, a grey ambling nag strayed from the stallion to which it had been taken, and stayed for about a dozen years before Henry officially claimed her. Also 'a black nag, pretty well shaped and buttocky, but very slow and dull, also stayed for about a dozen years. A grey gelding killed himself with shackle striving to leap a dyke.' Another grey mare he kept for seven years and eventually sold to his brother, who let it be stolen. There was another grey gelding 'which hath a kind of horn growing out of his hoof', and 'a dark grey, which I now enjoy, called the child horse.' Henry pulled down the ancient 'kiln house or furnis house' to make a 'beast house' and he built a cart house, swill-house and, 'at the end of the garden' a 'famous dove house' in and out of whose pigeon-holes flew sixty-three dozen plump birds.

While the children were young, wool prices high, Ellen busy and Henry able to attend his courts properly, he was a happy and contented man. But as his large and rumbustious family became more expensive to rear, while wool prices dropped and Ellen opened up fresh tirades of criticism over his extravagance every time he paid a bill, Henry turned more and more to his commonplace book for comfort, referring to himself as a man

> Who twenty marks was never known to waste,
> On cards or dice or dogs or hawks or whore
> Or any way with modest measure past,
> Yet by his wife in teeth is daily cast
> With wastefulness although to prove the same
> She never could (nor any) reason prove
> By all his life not twenty pounds he spent
> Whereof he did, or justly might, repent.

No man, he reassures himself on another occasion, could vouch and prove that he had wasted so much as a tenth of a year's revenue on apparel or retinue. And certainly there is no record of his having joined the rush to buy white velvet (or black 'for the graver sort') that the young gentlemen of the county were required to wear when Queen Elizabeth made her somewhat unexpected royal progress to East Anglia, in 1578. But however much Ellen may have objected on puritanical grounds, Henry would hardly have dared to opt out of attending the Queen. His loyalty was absolute. He adored the Queen, and composed a kind of private national anthem for her:

> For church our prince and peace
> This prayer never cease.
> Lord long preserve and grant our noble Queen
> True wisdom, faith, fear, love and earnest zeal.
> All heresies and secret foes – and seen –
> To quail as oft as light shall them reveal,
> Unto their own most glorious praise and name
> Thy churches good our prince and country's fame.

32

Ellen no doubt had something to say about the feasting that
went on during the royal progress. One menu alone included
meat, chickens, pigeons, quails, dotterels, peeweets and gulls, to
say nothing of horse-loads of oysters and four hundred and
twenty pounds of butter. Ellen held the purse strings and, as
Henry ruefully observed:

> When as he doth for any money ask
> For needful use as either debts to pay
> Our subsidy, town charges, or the tasks
> Which may not bid denial or delay
> Although she doth not flatly them deny
> Yet pays them not without some cross reply.

On the top of this, Henry found that he was going really deaf.
This may have been a convenience at home, but it made his
attendance at Court almost useless. He wrote a note explaining
his absence:

> By wanting wealth sufficiently
> For children to provide,
> And hearing matters in my power
> Well to adjudge and guide,
> My God of grace and world of right
> I hope will me excuse
> Though almost or yet equitie
> But slenderly I use.

He mentions a remedy for deafness tried by the miller of Great
Ellingham who had been deaf for three months through 'an
noyse in his head which letted him to hear his mill clapper being
in the mill'. In the month of May before the sun rose the miller
took the dew from the grass by skimming it with his hand and
pouring it into his ear, working it in with his little finger. This he
did for a month. Then, 'in a sudden rush or flash, the wind
breezed out of his head and he was cured'. Henry writes, 'Myself
never tried this because my deafness is not by a wynde.'

33

Another remedy was sent to him by Lord North, 'who was taken stone deaf so as he could not hear by no means any speech' but was healed by obeying these instructions: 'Bake a little loaf of bean flour and while hot rive it into halves and into each half pour into three or four spoonsful of bitter almonds – then clap both the halves to both the ears on going to bed and keep them close and keep your head warm.'

Perhaps Henry was healed, too, for his spirits took a turn for the better when the Norfolk coast was fortified against the Spanish Armada, whose defeat he describes with great verve soon after the event. The same year he sold 'Hingham Gournay's manor', the most ancient of his possessions, with all its cottages, farm buildings, charters, patents, court rolls and deeds. This must have solved the financial problems, as well as quietening Ellen's 'awle-like' tongue for a while.

Their eldest son, 'Tho's', marriage, when he was twenty-four, to Ann, the beautiful daughter of Sir Edward Lewkner, delighted Henry. He immediately set about restoring his birthplace for them. The last tenant of West Barsham hall had been his brother-in-law, who had now died, and Henry's sister had remarried and gone to Essex. Some of Great Ellingham's plans may have been used for the rebuilding of West Barsham, and even, perhaps, some of the same craftsmen, for old sketches show that the houses were not dissimilar. One wing of West Barsham Old Hall is still inhabited, standing upright and alone in a meadow, part of which had once been, as at Great Ellingham, a well-tended moat. It was as if Henry were living his own childhood all over again, without the irks of a dying father and an untrustworthy sovereign. He still had relations living within a couple of hours' ride from West Barsham, where he and Ellen and the younger children now frequently stayed. His aunt was still living in his manor of Harpley, with, only a mile away, the Walpoles,[3] who had owned Houghton manor for as long as the Gournays had

[3] John Walpole of Houghton was heir to his first cousin, Amy Robsart. She married Robert Dudley, later Earl of Leicester, who, it was believed by many at the time, was Queen Elizabeth's lover and likely choice as a husband. Amy died mysteriously from falling downstairs.

owned Harpley. Further on, at Sandringham, towards the Wash were the Cobbs who had also been there for generations, and on the coast itself at Hunstanton were Henry's dearest cousins, the L'Estranges, who lived in another charming moated ancestral home, which remained the seat of the L'Estrange family from the Norman Conquest until after World War II. Hunstanton Hall still lies in a tranquil park below the rising ground that shelters it from the North Sea gales. The family were devoted churchmen, and highly cultured, with a great love of music and a feeling for words. Alice L'Estrange, wife of the Sir Hammon of the day, was a granddaughter of a West Barsham Gournay, – in fact, the daughter of Henry's 'mine aunt Stubbs' gossip'.

Henry writes, the year after Tho.'s marriage, that his son 'Ant.' was 'hyer than his brother ffraunces at their age just of 16 by just four inches and lower than his brother Bass by three quarters of an inch; his voice was changed at Christmas before, but frankes voice is not yet changed.'

Frank was constantly with the L'Estranges at Hunstanton, as indeed were Tho.'s children when they arrived.

In the account books so patiently and methodically kept by his cousin Alice in her clear delicate hand, Frank is seen to be paying out for sweetmeats when her children were small, buying gunpowder, shot and other shooting requisites, and later bringing back a pair of silk stockings, costing two shillings, from London.

Frank's business sense incited his father to send him to London to make useful contacts; so, while his twin brother, Ant, was striding gruffly off into the bracing East Anglian countryside to learn farming, the smaller, later-developing Frank struggled as an apprentice, first to Mr. Tryme and then to Mr. Smooth. Bass was also a London apprentice, and bright, eccentric Edmund, after getting a good degree at Queen's College, Cambridge, soon became a Fellow of Corpus Christi.

Although Henry was liable to break out into heroic couplets against Roman Catholicism, he was not over-enthusiastic about excessive puritanism, as it was to be seen in the Blennerhasset family. At about this time he added a clause to his will that £400 should be disposed amongst his younger sons 'provided none of them held any fantastical or erroneous opinion so adjudged by the bishop or civil law'.

Edmund, at Cambridge, was already showing signs of puritanical leanings, but he was not included in this part of his father's will, for most of the latter's library was earmarked for him. The Master of Corpus Christi was Dr. Jegon, who was later to become Bishop of Norwich. Dr. Jegon's discipline at college was so severe that, with the fines he inflicted on the undergraduates, he repaired the college hall, on the screen of which was found written:

> Dr. John Jegon of Bennett college master
> Broke the scholars' heads and gave the hall a plaster.

To which the Master, seeing it, added:

> Knew I but the wag who wrote this in his bravery
> I commend him for his wit but whip him for his knavery.

It was suggested that Edmund was this wag.

Then there was the case of the Fellows' garden. The Master was keen to get the Fellows' garden to himself, and either by threats or persuasion he got all to resign their keys except Mr. Gournay, who absolutely refused to part with his rights. '"I have got the other fellows' keys," quoth the master. 'Then pray, master,' was Edmund's gleeful suggestion, 'keep them and you and I will keep them all out.'

Thomas Fuller referred to Edmund in his *Worthies of England*, a collection of biographical sketches published in 1662. 'He was an excellent scholar who could be humorous and would be serious, as he was himself disposed. His humours were never profane towards God or injurious towards his neighbours.' Edmund called on Fuller at Queen's College, Cambridge, and asked what he was studying. Fuller explained that he was collecting the witnesses of the truth of the Protestant religion through all ages. 'It is a needless pain,' Fuller reported Edmund as saying, 'for I know that I am descended from Adam though I cannot prove it.'

For one reason or another Edmund's fellowship was made void, the excuse being that he was not ordained, whereupon Edmund took holy orders, wrote the first of several learned theological books, and was reinstated as a Fellow.

His sister Anne's marrying Thomas Osborne, another Fellow of Corpus Christi, must have set Edmund off, for, after twenty years at Cambridge, he too, married, and accepted a living in Norfolk presented by his Stubbs cousin. He said he wanted to be nearer to his father. Whatever their religious disagreements, their affection for each other never wavered. As they raised their glasses to each other, Henry would chant

> To cheer thy stomach or thy sprite,
> Drink wine without a blame
> But in excess, or for delight,
> Breed sin, disease and shame

Henry loved to sit talking in the lofty parlour at Great Elling-ham or in the smaller panelled parlour at West Barsham with a son or son-in-law or fellow landowner, and would later turn his observations into poetry. In a lilting ballad, he summed up their talk with the conclusion that the great poverty and unemploy-ment in Norfolk at the turn of the sixteenth and seventeenth centuries was due, not to lack of 'all that served for belly, back or health' nor 'pleasure, ease or strength for to repel', but more from Norfolk's distance from 'rich London' where commodities 'sell deare' and are 'bt cheape', and still more from the fact that a third of Norfolk was common ground. This was supposed to 'herd both riche and poor', but in many cases the poor, unable to afford carts, hay waynes, waggons and horses, and even ploughs or spades, made a pathetic job of trying to produce their family's needs, sometimes with nothing more than their hands. Mean-while the new-rich from the cities seized on the summer hay and stocked it up for the winter, while the poor went hungry and 'with idleness did itch'. Laws intended to help the poor were merely helping the lawyers; more law-suits arose in Norfolk than anywhere else, not only between landlords and tenants but also between commoners themselves.

It was in Henry's early infancy that Robert Kett, who was eventually to become a co-ancestor, had been hanged as a result of the rising sparked off by Kett siding with the poor over the enclosure of common land. In fact, he had lawfully put up a few fences himself, with the approval of the villagers. It was not the locals who pulled his fences down, but the usual collection of thugs who joined in any trouble, encouraged, this time, by a tiresome neighbour. The result was that all enclosure was forbidden. Now, over fifty years later, Henry felt it had been a mistake to remove all of these newly-made fences. He advocated that land should be divided according to each parish's rating, so that established and trustworthy landlords, who could afford agricultural implements and knew how to make the best of them, could give employment to the struggling poor. Henry's hopes were gradually realised, the rights of commoners being limited to certain houses in each parish, and newcomers not being allowed to interfere.

Land, according to Henry's statements of his rents, seem to have increased little in value during the long and prosperous reign of Elizabeth. Even the rents of the pastures of the park had only reached that of meadows two hundred years before – about one shilling an acre. When he inherited from his grandfather his rents were about £100 a year. Very little money was then actually in circulation. But now, in the reign of James I

> Scarce two of ten of gentry by descent
> In fourth degree do hold their father's state
> I mean in lands of touching true extent
> Though in their rents they have a greater rate
> By racking them to three or four fold
> Though nothing gained as other things.

If Henry had inherited the commercial talents in which he had seemed to show such promise, something, perhaps Ellen's fierce puritanism, had prevented his using them. Of the estates he had

38

inherited from his grandfather, now only two were left – Great Ellingham and West Barsham. However, he had given all his children a good start in life and now, although he was certainly not impoverished, he had failed to multiply his fortune as might have been expected of him:

> A man who riches hast
> While they in life do last
> In giving do incline
> While they and choice is thine,

he observed by way of an excuse for the generosity he showed to all his family.

His grandchildren were as great a pleasure to him as his own children had been. At West Barsham there were six little girls and two grandsons. Frivolity ran high when they were with their L'Estrange cousins, Nicholas, Hammo, Roger and Ann, with whom they were close, affectionate and always lively. Nicholas was making a collection of anecdotes and jokes, and pressed everyone he knew to repeat any stories he heard, however long-winded or improper. With this encouragement the naturally garrulous Gournays burst themselves to help him to fill the MS. pages of his *Merry Passages and Jests*.[4] The darling of her generation was Tho's little daughter, Dorothy, referred to lovingly as 'my dear Coz Dot' and 'my dear co Do. Gu.' and again as 'doll gur'.

A long tale of Dot's is preserved in Nicholas' MS. about the Bishop of Norwich riding into the country to visit his godson and finding him cooped up under the kitchen table. The godfather tempted him to come out with fair words and promises of plums and such good things. 'I won't, good man Snotgall', said the boy, and the prelate could only beg his gossip to be of good comfort, 'for truly,' he said 'I can say nothing of my godson but that he may live long.'

If Henry had been skimming the dew at sunrise and pouring it

---

[4] *Merry Passages and Jests* by Nicholas L'Estrange. British Museum, Harleian 6395.

into his ear again he might have heard enough to cause him to admonish Dot with one of his own proverbs:

> As modest mirth contents thy guests no less than dainty cheer,
> So lavish words and too broad jests they scorn and cannot bear.

Dot's sense of fun was later recorded as illustrating the 'manners prevalent at this period' to the extent that 'some of the merry jests of this lady were of a description that could not be repeated.'

When his wife, Ellen, died, Henry gave up writing in his register. Perhaps there was now no need to seek refuge in it. There is not even a date given for her death. Such additions or alterations as Henry made to his will do not reappear in his book, as they had before. There are no new rhymes, but no doubt he continued to quote the old ones as they were needed. Young Ned, who was given to snobbish boasting, must have heard more than once:

> Much better is nobility by proper virtue won
> Than that which only do descend from father to ye sonne.

The decorative headings in Henry's book reveal a strong sense of design. 'A table for the journal matters' was the title of the index which he drew up, and added to towards the end of his life. As he grew older and less active, and perhaps even lonely for want of Ellen's scolding, he no doubt could have been heard quoting another of his tags as he sketched or painted by the bay window that he had long ago designed:

> The skill in arts or handicrafts will ever help and laste
> When wealth, friends or offices by divers means do waste.

Henry Gournay was sixty-seven when he died on 23rd February, 1615. In his will he asked to be buried beside his wife and daughters. To Amy and Abegail, he left £200 each on their marriages (or two years after his death if they were still unmarried) and £20 a year meanwhile. Most of his children had already received their portions. Edmund inherited his Latin books, while his younger brothers presumably managed to keep any fantastical or erroneous leanings to themselves, and so received the promised bonus. Henry's servants and the poor were not forgotten, and finally Thomas inherited the Great Ellingham and West Barsham estates, Henry's silver ewer and basin, his gold chain and all his wordly goods. But alas, before Henry's will had been proved, Thomas hurriedly made his own will, and died, a year and a day after his father. Once again a small boy became head of the family.

Slipped into the last page of Henry's commonplace book, on a small piece of vellum its new owner signs his name three times: 'Edward Gurnay, Edward Gurney, Edward Gourney his book'.

Edward, always to be known as Ned, was ten years old when the book and everything else became his. Spelling was still completely inconsistent, particularly of names, but the head of the family may have been trying out variations with the intention of stabilising one of the spellings. Edward's 'Gurney'[5] will be used now in this book, though the family were not always consistent.

[5] The spelling of Gurney was stabilised about 1700 by John of Norwich. This spelling was about the only one not chosen previously by the family.

Chapter Two

Edmund and Ned
1617–1648

'I like a Holy-rowly-powliness,' said Parson Edmund Gurney concerning equality of behaviour in church, 'for there sure, if anywhere, we ought to be haile fellows well mett.' His young nephew, Ned, of West Barsham, explained that his uncle was 'inveighing against the common fault of the menial sort of people, who are too prone to perform civil and outward respects upon the coming of greater persons into the church, by rising, bowing etc. even in the midst of their devotions and of divine worship.' Ned told the story playfully, for he was of a playful disposition, despite his attention to his books, with an emphasis on the sciences. He and his brother and sisters, particularly Dot, were all devoted to their uncle, who tried to replace their father as best he could. In 1611, he had moved over to the other side of West Barsham after his brother Thomas's death, to become rector of Harpley. Here his aunt lived at the manor which his grandfather had left directly to her. Harpley was under an hour's ride from West Barsham (at Ned's impetuous pace – longer at Edmund's) and a mile from the Walpoles at Houghton. Houghton Hall is now the most magnificent of all the Norfolk stately homes that later replaced the more modest manors of Edmund's time. Harpley church still rises above its little village, as truly a beautiful guardian and place of worship as ever it was. It had been rebuilt by Edmund's ancestor John 'de Gournay', who was patron and rector between 1294 and 1332, as were subsequent Gurneys. Its carved angels in the roof beams, the hand-smoothed animal carvings on the pew-ends, and the sumptuous sedilia certainly date back to Edmund's day and probably much earlier. He would have had to stoop to pass through the low, elaborately-cusped priest's doorway, as had the ancestral priests before him.

The living itself was worth £22 a year. Thanks to a legacy of land, Edmund was able to build his own rectory, into which went his Latin library and the beginnings of a family of his own. Unfortunately, his wife's personality and even her name are left unrecorded.

At Cambridge Edmund had never toed the line, nor did he now. He continued to tease Bishop Jegon, who had previously been the Master of his college, and to taunt the bishops who followed him after Charles I came to the throne.

The first of Archbishop's Laud's supporters to be sent to Norwich 'to impose order and uniformity in the diocese' was Richard Corbet. Despite their obvious disagreements, he and Parson Gurney could understand each other, for Corbet was a man with much the same easy humour as Edmund's. As a young man he, too, had been fond of poetry, good wine and practical jokes, and as bishop, though always courteous and careful not to offend, he did not entirely abandon these qualities. He ridiculed Puritans, but without malice, and countered Edmund's jokes with cheerful but never hurtful mockery. Edmund was reported for refusing to wear a surplice in church. He appeared before the bishop, who quoted back at him from Edmund's own parody of the cries of 'the Destructive Puritan':

> Boldly I preach, hate a cross, hate a surplice,
> Hate mitres, hate copes, and hate rochets,
> Come hear me pray nine times a day
> And fill your head with crotchets.

He then told Edmund more seriously that he really must always wear a surplice. Edmund produced his surplice at once, put it on, mounted his horse and rode home in it. Fortunately the Bishop was as much amused by this exhibition of the absurdity of obeying an order without any regard for its context as the onlookers were by the unexpected sight of a side-saddled ecclesiastic.

Parson Gurney was popular wherever he went, and all was 'Holy-rowly-poly' even in the later days of the reign of King James I. Nicolas L'Estrange's collection of anecdotes gives a vivid impression of the life through which Edmund moved wittily and contrarily. He and his brothers and nephews and nieces appear again and again in the *Merry Passages and Jests*, with or without their L'Estrange cousins and other Norfolk personalities, notables and non-notables. 'Nicho.' L'Estrange brings them all to life in his collection. There they are at the dinner-table, cracking doubtful jokes about the rape vinegar and slip-coate cheese, and how young Bacon said the Pastons' Venetian glasses, though beautiful, failed to hold enough sack. Alice, Lady L'Estrange herself, had a keen indefatigable tongue and far-reaching memory for tales retold of her Gurney great-grandfather who began to rebuild Great Ellingham Hall. There is Edmund in the market-place, buying an axe, he says, to crack an egg, and both his twin brothers, one out hunting and the other halfway down a rabbit-hole, and there is Dot calling on the poor and receiving comical if not always actually obscene rebuffs for her trouble, while her brother Ned is being told off in the stables by a lad who failed to recognise his master. Much of the dialogue is in broad Norfolk, studded with technical and long-obsolete terms used in falconry and farming. On the open heaths, in the peat marshes of the Broads and on the blustery north Norfolk cliffs, Edmund lived as full a life as any of the Gurneys. In farm kitchens, inns and parlours, in churches, law-courts and custom houses, he exchanged news and good cheer with everyone, and at West Barsham and Hunstanton Halls, where there were dancing and music and much literary discussion, he joined in with enthusiasm.

Nicholas L'Estrange's *Merry Passages and Jests* serves as a useful visitors' book to Hunstanton, revealing that among the not infrequent guests was the composer Henry Lawes, who suggested *Comus* to John Milton and wrote the music for it and other masques for which Milton wrote the words.

Nicholas L'Estrange never appeared in print, but his father and brothers published various well-phrased pamphlets and prefaces. At about the same time Edmund Gurney dedicated his first religious book[1] to Alice, Lady L'Estrange and her father, Richard Stubbs, to whom he writes, 'Sir, I request you to be godfather to this infant as you have been sometime unto myself.' It is a charming and interesting little book, explaining his inability to accept the conversion of eucharistic bread and wine into body and blood.

His later published works (of which there were several 'to be sold in St. Paul's churchyard') show that his feelings against Roman Catholicism, or even any doctrines or ceremonials faintly approaching it, were even more vehement than his father's had been. When his baby daughter died he did not bury her 'fayre corse' with her feet towards a chapel or pew, but in the grassy churchyard at Harpley. On the outside wall of the church he set up a memorial to this fortnight-old babe as a warning to passers-by. He had christened her Protestant.

> Protestant (Gournay) hereunder I lie,
> Such name at first was I christened by
> And as soon as my days doubled seven
> My name forever was written in heaven.
> Then still be bold, both young and old,
> Thus to protest against anti-Christ;
> And should all fail these stones should cry
> Perpetually we do defy Rome's heresy; idolatry,
> Bloodthirstiness, and boundless soveraynty.
>   A.D. 1623

Fond as the L'Estranges were of Edmund, he was either not asked or else refused to solemnise the marriage between Nicholas, the Merry Quipper, and Ann Lewkner, a first cousin of Ned and Dot on their mother's side. The L'Estranges adhered strongly to the conformist Church of England, and may well

---

[1] Edmund Gurney's short explicit book on Transubstantiation was published in London in 1630. The belief was later to become the main issue of the Test Act of 1672, over which Quakers refused to take oaths.

have feared some eccentric outburst from their more Puritan-minded relation, or equally Edmund may have objected to the extravagance of the plans for the wedding. Anyway, ten shillings was paid 'to getting leave for Lady L'Estrange's cousin Stubb' and one-and-six for their 'not being married at Hunstanton'. Other wedding expenses included dressing up the church of St. Gregory, Norwich, bell-ringing, singers, and costs for the refreshments at the town house in Chapelfields, Norwich. But by far the largest item recorded is £21 9s 'for gloves, poyentes and garters for his two brides maydes'. These 'pointes' were the elaborate pointed lace fastenings so despised by Puritans, whether they trimmed ladies' gowns or gentlemen's jerkins.

Nicholas took the opportunity to add to his collection fresh stories about clergymen, doctors, Welshmen, Dutchmen, the King and other people's horses and dogs. Frank, the 'lower' Gurney twin, contributed, either at the wedding celebrations, or soon after them. 'A Welshman had sentence of death passt upon him for having two wives, but he stormed and swore and splitt his nailes, he saw no reason why they had to hang him for two wives when the priest told him before a creat people he must have 16 – foure better, foure worse, foure richer and foure poorer.'

In London, Frank had become a member of the Merchant Taylors' Company, but now the meticulously kept household accounts of the L'Estranges suggest that he was more often at Hunstanton, working for them as their agent and even as their banker, for besides the commissions he carried out for them, he invested their money, borrowed it, and sometimes lent them money, too.

For Frank's own wedding to Anne Browning of Maldon, Essex, Lady L'Estrange ordered a dozen barrels of oysters to be sent to his house. He returned to London, but remained in close contact with the L'Estranges, calling his eldest son Roger, after their youngest child. His eldest daughter was christened Dorothy after his beloved niece, Dot, and his next son was named Francis after himself.

Not long after Charles I came to the throne, Sir Hammon L'Estrange put a hundred pounds into a company that Frank and

another cousin set up in Lynn (now King's Lynn) in a deconse-
crated church which an earlier Blennerhasset had already,
according to Frank's father's old friend, Sir Henry Spelman,
'perverted to be a town house for the manufacture of stuffs, laces
and tradesmen's commodities'. But despite contributions from
other country gentlemen, the business had failed and the deso-
lation of the church was only increased by the efforts to trans-
form it. Frank, with his London connections, was expected to
make a great success of the revival, but alas he fared no better
than his predecessor, and Sir Hammon had to rescue him from
his plight.

Once again Frank's name appears regularly in the Hunstanton
accounts, investing money for the family in the East India
Company and various Dutch firms, and less formally in connection with young Roger L'Estrange, who was now at Eton.
Frank advanced his pocket-money, bought his books and paid
for his 'dyett' on his journeys to and from school. When Roger
left Eton, aged eighteen, Frank went and collected him and
shipped his trunks and bedding back by sea to Lynn and then on
again to the nearest quay to Hunstanton Hall.

There was trouble over a horse which Frank bought for the
L'Estranges for £6 from his nephew, Ned, at West Barsham.
Frank's man, Henry Balls, was sent to collect the horse, for
which he was paid a shilling. These 'riches' so went to his head
that he rode off to Norwich, twenty miles out of his way, to
spend them. Here 'Henry Balls did lame the horse' which involved paying fees to two farriers to get the horse home.

Ned's life was much taken up with horses. He delighted in
telling the bright young ladies of Norfolk, brought home by his
six sisters for him to dance with, of foolhardy feats out hunting,
particularly the failed feats of those who had only recently made
their fortunes in the city of Norwich and moved out to the
country. A favourite butt, perhaps not unnaturally, was the
purchaser 'for his own use', of the last piece of ancestral property
that Ned's grandfather, Henry Gurney, had sold the year after
Ned was born. The manor of Harpen (now known as Hargham),
bordering on his Great Ellingham land, was set in a garden and

orchard with over five hundred acres of arable, meadow, pasture, heath and woods, with four cottages and a windmill, all of which Ned would dearly have liked to be still in the family. Thus Richard Hovell, the comparative newcomer, was, in Ned's eyes, a complete outsider, a hopeless rider, and his son, 'Dick Hov.', as according to Nicholas L'Estrange, Ned called him, even worse. Neither was able to stay on a horse. Dick Hov. lacked any musical ear, and when he tried to dance 'never footed to the musicke, nor could distinguish betwixt the beginning, end or middle of any dance or betwixt one tune and another.' 'Young Mr. Hov.' refused to accept the necessity, observing 'dost thinke we have nothing else to doe but to listen to the fiddles when we should dance?'

Once when Dick Hov. was out hunting near the place where the local landlord, Sir John Pooley, was fishing, a hare was by accident forced into the pond and fell foul of the net. Nicholas reports Ned as saying that

> Hounds come almost at a dead fault and Dick Hov. gallopps down to the company, and meeting Sr. Jo. Poo. there salutes him and askt him what he fisht for. 'For hares,' says he, and wagers he will find one, offering to put stakes into a third hand. 'That's very likely,' sayes Hov., taking it for a frump and jeere. 'I am sure 'tis very true,' says Sr. Jo. 'and that you'll find presently. Pull pull,' says he, and withdrew the net with a huge hare sprawling in it. 'Look you here,' cries Sir John, 'did I tell you as much?' 'Yes, faith,' says Dick, 'and now I see the old saying is true, that there's no creatures upon earth but the water has the same: and what a wonderful thing it is!' 'Not to me,' says Sir Joe Poo, 'for I have eate many a good hare oute of this pond in my time.'

And so the stories against the Hovells were spread abroad in increasingly preposterous vein.

Suddenly Ned changed sides and asked to marry 'old Richard Hovell's' daughter. It can hardly have been for the windmill and all that went with it, for Harpen had already been sold again. The Hovells approved of the marriage but, once it was achieved, old

48

Mr. Hovell set about Ned for his high-handed ridiculing of his son, and told him the Hovells were already country land-owners at the time of the Conqueror, and the so-called re-spected ancient family of 'de Gournays' were not respected at all; indeed he even doubted their antiquity. Ned was appalled by the suggestion, and appealed at once to his uncle Edmund, who merely reminded him of the untraceability of his pedigree from Adam. Ned then tried his uncle Frank, who had only recently deposited a family tree in London with Sir Henry Spelman, who had approved it after comparing it favourably with original deeds. An incensed letter survives from Ned to his 'ever hon-oured father in lawe Richard Hovell Esq. at Hillington', in which he says, 'I purpose and intend (God willing) to sett forward to London on ffryday next where I shall to the uttermost of my power seeke to recover my birth and family from that unworthy esteem some have surmised.'

This touchy matter disposed of, Ned bounds straight on in his letter to having seen '44 goodly horses landed at Blackeney, which were intended for Dover and so for London but seeing there accidently cast upon that shore they resolved to make sale of them there. Their colours are greys and bays. You may have admirable choice for your coach and hap'ly worth your money.' Ned sends dutiful remembrances to both his parents-in-law, and remains their obedient 'son-in-law, Edw. Gournay', adding an urgent P.S. 'The horses I suppose stay there not longer than 3 or 4 days. West Bash'm April 7th 1638.'

Before the draining of the fens and marshy land to the east of Lynn, there was much winter flooding, making hunting almost impossible. Thus Ned and his sporting friends substituted wild-fowling with heavy guns mounted on punts, which, when the floods were frozen over, were turned into sledges. In the long icy winters of the period, Ned abandoned all serious pursuits for the excitement of winter sports, seventeenth-century style, with 'sleadse and gliding on our skeats'.

He quietened down after his son was born. He became known as a good and generous churchman, giving freely not only to his own church but also to the poor and aged of other parishes.

Although he could not go along with all of Parson Edmund's inventive bishop-teasers, he did agree with him that Bishop Matthew Wren, whom Archbishop Laud sent to Norwich when the more humorous Bishop Corbett died, was unbearably obsessed with his love of ceremony and rigid discipline. Wren had inherited a passion for attention to detail, a family trait that must also have been passed down to his nephew, the great architect, Sir Christopher Wren, with happier results.

The Archbishop was determined to subdue all non-conforming ministers and lecturers in order to promote absolutely consistent 'reverence, decency and good order throughout England and Scotland'. The exact form of the Prayer Book was to be observed; detailed instructions about services, liturgies, baptisms, marriages, prayers for the sick, churching of women and, above all, holy communion were to be followed to the nth degree.

In the diocese of Norwich, Bishop Wren sent out a printed pamphlet of 897 questions asking how services were being conducted, and what was the condition of the church fabric, the behaviour of the minister, and the morals of the parishioners. Minute details were given, such as that 'a communion rail be made reaching from the north wall to the south wall, near one yard in height, so thick with pillars that dogs may not get in', which certainly seemed ridiculous to Ned, whose dogs had always had the run of the chancel, including the legs of the communion table, and, on some occasions, the communion bread. Were they not also God's creatures? Bishop Wren ordered that, in the administration of the Lord's Supper, the minister was to consecrate bread and wine standing at the west side of the table and with his face to the east and his back to the people, elevating the bread and wine so high that they could be seen over his shoulder. These geographical gymnastics were particularly irksome to Edmund, as were to Ned the rulings to all squires accustomed to privacy in church that their room-like box pews were to be removed. Pews were to be built so that those inside them could be 'seen how they behaved themselves'. No pew must exceed a yard in height. But despite this levelling, the most important people in the parish, arranged in order of importance, were ordered to form the front row of the ranks of kneeling parishioners taking communion.

Parson Edmund regarded what he called these 'Popish Practices' as the very antithesis of holy-rowly-powlyism.

Things came to a national head when Archbishop Laud and King Charles I tried to force the Anglican prayer book (known abusively by the same nickname as is used today for prison – 'porridge') on to the Scots. The King felt compelled to raise an army to oppose those who refused to sign the Covenant, insisting on the absolute use of the Prayer Book. Ned immediately dashed to add his name to the roll of Norfolk knights and gentlemen sending horses, men and money to the royal cause. He contributed one harquebusier complete (named Thomas Baker), and £20 in money. The army was led by his neighbour and family friend, the Lord Lieutenant of Norfolk, Thomas Howard, Earl of Arundel. To the young Norfolk sportsmen it was as good as a day's hunting. Roger L'Estrange, now aged twenty-three, took part in the expedition as did his father, Sir Hammon L'Estrange. Ned was now thirty-one, and his brother-in-law, Dick. Hov., was about the same age.

At Berwick the King placed himself at the head of the troop, but Ned never even saw the skirmishes that took place before peace was concluded and the King's forces disbanded. Camp fever had broken out. Ned caught it, and made his will in his own hand (witnessed by Sir Hammon L'Estrange). He recovered sufficiently to go home, but he was never fully restored to health. He spent most of the next two years at West Barsham Hall, in his 'closet now above the kitchen' where he kept his father's English books, his globe and his mathematical instruments. Although he insisted that he was in 'perfect health, memory and understanding', he cannot have expected to live until his son came of age, for he devoted such energy as he had left to trying to arrange that as much as possible of his inheritance should be 'improved' to cover the high charges that would be made on yet another wardship, as he knew from his own experience and his grandfather's.

Ned died on 6th August, 1641.[2] This time the boy heir, his elder son, Henry, was nine when the depleted Gurney inheritance became his.

Dot died only three months after her brother Ned, leaving a warm and affectionate will which included generous sums not only to her brother and sisters but also to all her nephews and nieces and many of her 'deare and loveinge' L'Estrange and Lewkner cousins. She left her two best gowns, her best petticoats and best linings to her god-daughter, and to her aunt her gold dagger and cornelian ring. To her newly widowed sister-in-law she left six silver plates, her silver maudlin (tippling) cup with the cover, and her cabinet 'but nothing in it'.

Dot had clearly been a woman of substance. Her uncle Frank had invested several hundred pounds of hers on various occasions. She was living in Tombland, Norwich, when she died in her early thirties, unmarried. Had she, like her uncle Frank, a financial bent and consequently, perhaps, a business of her own? Her sisters had married well, and could have given her a home – one was living with her husband and daughter at Great Elling-ham Hall, first as a tenant and later as its owner. But Dot had preferred to live and die alone.

This was the year when the people turned against the King,[3] crying 'No bishops! No bishops!' and threatening to disembowel them as they went by. Bishop Wren of Norwich was accused of 'superstitious and idolitrous gestures and actions'. Twenty-five acts of impeachment were brought against him and he was sent to the Tower.

But despite Wren's replacement in Norwich by the much more tolerant Bishop Hall, peace for such clergymen as Edmund Gurney was short-lived. When war broke out the following

---

[2] Only two of Ned's children survived to maturity, little Henry of West Barsham and his sister, Frances. Little Henry married Ellen Adams but died, aged twenty-nine, in 1661, leaving no children. Ellen lived on at West Barsham till 1674, when she sold it to Sir L'Estrange Calthorpe, a cousin by marriage.

[3] The Act of Uniformity, 1662, demanded that before the ensuing St. Bartholomew's day, 24th of August, all ministers and schoolmasters were to make a declaration of the illegality of taking up arms against the King and to repudiate the National Covenant.

year, the King, at Oxford, encouraged Royalist army attempts to take Norfolk seaports. The L'Estranges took and held Lynn for nearly a month. Roger L'Estrange fought beside his father while the town was assaulted from across the river. When Sir Hammon was persuaded to make terms, Roger went straight to the King at Oxford and convinced him that the spirit of resistance was much stronger in Norfolk than it really was, and the King sent him back with the promise of £5,000 and the governorship of Lynn if he could retake and hold it.

Roger returned to the north Norfolk coast, hoping to bribe local fishermen to follow him. But he was tricked into arrest by the parliamentarians near Sandringham, and carried off to London, where he would have been executed but for the intervention of the King's dashing young nephew, Prince Rupert of the Rhine, who had come over from Bavaria to fight for him. Instead, Roger was imprisoned for three years in Newgate, refusing throughout to sign the Covenant.

This Covenant – 'to use the official prayer book only' – was enforced with such appalling harshness in Norfolk that signing it was almost unavoidable. Bishop Hall, in whom so much hope had been put by broader-thinking people, was himself turned out of his palace to make room for the new committees of sequestrators. Some of their earliest work was plundering Hunstanton Hall of 1,600 sheep, all the corn, and most of the horses.

From then on the L'Estranges were over-taxed and subjected to gross financial insults, as Alice, Lady L'Estrange, showed in her ledgers, adding her own indignant opinion of the financial claims made by the oppressors. The Hovells at Hillingdon suffered in the same way, and at West Barsham Ned's son was forced to pay even more in taxes, owing to Ned's attempted loyalty to the Crown, than his father had calculated the wardship charges would involve.

For the clergy who refused to sign the Covenant there was nothing but starvation; ejection from their livings was the lot of over 200 Norfolk priests. Edmund Gurney, owning his own rectory as he did, and with generous relations (Alice, Lady L'Estrange lent him £20) would not have starved had he refused to sign the Covenant, but he would have lost what he no doubt considered his much more valuable 'right to preach' and to conduct services. As he retained his living at Harpley, it has been assumed that he signed the Covenant in 1643.

In January 1647, when the Civil War seemed to be safely over and Roger L'Estrange had been released to return to live at Hunstanton with his parents, the L'Estranges were able to go on 'a London journey' via the port of Maldon, on the estuary of the river Blackwater in Essex. Their expense-sheet shows how they stopped at Colchester for oysters and wine for 1/11d, while their horses were being held for 3d. When they reached Maldon, their expenses rose steeply at the inn where they stayed and put up their horses, suggesting an evening of entertaining.

Frank Gurney's brother-in-law, Jeremiah Browning, was an alderman of Maldon. Frank's second son, Francis, later married his cousin Jeremiah's daughter Anne, and settled in a house in Maldon near the river. The L'Estranges were evidently on this occasion visting the family, possibly on the occasion of young Francis Gurney's betrothal.

By the time they reached home, King Charles had been handed over to Parliament by the Scots, and both countries were in chaos again. The King escaped, was kidnapped, and escaped again to rally a new army against Parliament. Fears of a new Presbyterian uniformity were mingled with further fears of the renewed horrors of inter-family fighting. Many bewildered people found solace in the independent-minded preachers of the marketplaces. Parson Edmund would certainly have stopped to listen, and may well have preached himself beside the market-crosses. News was passed on of any exceptional preacher, and so George Fox, founder of Quakerism, would have been known to Edmund as a young man who had left the grazier he was apprenticed to and the sheep he was learning to care for to travel the road and join in with religious discussions wherever he found them. Fox listened to all the arguments, and resolved to forsake all religions and to attend to the teaching of the spirit. The message he preached was direct communication with God without the intervention of priests. Edmund may well have been among those who resented this claim to direct inspiration without ecclesiastical sanction, or he may have sensed something of the quiet beauty and purity that this outwardly ranting and furious young preacher strove to teach in his new approach.

The year 1648 is a significant one in the movement known as 'Children of Light' or 'Friends of the Truth', later to be known as 'The Society of Friends'. They were called Quakers because, on one of the many occasions when Fox was brought to court for preaching against the 'Steeplehouse', as he called the church, and 'hireling ministers', as he called the clergy, he bade the judge 'quake and tremble at the truth' as revealed by him.

Much of what Fox taught was in line with Edmund's own holy-rowly-powlism which his nephews and nieces and their children would have learnt from him. Those of them who later became Quakers may well have been searching for the kind of spiritual love indoctrinated in them by Edmund, who died in May 1648, the year in which Quakerism was founded. He was buried in St. Peter's Mancroft, Norwich, where his Cambridge friend and brother-in-law, Thomas Osborne, had been minister.

The date of his brother Frank's death is not recorded. It is merely observed that Frank was not living in 1660, the year of the restoration, when Ned's only son, the last of the West Barsham Gurney squires, died, aged twenty-eight, leaving his wife without children.

No traces after that date can be found of the taller twin, 'Ant.', nor of Bassingborne, nor of any of the male Gurneys of this line except young Francis the 'lower twin', of Maldon (married to Anne Browning) who set up as a general merchant, and begat ten children, five of whom were raised to adulthood.

Chapter Three

John and Elizabeth
1665–1721

In 1667, seventeen years after the death without issue of Ned's only son, a young Gurney turned up alone in Norwich and, from the humblest apprenticeship in the leather trade, became eminent as a Quaker, city merchant and financial adviser to the first prime minister. He is believed to be John, the eldest son of Francis Gurney and Anne Browning of Maldon, and a grandson of the 'lower twin'.

This John Gurney was born at Maldon on 7th October, 1665 and christened there three weeks later. He and his nine brothers and sisters were all christened at St. Mary's church, where their parents were registered communicants. Anne's brother, Thomas Browning, was a doctor of divinity and rector of a nearby parish. However, as his house was 'untenanted' in the year after the Covenant was forced on the clergy in 1662, Dr. Browning had probably refused to sign and thereby lost his living, though he was still in the neighbourhood. Later, other Browning relations appear in Quaker records in these parts. Thus puritanical ideas would have come into the family not only through teaching passed down from John's great uncle, Parson Edmund of Harpley, but also from his maternal uncle.

John's parents continued to attend communion at St. Mary's for several more years, but neither John nor his brothers and sisters became communicants. They were all brought up in an already ancient house, which stood on the banks of the river Blackwater, near enough to high water for all outside doors to be built above short flights of steps against flooding. It was an irregular, sprawling gabled house which Francis Gurney rented from Maldon corporation, of which he was an alderman and later one of the two bailiffs. He had also bought long leaseholds on other buildings in Maldon, and a salt-cote on farm lands outside the town. The Gurneys had a boat, a cart, several horses and numerous farm animals. Here was a good life for a bright and amiable boy, with much to be learnt from the varied interests of his father. There was not only the farm, some forestry, and the salt-cote but also a small foundry, warehouse, and the Gurney quay from which, it is recorded, were loaded salt, corn, hay, wood and timber and onto which were unloaded coal, stones and pipeclay and no doubt much else besides.

When John was nine, the heralds' visitation for Essex entered him as Francis and Anne Gurney's 'sonne and heir', with three younger brothers and a sister still living. His father, styled 'gentleman', bore arms (argent, a cross engrained gules, a crescent for difference). Francis signs the attestation 'Ffra. Gournay' despite the spelling throughout the heralds' account being 'Gourney', including that of his son and heir.

John was twelve when the youngest of the ten children (only six of whom were to grow up) was born. It was not long before John was helping his father with his business letters and learning something of accounting, which his father, in turn, had learnt from his own father, Frank, who was also the source of many useful business contacts in London and the provinces.

In the same way as not all of John's grandfather Frank's ventures had prospered, nor did all those of John's father. During the third Dutch War, when John was seventeen, his father, noticing an extra demand for clay pipes for the expanding navy, wrote to a dealer, Cornell, whom he knew in Poole Harbour, ordering a boat-load of best quality fuller's earth or pipeclay. If, he said, none could be delivered immediately, then the order was to be cancelled. Cornell replied that it would be too dangerous to ship any such commodity by sea during wartime, and father and son thought no more about it.

Over a year later, and three months after peace had been declared, Francis Gurney was surprised and annoyed to find that several ship-loads of Cornell's clay had been sent to Maldon with an account addressed to him, charging him the high price of twenty-two shillings a ton for it. The price for best clay had now dropped by half, and this clay was of the worst quality. 'Its badness, roughness and coarseness,' Francis said, made it impossible to sell. Several people more skilled in the commodity than he, he said, declared it unworkable and unfit to use, and they could make no use of it even if it were given to them for nothing. Francis tried mixing better clay with it, but could still only get a poor price, moreover he lost customers who had previously dealt with him. Cornell then followed up the consignment with a parcel of Purbeck stone and a bill for both clay and stone. John's father paid him £30, considering that 'in view of the badness of the clay' he had paid enough, indeed, he was 'much demnified by Cornell', whereupon Cornell turned up in person in Maldon to collect what he considered was still due to him. John's father produced some of his dissatisfied customers and told Cornell, in no gentle terms, to take back the clay. This tirade left Cornell begging him to sell the remainder as fast as he could for what he could get and to keep whatever he made; indeed Mr. Gurney was to refund himself for any difference between the actual value of the stone and the £30 which Cornell now admitted had been overpaid to him. Any balance should be applied to Mr. Gurney for the charges of freight, sales and warehousing. Cornell left Maldon full of apologies and there the matter might have ended.

Unhappily, not only was the stuff still blocking the warehouse a year later, but also news reached Cornell that John's father had been involved in a lawsuit in which an action was brought against him and others for trespassing. Had the pipeclay and its worries not remained piled up, and had Nicholas L'Estrange been there to retell the tale, the whole thing would have ended as a merry passage and jest with a jolly laugh round the fireside. But now the family sense of fun had deserted it, and Nicholas was dead.

The fresh incident began with John's father, two of the borough's sergeants at mace and two other men, filing a case against a wool-comber called Dabs and eight of his relations for a debt for a bargain of wool of £14. 8s. 4d. The whole family promptly disappeared except for Dabs's wife, whom he left in

58

charge of his house and belongings. The two sergeants at mace then took part and removed from Dabs's house goods later valued at £11. 12s. 6d. Dabs and company returned, nonplussed. Presently they were advised to bring an action against the two sergeants, the two other men, and Francis Gurney, which Dabs & Co. won.

Cornell followed up this Gurney defeat by denying all agreements and payments from Francis and ingeniously brought about his arrest upon a supposed debt of £43.

There is no evidence that John's father was actually detained at any time and, no doubt, such was the strength of his supporters both in Maldon and in London that nothing more physical occurred than the addition to his already overtaxed irritation. This incited him to file a bill against William Cornell in order to bring his whole four years of dishonest and tiresome behaviour into the light.

At what point Samuel Pepys became a friend of the family is not clear. Pepys was at this time surveyor-general of the victualling office, in which capacity he showed himself an energetic official and a zealous reformer of abuses. He may have been asked to investigate the mixing of the pipeclay. Or he may have met Francis Gurney earlier through their mutual interest in shipping. Nor is it known what, besides the disheartening piles of pipeclay still lying about like unmelted snow, precipitated Francis Gurney's final burst of despair. For over two centuries the Gurney family was perplexed by the absence of any kind of will or last testament being proved pertaining to a man of Francis Gurney's comparative wealth. Then, early in this century a series of caveats was unearthed, all entered within a few days after John's father's tragic death twelve weeks after filing his bill in Chancery.

'Let nothing be done in the estate of Francis Gurney of St. Mary's, in the town of Maldon in Essex, deceased,' states Dr. Thomas Browning, calling himself 'the chief creditor', probably as a legal fiction to try to protect his widowed sister and her children. On the same page another plea, dated August 21st, 1677, is entered 'that no grant pass to the estate of Francis

Gurney, of Maldon in Essex, who drowned himself in his own well on Sunday night the 12th of this instant August. At the desire of Samuell Pepys Esqr.' Pepys makes a note in his diary that 'Fra; Gurnee of Maldon in Essex dron'd himself the 12th of instant Augt,' Three other caveats are entered in an effort to try to save the property of the family, for at that time the personal estates of all suicides were forfeited to the Crown. If the tragedy could have been recorded as an accident or even as 'suicide during temporary insanity', the widow and six children could have been saved from eviction and removal of their belongings. But a jury stated that Francis Gurney committed suicide on 12th August, 1677, on which date he was possessed of goods to the value of £560. 13s. 4d besides his houses and land. There were also eleven sums owing to him, ranging from 11/8d to £78 owed by the Duke of Albermarle.

A commission was appointed to enquire into the whereabouts of Francis Gurney's goods and chattels and to take the same for the King's use, selling some of the goods when valued, the money arising to be paid into the exchequer. Thanks to some unknown help, the Gurney assets were most generously under-valued, for all John's father's stock-in-trade as well as his farm implements, his cart, boat, horses and farm animals were included in the total value of £34. 13s. 4d. Perhaps Mr. Sam Love had lived up to his name, for he it was who was taking charge of 'lumber', which might well have covered Anne's favourite things and essential equipment which she could have bought back for a few pence. Only one flock bed and brass pot appear in the sale to represent household goods.

But whatever the financial situation, the disgrace must have lain heavily on this Christian family, the youngest of whom were still only ten and eleven. The funeral of Francis Gurney does not appear in the records of St. Mary's church, for suicides were not allowed Christian burial, and there is no further reference to Francis Gurney to be found in Maldon after the inquisition taken at Chelmsford on 11th October 1677.

On John the greatest responsibility seems to have fallen for he was the only one old enough to go out and earn enough to keep them all, The injustice of the whole horrible affair was enough to determine a young man of John's brief but thorough experience to go out and start life again. There are no further references to John Gurney, born in Maldon, 17th October, 1665. However, within months the name of John Gurney appears for the first time in the Norwich Quaker registers, among the witnesses at one of their weddings. From then on his presence among the Norwich Quakers was increasingly noticeable. It was a time when every thinking person sought a religion in which he could believe whole-heartedly. There had never been such a time for fierce religious argument and probing discussion. The stark finality of Calvinistic Puritanism, with its threats of hell-fire and the noisome pit would have been as comfortless to John as the elaborate arguments of the High Anglicans and Roman Catholics. Quakerism was strong in Norwich, whose earlier citizens had been among the Pilgrim Fathers who sailed to America in the *Mayflower*. After the suspicion and misery of the Maldon tragedy, with the hounding by Dabs and his confederates, the repeated attendances in court, the deprivations and final refusal of Christian burial for his father, how the stillness and quiet of a Quaker meeting, with its underlying trust and kindness, could have soothed and healed! What greater restorative, when recent experience had suggested the opposite, than the Quaker belief that there is something of God in every man? In Quaker meetings, free from formalities, people of widely different views could unite to worship without being called upon to accept anything they found unacceptable. Peace on earth and good will towards men – if only they would receive and distribute love!

Perhaps it was the practical as well as the spiritual appeal that drew John Gurney towards Quakerism, during his first few months in Norwich. Soon after the wedding his name appears again as one of the young men 'nominated to have the care in looking after the back garden' on some ground which the Friends had lately bought.

There are no pictures of John to show the family likeness that successions of his descendants carried, but there are pictures of his sons, including one at about the age which John was at this time. Fair or reddish-tinged hair, rosy complexion and a curiously childish formation of the chin (later developing into a firm square jaw) occur again and again in family portraits, with every sort of variation of nose and mouth. Since this John Gurney's age tallied with that of the eldest son and heir of Francis Gurney of Maldon, it has generally been assumed by his descendants that he was the same person.

What could have been more natural, it was suggested, than that John of Maldon should have gone to Norfolk to seek work among his father's well-to-do relations? He would certainly have heard his father talk of his own grandfather, Henry Gurney of Great Ellingham and West Barsham, and of his grandmother Blennerhasset. John may well have known some of the quips and jests by heart. Norwich would have seemed a place full of his father's cousins and friends.

In fact, by 1578 there was not a Gurney, Gournay or Gourney of the West Barsham descent left in Norfolk. It was only four years before this that West Barsham Hall had been sold by Ned's childless daughter-in-law to his cousin, Sir L'Estrange Calthorpe. Harpley Manor had been bought by the Walpoles in 1642, before John was even born. Great Ellingham Hall had descended through a Gurney daughter to a first cousin of Francis of Maldon. She and her husband, Sir Roger Potts, usually lived at Great Ellingham, but Sir Roger also owned the then somewhat dilapidated but romantic and entirely moated Hall of Mannington, twenty miles from Great Ellingham. There were still other cousins in Norfolk, but none bearing John's surname. Somebody, either related or of a friendly disposition, must have helped this young man. Apprenticeship demanded not only introductions but also payment. Possibly John had salvaged enough from the disaster in Maldon, after resettling his mother and the younger children elsewhere, or he may have shown sufficient promise in a humble job to have won a high enough approval from his master to be given a free apprenticeship. The Norwich corporation books show that John Gurney was apprenticed to Daniel Gilman, citizen and cordwainer. In Norwich, cordwaining – tanning, curing and buying and selling leather – would almost certainly have involved boots and shoes.

Whether John Gurney was in touch with Samuel Pepys after he went to Norwich and became a Quaker is not recorded, but certainly Pepys was, in his own way, in sympathy with the Quakers who went to prison for their cause, 'They go like lambs,' he writes 'without any resistance. I would to God they would either conform or be more wise and not be catched.'

Probably John's show of determination and integrity as a staunch and active Friend impressed his master as much as his knowledge of percentages or handling freight on an awkward quay. When the test came, John showed all the spirit of the earlier Quakers. It was now some thirty years since the rise of Quakerism, but still there was a long way to go before Quakers were to be loved for their tranquillity, as Charles Lamb later entreated that they should be. The idea that they were passive, silent men and women outside their meetings was far from the truth. The truth to George Fox himself meant going up to a man and saying 'My fat-faced man thou are a damned lie. Thou are pretending to serve God Almighty and art really serving the devil.' But swearing at another man, or any form of swearing, using God's name, even in the coldest of blood, counted to Fox and his followers as a direct breaking of the commandment against taking God's name in vain. Quakers, then, were to suffer persecution, prison and even death rather than take an oath in court. This 'damnable sect deluded by Satin' of 'scandalous persons' was still regarded as politically dangerous.

Like the early Christians, as well as meeting to worship together Quakers met to eat together and talk of the progress they made in their faith and recount the trials that they and others had suffered. But unlike the early Christians, who met in the catacombs of Rome, the Quakers did not meet in secret. They openly built meeting-houses, and, if kept out of them, they met in streets and public squares. They carried their physical and mental wounds with joyous smiles (which were not always interpreted as showing how beautiful their lives were rendered by so much love).

Since the Scriptures contains the record of the life and teaching of Jesus Christ and of many men and women inspired by God, Friends regarded the Bible as of great importance for the understanding of the will of God, but not as the final authority. The Apologist, Robert Barclay, believed Scripture to be inspired by this spirit as 'a declaration of the fountain and not the fountain itself'.

In the third year of John's apprenticeship, on 29th November, he was among 'Friends who had been kept out of their meeting House' and who had 'met together in the street to wait upon the Lord'. John and another Friend were 'violently pulled out from among the rest as if they had been malefactors', and taken before a J.P. who, as they declined the bail demanded, committed them to prison until the next quarter sessions.

John was in prison for nearly three of the seven years required as an apprentice to gain the freedom of the city. Religious prisoners are well known for making use of their time with prayer, meditation and, when possible, reading. Quakers were said to have been particularly barren in their writers to start with. Though founded on logical interpretations of the Scriptures, the writings of the early Quakers were often fanatical in content as well as chaotic and inconsistent. Extracts from Fox's *Journal* show the Society's history and origin; William Penn published a pamphlet *No Cross, No Crown* illustrating their practice. Then the young Scots Quaker, Robert Barclay, wrote his *Apologia* in Latin which was later translated into English as *The Apology not as a regretful acknowledgment of offence but as an explanation of the faith preached by the people called in scorn Quakers*. In it, Robert Barclay frequently employs a modern, almost breezy touch to explain customs and phrases accepted but by no means previously understood before by most Quakers. He cheerfully explained the Quakers' objection to such titles as 'your excellency, your majesty, your honour, your eminence', which had nothing to do with obedience due to magistrates and superiors. No such titles were used in the Bible. 'In speaking to rulers they only used a simple compilation such as Oh king or oh king Agrippa.' Barclay explained that *your excellency* may be a person of no excellence, *your grace* may be an enemy of grace and *your honour* known to be base and ignoble. He objected to *holiness, eminence, grace, lordship,* and *worship* as 'blasphemous usurpation. Ought not holiness and grace to be in every Christian, and how can they claim any more titles than were practised by the Apostles and primitive Christians? The Apostles were not called *your grace* nor *your worship* neither *my lord* Peter nor *my lord Paul* nor *master Peter* nor *master Paul* but simply *Peter* and *Paul*.'

In Norwich gaol five women Friends were imprisoned in a room so smoky that they could scarcely breathe. In another prison they took turns to put their faces down by the crack under the door to catch the incoming draught.

In 1685 John and his fourteen fellow prisoners belonging to the Society wrote an impressive address to the city, explaining that they were not dangerous rebels and that, if they were allowed to go free and their persecution ceased, they could be of more use to others. At the summer assizes the oath of allegiance was tendered to them again; they refused it and were recommitted.

After John's release from prison during the relaxation of severe measures against Dissenters early in the reign of James II, he finished his seven years' apprenticeship, and then began to set up a general trading business of his own. There was nothing in the movement against making a success of business. Indeed, it was to be commended by the Society of Friends, and later Friends who failed in business were temporarily or permanently disowned according to the efforts they made to recover themselves.

In the early years of the movement, sticking to their religious principles had meant that Quakers in all walks of life had been deprived, if not of their liberty, at any rate of their livelihood. But gradually the personal integrity of the Quakers earned them a reputation for absolute incorruptibility and honesty. In his journal George Fox left support of this:

At the first commencement when Friends could not put off their hats to people, nor say 'you' to a particular person but 'thee', and 'thou' and could not bow nor use the words of salutations, nor fashions nor customs, and many Friends being tradesmen of various sorts, they

65

lost their custom at first, for the people would not deal with them nor trust them. For a time they could hardly get money enough to buy bread, but afterwards when people came to see Friends' honesty and truthfulness and 'yea' and 'nay' as a word in their dealings they knew and saw that they would not cozen nor cheat for their conscience sake. So then things altered, and drapers, shop-keepers, tailors, shoe-makers and other tradesmen who were Quakers found that trade had doubled beyond any of their neighbours.

When Friends moved from one area to another they 'were to carry a certificate from their monthly meeting which was to testify to their sober and orderly conversation and, if single persons, to signify also their freedom to accept marriage engagements'.

Although John's application to become a freeman of the city was turned down, such was the respect of his fellow citizens that he was allowed most of the privileges of a freeman, and was allowed to carry on his mercantile affairs within the city of Norwich without taking an oath.

On 7th September, 1687, John went to Woodbridge in Suffolk, bearing a certificate written in his mother's own hand signifying her goodwill and free consent to his marriage that year. This was recorded in the Woodbridge Quaker records together with his marriage that day to Elizabeth Swanton. Elizabeth had not been living in Woodbridge, and her family was believed to have come from one of the Swantons in Norfolk, Swanton Morley, Swanton Novers or Swanton Abbott. Two of her brothers were merchants in Wells-next-the-Sea, then a thriving port of the same size and importance as Maldon.

Quaker weddings were not recognised by the church, which regarded the children of Quaker marriages as illegitimate. Successive judgments in the civil courts, however, implicitly considered them as good marriages provided they were open and before witnesses. Quaker marriage was and is still almost completely without ceremony. A silence 'for a reasonable time' ended with the bridegroom, in this case John, taking Elizabeth's hand and saying 'Friends, I take this Friend, Elizabeth Swanton, to be my wife, promising through divine assistance to be unto her a loving and faithful husband until it shall please the Lord by death to separate us.' The bride repeated the words naming John and the couple were man and wife in the sight of God and the assembled company. Unless anyone felt moved to speak, that was the marriage. As many witnesses as possible signed the marriage certificate, which must have given the bride considerable confidence.

The couple returned to Norwich which, outside the castle which was then the town jail, was a delightful place to live in. Almost every seventeenth-century account of Norwich includes some reference to the beauty of its gardens and the skill of its gardeners. Thomas Fuller writes at that time, 'Norwich is as you please either a city in an orchard or an orchard in a city so equally are houses and trees blended where the pleasure of the country and populace of this city meet together.' He attributed the Norwich cult of flowers to the Dutch immigrants who were encouraged to settle in the city during the sixteenth century. 'They brought here with them not only their profitable crafts but pleasurable curiosities' not forgetting the canaries, forerunners of the Norwich prize breed.

John Gurney's house stood almost in the middle of the great kite-shaped city, surrounded by its ancient twelve-gated wall, with a steep cobbled street running down to his quay between St. Miles bridge and Duke's Palace bridge on the river Wensum that circles three sides of the city. The house was large and solid, commanding an important position at Charing, or Shearing Cross, which marks the 'plain' where the main sheep-shearing had taken place for centuries. Open spaces and town squares are still known in Norwich today as 'plains'.

A sketch exists of 'the sign of the three pigeons' in which the John Gurneys lived and from which they operated. It shows a large fifteenth-century mansion standing in the fork of two streets of different levels. Though the names of the streets have been changed (in John's day they were Over and Nether West-wyke, and now are St. Benedict Street and Westwick Street), there is no mistaking the site. The house itself has been replaced by a wedge of red brick dated 1878. St. Gregory's church still stands opposite the ancient houses propping themselves up against the modern ones. There are still thirty-six medieval churches in Norwich, as well as the Norman cathedral whose spire can be seen twenty miles away, and the Norman castle, now much restored, in which John had been jailed. His house is conspicuous in the perspective map of early Norwich compiled by Richard Taylor, in which it can be seen facing the clearly-marked Charing Cross.

Elizabeth had many but not quite all the qualities of the proverbial woman whose price was far above rubies. Her husband trusted her and as a result his business prospered. She was not merely '*like* a merchant ship bringing food from afar', she kept the books and made sure that the merchandise carried in the ships which both her husband at Norwich and her two brothers at Wells-next-the-Sea dealt with was profitable. She was kind to the poor and needy, and not afraid to go out in the snow on errands of mercy. She planted fruit trees in her Norwich garden and, living in the heart of the weaving industry, she certainly bought wool and flax, and handled distaff and spindles. She could never have dressed her household in scarlet and herself in purple, for quiet shades and pale colours were favoured by the Friends. She very likely 'made linen garments and sold them and delivered girdles unto the merchants'. Elizabeth certainly never ate the bread of idleness but, though she opened her mouth with wisdom, the law of kindness was not always on her tongue. There were times when she spoke very sharply. But, nevertheless, her children still called her blessed and her husband praised her 'many daughters have done virtuously but thou excelleth them all.'

Elizabeth not only acted as chief clerk to the firm but she also had eight sons, the last of whom were twins. John records in his own hand that four lived to man's estate. 'John born in the 5th month called July 1688; Joseph born in the 1st month in the year 1691; Benjamin born in the 12th month called February in the year 1693 and Edmund, the second of that name, was born in the 9th month called November in the year 1697.' The Quakers had their own method of dating in which they ignored the pagan names of the months and the days of the week. Until 1751 the

English year began on the 25 March (Lady Day). The days of the week were called first-day (Sunday) to seventh-day (Saturday).

John was called after his father; Joseph and Benjamin were named from the Old Testament, and Edmund, no doubt after the beloved Holy-rowly-powly Parson Edmund of Harpley.

Norwich now vied with Bristol as the second largest town in England and the third in Europe. Trade expansion was heading towards an unparalleled peak, and John Gurney was constantly consulted by the corporation on matters of commerce. Among those who also sought his advice – and not only on finance – were the two brilliant old Etonian grandsons of Parson Edmund Gurney's friend and neighbour, Mr. Edward Walpole of Houghton. Both Robert and Horatio Walpole went early into politics, in which John Gurney, as a Quaker, could take no part. But Quakers could and frequently did advise politicians, and Sir Robert Walpole, the first prime minister to bear that title, was to regard John Gurney, and later his sons, as 'among his most valued political allies, exerting on his behalf the full weight of their influence in Quaker and merchant power circles'. They had much in common. The Walpole family had suffered persecution as Roman Catholics. Sir Robert, who became an M.P. soon after inheriting his father's baronetcy, made a special study of commerce, with particular emphasis on colonial trade. He entirely agreed with the Quakers in advocating peace. In the old family manor house of Houghton he began to hold 'congresses', at which he mixed his government colleagues with his Norfolk hunting friends and his Norwich advisers.

Soon after the first Norwich newspaper, the *Gazette*, had been launched (after printing had been abandoned in the city for over a century) John's appointment was announced at last, as a freeman of the city, without his having to take oaths. It was in this year, 1709, that his eldest son was married to Eliza Hadduck. Among the witnesses were two more Great Ellingham relations. Witnesses were not necessarily themselves Quakers.

Four years later John's second son, Joseph, married Hannah Middleton. Peace with France was being celebrated that summer with pomp and joy in Norwich, but the wedding party, as

Quakers disapproving of war, had to ignore this and turn their attention to the long, silent non-ceremony of the wedding in their meeting house in Goat Lane. Hannah was a particularly lovely bride, tall and slim with wavy fair hair tucked almost out of sight under her simple white muslin bonnet. She had come to Norwich from her home at Newcastle-on-Tyne to stay with her sister, who was married to Peregrine Tyzack, of a French glass-making family, then working in Norwich.

A pencilled note beside family records suggests that John's wife, Elizabeth, whose price was above rubies, was not herself above 'something of family pride, although not in affluent circumstances at the beginning herself'. It was rumoured that, despite the equality of all in the eyes of God, as pointed out by the Quakers, 'she did not at all like her eldest son's marriage with Eliza Hadduck, although she was an heiress, because she was not a woman of family. On the contrary, Elizabeth's second son Joseph's marriage to Hannah Middleton greatly delighted her, because of Hannah's belonging to an ancient gentleman's family stemming from Belsay Castle, Northumberland.' It was also difficult to avoid comparing Hannah's slim and comely figure with Eliza's shorter, more solid appearance. Indeed, Hannah was so lovely that she was known as the Fair Quaker.

But the Hadduck inheritance, if not the Hadduck physique, was very beautiful too, consisting of undulating land lying south-west of Cromer. The network of lanes in the hinterland of the north Norfolk coast still disintegrates in places into tracks leading to fields identifiable on the old maps as once being Hadduck property. Hempstead mill-pool must be almost unchanged, with wild duck coming in at dusk to alight on its unrippled surface. Its water-mill is now silent, but the mill-house itself, in which Elizabeth Fry spent her honeymoon in 1800, is still inhabited.

John and his sons were in the habit of attending the yearly meeting of the Friends at Old Devonshire House by Bishopsgate, in the city of London, which the Quakers had rented since their earliest meeting-place, at the sign of the Bull and Mouth in Aldersgate, had been burnt down in the Great Fire in 1666. Yearly meetings had begun, in order that local quarterly meetings should report the deaths of ministers and of Friends who had died in prison, and how the truth prospered, but gradually the range of subjects widened and the purpose changed. Friends no longer came merely to provide factual information, but as an important disciplinary condition. Other lesser meetings were held, too, and there was a great deal of informal discussion in between, concerning the truth not only in religion but also in commerce.

Since a new length of turnpike had been made on the London to Norwich road, delivery of the mail could be, and often was, no slower than today's. Travelling in the heavy, lumbering stage wagon still took two or three days, and longer for John Gurney and his sons, who liked to linger on the way to talk 'business and the Lord.' One letter to John survives from such an occasion:

Ffor John Gurney, Senr. att
Theodore Ettleston's,
In Crown Court,
In Gracechurch Street,
London.

Norwich, yᵉ 17 of 3ᵈ mo. 1716.

My Deare,

Theise are to acquaint thee that I have drawn a bill on John Ettleston to William Crowe, or order, for James Paynter. Thou told me he nor his father would want no money, but he have been with me twice for sum, but I had none for him nor nobody else. I never knew such a week of trade all the hard weather as I have known this week. I could have had some if Richard How had sent culord and the book muslin, and those goods I sent for; but when we have served all his customers, so that they have forestalled the market, then I shall have the rubbish they leave. I take it very ill that thou tye me those people, for I am sure we are both sufferers by it. He know right well if there be any thing to do it is att this time of yeare, but I have been served so severall years. Branthwait have not sent me the money, nor Lilly have paid none, nor the country have sent none, nor I have taken scarce any, so I know not what they wil do att John's. What pleasure

71

thou meet withall at London much good may it doe thee; but I am sure I am in trouble enough. I can hardly tell how to forgive Richard How, to think how he have done by me. My neibour Alice desire thee to buy her 2 hundred of gold, and 2 pound of the best coffee. Pray desire John to think to buy me sum silk gloves of the maker, as I ordered him by my letter. So with deare love to thee and my children, I conclude,

Thy discontented Wife at present,
ELIZ. GURNEY.

My daughter Hannah have now sent for me strait. Her child is taken very ill.

This letter to John Gurney from his admittedly harassed wife suggests something much more modest than the eminent merchant and financier he was said to be. The business might well have been a corner shop combining selling domestic commodities and muslin, with some over-the-counter lending and borrowing. One thing is clear, however: transporting £200 worth of gold safely must have presented some anxiety, whatever position the family had reached. Quakers were always unarmed, and so the superstition growing up – that it was unlucky to attack a Quaker – must have been greatly to their convenience.

This letter was written within John Gurney's last five years, by which time he had bought another house for his eldest son's branch of the business, 'att Johns', a few streets nearer to the country lanes leading to the Hadduck property. For his second son, Joseph, he had bought a house at the Sign of the Dog in Magdalen Street, with a courtyard round which the wings served as business premises, home and birthplace of a great many Gurneys, including Elizabeth Fry. It has recently been restored as Gurney's Court by the city of Norwich, and is now back in Gurney hands again. In Richard Taylor's picture map, the main house (with the other two houses in the court) can be seen standing exactly as it does today, midway between St. Saviour's church and Fie Bridge. This area was already known as 'over the water'.

At nearby Stump Cross, John rented another warehouse in Cat and Fiddle yard. Now that Benjamin was married, too, he may have bought yet another house. He certainly left Ben his fair share of the family fortune.

There are no asides left suggesting Elizabeth's opinion of Mary Pearce of Norwich, whom her youngest son, Edmund, married eighteen months after she wrote her disgruntled letter. For this couple, a house was bought at Mile End, outside the city walls. Edmund took after his namesake in becoming a devoted minister. Moreover he became clerk (the presiding officer and secretary combined) to the local Quaker business meeting. He had to name three of his sons Edmund, before one survived to grow up and, through trade with the Netherlands, bring a succession of Dutch brides into the family.

By the end of the second decade of the eighteenth century, the Norwich wool trade began to suffer a setback following the great boom. The import of cotton and calico from the West Indies was undercutting the finer woollens and silks of England. Increasing unemployment in Norwich led to rioting and tumult. Sir Robert Walpole had also suffered a setback. From first to last he had favoured religious tolerance; he was recognised as a great financier, and had become as keen as a Quaker on colonial settlements. But his love of peace, together with his opposition to King George I's demand for war, had cost him his power. Now, however, in 1720, he was recalled to help the government through the South Sea Bubble and a spate of other financial explosions, including the near-disaster in the woollen industry. John Gurney's eldest son was already known as The Weavers' Friend for the interest he took in their welfare. Robert Walpole, as the Friends called him, now persuaded him to give evidence, to a committee of the Lords in Parliament, of the crisis in Norwich; this he did with an unexpected burst of oratory.

In reply to the suggestion that our woollen manufactures were not suitable to be exported to our plantations because of a worm that ate them there, young Gurney said 'We have a sort of worm called a moth in England and they probably have moths in the West Indies.' He knew of another worm that was a great devourer – namely calico – which, if importing it were not prevented by law, would eat out the wear of the woollen stuffs in England. The Lords were much entertained by his rhetoric. He then enlarged on the subject of smuggled calico, using experience gained on his wife's Hadduck estates near Cromer, to observe that 'drapers go in their coaches on sundays and load them back with enough "run" calico to keep both coach and horses.' He went on to describe the deplorable conditions of the unemployed, reducing the Lords first to uncontrollable laughter and then to tears.

On Gurney's return from the mission, the people of Norwich arranged to meet him twenty miles outside and escort him home in triumph. However, this did not suit his Quaker modesty and when he heard of their intentions, he avoided their ovation by arriving much earlier in the morning than was expected. This did not prevent them, however, from engraving his portrait as their public hero with the inscription 'The woollen manufacturies' glory. To the immortal praise of John Gurney of Norwich, who by his celebrated extempore speeches, February 1720 before ye honourable House of Commons, turned the scale of contention between the linen and woollen manufacturers.'

His father was able to read his son's speeches in full in the *Norwich Gazette or Loyal Packet*, and to hear that 'in consequence of the talent he displayed', he was offered a seat in the House of Commons by Robert Walpole and his brother Horace, 'with both of whom he lived in terms of intimacy'. But the offer was declined as being incompatible with his son's religion.

An Act of Parliament was passed to save the woollen and silk manufacturers; it prohibited the wear of calico, with a penalty for each offence on the wearer, and of £20 on the seller. With four sons coming up to be master weavers, the old Quaker must have had a long quiet chuckle, while hopefully thanking God that the weavers' families also would now be fed.

The following year Sir Robert Walpole began to convert his old manor house of Houghton into the magnificent palace that it still is today and the Weavers' Friend bought land near the Hadduck estate, including some at Mannington, in whose moated hall, 'Old Lady Potts' still kept the late Sir Roger's liquor, even if she did not live there herself. Sir Roger had constantly quarrelled with his son over debts, and told him it was 'perfect nonsense that he should divest himself of his estate', and he did 'not propose selling Great Ellingham'. However, he eventually did sell it to Francis Colman, an ancestor of the great mustard family of Norwich, which gave rise to the quip that 'old Lady Potts had sold her birthright, not for a mess of potage but for a Pott of Mustard.'

During John Gurney's last year he became obsessed with certainty ('although inaccurate' as the pencilled note describing the aberration points out) that, had he not joined the Society of Friends, he would be known as Earl Gurney. He was probably confused by his son's success and his speech to the Lords, but the writer of the note preferred to suggest that the old fellow referred to his own ancient line, adding with his pencil that his un-Quakerly son, Benjamin, was seen to keep a very long family tree inside his herbal. He left it to his daughter, who lent it to her more Quakerly cousin who, no doubt very properly in the circumstances, lost it.

John Gurney died on 12th December, 1721, aged sixty-six. He was buried as silently as he was married, in the old Dutch garden that the Friends had bought as their burial ground, the Gilden-croft or Buttercup Field. This was the garden John cared for when he first came to Norwich as a lad, ten years before the capacious Gildencroft meeting house was built at one end of this peaceful garden.

Chapter Four

Joseph and Hannah
1727–1761

The two Norfolk houses that Joseph and Hannah Gurney lived in are still standing. To the Court House, Magdalen Street, they added Keswick Old Hall, the country house where nine generations of Gurney descendants have lived, thus accumulating the kind of personal papers, pictures and furniture that bring more light to this particular line than to any of John and Elizabeth Gurney's four sons, all of whom were admitted to the freedom of the city of Norwich within two years of their father's death in 1721.

Joseph's elder brother, John, the Weavers' Friend, made the most money, aided by the lion's share of his father's legacy, together with the Hadduck property. Joseph was not far behind. Their youngest brother, Edmund, was the most Quakerly, believing in high thinking and low living, though not so low as to go without a horse and carriage. Brother Benjamin was always the most independent. With his share of his father's inheritance, he set up his own loom, but was always more interested in new techniques than in making a fortune. He experimented in making a glossy finish to woollens, bringing them up to a high glaze with hot irons. Sons and grandsons of Benjamin won their freedom of Norwich as hot pressers rather than as weavers. Unlike the rest of the family, none married cousins, and some went off to become cutlers in Sheffield, watchmakers in Bristol, and general merchants in New York and Beavoir Town, U.S.A. Indeed, it was only when visiting their grandmother at the old corner house in Norwich that Benjamin's children appear to have met their cousins at all. Her other grandchildren met frequently, liked each

76

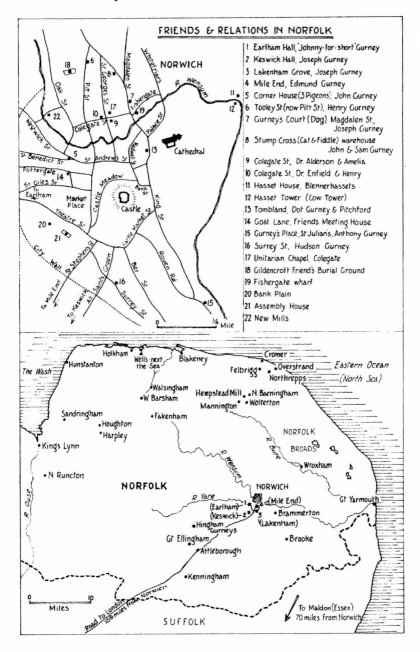

FRIENDS & RELATIONS IN NORFOLK

1 Earlham Hall, 'Johnny-for-short' Gurney
2 Keswick Hall, Joseph Gurney
3 Lakenham Grove, Joseph Gurney
4 Mile End, Edmund Gurney
5 Corner House (3 Pigeons), John Gurney
6 Tooley St (now Pitt St), Henry Gurney
7 Gurney's Court (Dog) Magdalen St., Joseph Gurney
8 Stump Cross (Cat & Fiddle) warehouse John & Sam Gurney
9 Colegate St., Dr. Alderson & Amelia
10 Colegate St, Dr. Enfield & Henry
11 Hasset House, Blennerhassets
12 Hasset Tower (Cow Tower)
13 Tombland, Dot Gurney & Pitchford
14 Goat Lane, Friends Meeting House
15 Gurney's Place, St Julians, Anthony Gurney
16 Surrey St, Hudson Gurney
17 Unitarian Chapel, Colegate
18 Gildencroft Friend's Burial Ground
19 Fishergate wharf
20 Bank Plain
21 Assembly House
22 New Mills

other and, in the case of the Weavers' Friend's son and Edmund's daughter, eventually married each other.

Of Joseph's and Hannah's ten children, only four grew up. 'Young' Hannah was the eldest. She was not so good-looking as her mother, but she was full of 'kind and lively affection'. The second child, Johnny, for whom his grandmother 'was sent for strait' when he was a baby, cast off his infantile disorders and waxed strong and 'very remarkable for the beauty of his person of face and figure'. His brother Sam, seven years younger, was not so fortunate. He was born lame and remained puny and often poorly throughout his life. Johnny adored him. Everybody adored him. A note to Joseph signed 'thy most affectionate loving wife Hannah' mentions that their daughter sends 'dear love to Sam; as is also mine. Accept the same (my dearest) to thyself.' No 'settlement', as the family called the settling down for reading, talking, or quiet, was complete without Sammy, whose chair, evidently a light open form of sedan, was borne into place by the willing hands of father, brother or Quaker servants. A long garden stretched right back to the street behind it, and in the summer the family sat here under the trees, with the children playing about them. Their kitchen garden lay behind the next house to theirs.

In 1728 the down-to-earth grandmother, whose price was above rubies, was laid to rest in the Gildencroft garden. No stone marked her grave or that of her husband as it was believed that headstones tended to 'exalt the creature'.

A year later the last of Hannah's children was born, 'young' Joseph. Despite her ten confinements over fifteen years, Hannah kept her good looks and figure. A painting survives of her at this time, wearing, strangely for a Quaker, a rose-coloured silk gown with a braided bodice over a white fichu in a style that, like the inner cap to her bonnet, must have been considered simple then, compared with the elaborate fashions of the day. The portrait shows a strong, serene and lovely face and a graceful figure. An engraving of it was made and printed with a rhyme beneath it intended to encourage the young to make themselves attractive without the aid of external deckings.

No gold nor Gems are wanting to the maid
In neat simplicity, like this array'd;
Plain native beauty more delights the heart
Than all the glittering ornaments of the art.
The fair Quaker.

Besides bringing up her family, attending to her housekeeping
in a pure and wholesome manner, taking the children to Meeting
and caring for the poor, Hannah was the first Quaker to introduce the arts into the family. Her brother-in-law's glass-making
brought other craftsmen and designers into her and her sister's
lives. French and Dutch craftsmen in many mediums tended to
congregate in Norwich. Scientists and medical doctors also
gathered 'in high proportions'. Science was considered a safe
subject for Quakers to discuss, and they were urged to study
nature as a proper way of involvement with the inscrutable ways
of the Creator. Friends were encouraged 'to visit one another, to
hear or read history, to speak soberly of the present or past
transactions; to follow after gardening; to use geometrical and
methematical experiments, and such other things of this
nature'.

A companion piece to the engraving of Hannah was one of her
more portly husband, Joseph, whose Gurney mouth and chin
still bears the innocence of a child, and not yet the forcefulness of
later years. His fair hair is covered with a black Quaker hat and
curled wig. The plain, well-cut coat is of shining silk. Each shirt
sleeve is minutely gathered into a slim band. His cravat is neat,
and he carries gloves and a silver-topped walking-stick. Here was
a well-to-do comely fellow in early middle age, answering, it
would seem likely, to the lines inscribed below his portrait:

Virtues unfeign'd, simplicity and truth,
These are the pride of age, the grace of youth – A Quaker –
'Tis not the hat, or coat, the wise will scan
What dwells within, this recommends the man. – A Quaker –

There is a tantalising reference to 'a very interesting manuscript account of him' which 'testimony is remarkably well

drawn up, and gives a high idea of Joseph Gurney as a man of principle and devotedness of life'. There might have been much more to tell about him if only his great-grandson could have left the trunk alone which, he writes, contained not only Joseph's papers but also those of his father. 'They are of all sorts, many about the Friends of those days, giving pictures of a set of people living amongst themselves. They seem to have corresponded and lived among their own – Friends and brothers, uncles and cousins. There are seventy-nine yearly retrospects of the march of Joseph's fortune.' Later, this great-grandson notes that he would see what room there might be 'in the bank rooms for such of the old papers as well may be kept and burn or destroy, at some paper mill, the rest.' Alas, it was the march of fortune that most interested the bank.

However, not a birth, marriage or death went unrecorded within the practising Quaker families, and to some extent much of the restrained joy, pain, anguish, delight and sorrow can be read into these, when backed by the few surviving personal letters. Many questions will still go unanswered. How much were the first-cousin marriages (which the Quaker Yearly Meeting advised against as early as 1675) against the wishes of parents and how much were they contrived to prevent fortunes marching out of the family?

It was now not unusual for whole families to go together to London to attend the Yearly Meeting[1] in the City. London Quakers offered hospitality, which was returned if the host's family visited their guests' areas. Did Joseph and Hannah's only daughter, 'young' Hannah, meet the forty-six-year-old widower of her choice in London or in Norfolk? Nathaniel Springall (who had a grown-up son, known as 'Nat',) was the widower of one of the ten Barclay sisters, 'all singularly beautiful except for a slight

---

[1] In an effort to avoid making any hard and fast rules, it was not until 1738 that any centrally agreed 'collection of council' was made available for quarterly meetings. *The Book of Extracts* was now prepared for each quarterly meeting. 'Advice collected from reports at yearly meetings was recorded in chronological order under subject headings, alphabetically arranged, although such an arrangement was not permitted in any list of persons, which had to be haphazard.'

defect of the figure' (rounded shoulders and drooping bosoms). Their father, David Barclay, Quaker, merchant, tycoon, was renowned for his hospitality in his great house in Cheapside. David Barclay may well have invited the Joseph Gurneys to Cheapside, or he may have taken his own young to Norfolk. Caroline, another of his ten ineptly nick-named 'hunch-backed beauties', married John Lindoe of Norwich.

The majority of Quakers met their matches coming out of Meeting or at the great solid meals in Quaker houses afterwards. But another age-old opportunity for engagements to be made, which was not banned to Quakers, was in the field of sport. Hunting, shooting and fishing were still regarded not only as necessities for filling the pot, but also as 'innocent divertisements which may sufficiently serve for relaxation'. Hunting was looked upon as a normal form of husbandry and exercise. Fishing was seen as a means of practising a skill while giving an opportunity for peaceful meditation.

Thus Joseph and Edmund conscientiously enjoyed shooting with their elder brother, the Weavers' Friend, on the Hadduck estate, where Little Barningham manor was becoming more of a shooting-box than a farmhouse. The ancient moated hall of Mannington, whose land marched with the Hadducks', was in the process of being sold by the current Lady Potts to Horatio Walpole, who had nearly finished building his great house of Wolterton Hall a mile from Mannington. He used the same architect as Thomas Coke was employing to raise his palace at Holkham an hour or so's ride away. Shooting was not then the highly organised pursuit it later became. It was more of a stroll or a ride across parts of several gentlemen's estates by previous arrangement, with servants rather than beaters in attendance, with spare ponies and game-carts. These informal business and political shooting-days often combined Walpole, Hadduck and Potts properties, sometimes extending in the other direction as far as Felbrigg, where Ash Wyndham's romantic house (now a National Trust heritage) was enjoying a lull between Jacobean and Georgian rebuilding. Such shoots, according to the vagaries of the quarry, were sometimes continued on to land marching

81

with Felbrigg owned by another sporting Quaker landlord, Richard Kett[2] of Roughton. Here the usual Quaker hospitality was shown, whether after a religious meeting or a meet of hounds.

Richard Kett was an indisputable direct descendant of Kett the Rebel, who was hanged in chains from Norwich Castle in 1549 as was his brother hanged from Wyndham Steeple. The family of Kett (pronounced Kit, and spelt, almost up to the time of the hangings, 'le Chat') had held farms in Norfolk certainly since the thirteenth century. Robert the Rebel has always been regarded by his family as a martyr to a worthy cause – in this case the poor. The fighting he incited in Norwich during that hot summer of 1549 was skipped lightly over by even his strictest Quaker descendants.

Richard Kett's wife was a Hope, of the merchant family of Amsterdam, that long-recognised haven of the fleeing persecuted. Their new neighbour, Horatio Walpole, became ambassador to the Hague on two occasions, one lasting seven years, which may have had some bearing on his friendship with the Ketts.

Inevitably the young, meeting at shooting-picnics and on mere- and sea-fishing expeditions, fell in love. But the penalty for Friends marrying out of the Society was expulson. Thus the Ketts, Hopes and Gurneys were left to marry each other.

Like his brother the Prime Minister, Mr. Walpole combined politics and business with sport. Consultations with the Weavers' Friend and his brother Joseph Gurney on finance and with Edmund Gurney on the problems of the American colonies went hand in glove with pleasant days out in the woods lying inland from Cromer and Sheringham. Serious Quakers were much concerned with the iniquity of the slave system which was still being carried on in their own colony of Pennsylvania. Although they regarded war as ungodly, they were content

[2] Several Ketts had married into the family of le Neve, distinguished heralds and genealogists, including Peter le Neve (1661–1729) Rouge Croix pursuivant (F.R.S.), whose copious notes form the backbone of the *History of Norfolk* begun by Parson Blomefield (1705–52).

enough to be protected by the arms of others, and paid towards the fortification of New York. Horace Walpole, who had been made surveyor of plantation revenues for life, admitted that he had much to learn from the Quakers' knowledge of this particular colony and the lines on which it was run – free ownership, democratic assembly with universal suffrage and vote by ballot, trial by jury, no imprisonment for debt, state education for orphans, the severest laws being against intemperance, swearing, card-playing 'and other evil sports and games'. There was no suggestion yet that there was anything un-Christian in owning slaves. William Penn himself had owned them, only leaving them their freedom in his will which they gained after his death in 1718.

Edmund admitted that the very virtues of the Quakers, their stubborn determination and consistency of purpose, made them a difficult people to govern even by their own laws. Edmund, (of the second attempt at the name) married first a Kett, then a Hope, and thirdly a van Vliereden, also of Amsterdam origin (although the 'van' was considered too titular for Friends, and became plain 'Fleurden'). 'Young' Hannah Gurney married Nathaniel Springall, who was a nephew of Richard Kett, in 1739, the same year that her handsome brother Johnny married another of Richard Kett's daughters, Elizabeth, known as 'Bett Kett' (pronounced 'Bit Kit'). Nathanial Springall only survived two years of his marriage to 'young' Hannah. Their baby died a year later. Johnny and Bett also lost their first baby, but a sturdy son, Richard, was born to Bett, three weeks after baby Springall's death.

Reaction to all this can only be surmised from accounts of other occasions in the family when joy and relief, mingled with sorrow, were all faced with the same quiet equanimity. It was ten years before Hannah remarried. All three generations continued to live together in the Magdalen Street court house over the business premises where Joseph had placed his son, Johnny, and later Sammy in his carrying chair, in the counting house. Their young brother, Joseph, was still a schoolboy.

Johnny was exceptionally well-equipped to go into a thriving firm that was all ready for expansion. He was naturally astute, but, for him, the Quaker code of absolute integrity in business was inflexible. Integrity came before all else. He was a man of great activity and energy and, in spite of extensive business engagements, devoted much time to the Society of Friends, attending meeting regularly, and four times he served as clerk of the Yearly Meeting in London, an office also filled by John Fry, who was to become grandfather of Elizabeth Fry's husband.

It was said that Johnny Gurney took his good looks from his father, his opportunities in business from one uncle (the Weavers' Friend), and his status in Quakerism from another, Edmund. Perhaps he also took a little independence from his third uncle, Benjamin. For he now started to branch out in the yarn trade. Machine-spun yarn was still unknown, and since, as a result of his uncle's advocacy, the law had been passed to help the woollen industry, hand-spun yarn from the Norfolk and Suffolk villages was inadequate for the, again, clattering Norwich looms. Johnny searched for a surplus source of hand-spun yarn and found it in southern Ireland. He arranged for it to be shipped from Cork to Yarmouth and then brought it by river to Norwich, where it was unloaded on the Gurney quays. Far from being accused of under-cutting local spinners, Johnny and his brother Sam were later applauded for giving more employment not only to the Norwich weavers but also to the hitherto impoverished southern Irish. It came as a genuine surprise when Sam pointed out to their father that they were already making a fortune for the family.

On Johnny's first appointment in 1745 as clerk to the Yearly Meeting for Great Britain, held in London, his father and sister, Hannah and Springall, accompanied him. When the meetings were over Johnny went to Amsterdam to investigate the state of trade abroad. Much of the worsted damask and light-weight cloth, dyed in alluring colours, was exported from Norwich to Holland, then often on to France, Spain, Italy and Portugal under the trade mark enforced by the Norwich Worsted Weavers. Few of the principal merchants and manufacturers of Norwich were strangers to Holland, for many had been sent to Amsterdam or Rotterdam for their commercial education.

Joseph wrote to his wife from London

84

'8 4th month 1745

My dear, Notwithstanding Hannah's writing otherwise, Johnny went from thence this morning [this was the same Johnny for whom his grandmother was 'sent for strait' when he was only three months old] wish ye may have a safe journey. Weather being extream wett and some danger of the water being out, but he promised would run nor risque. I likewise would have set forward this day but Hannah could not well get ready. Hope today we shall be moving homeward and I should well reach home 5th or 6th day. This with my endeared love ends from Thy affectionate husband Joseph Gurney.

Joseph and his daughter Hannah, when she was ready, returned to Norwich in time to see, and, as good Quakers, to ignore, the great archway erected in the market-place, and the illuminations all over the city in thanksgiving for the suppression of the '45 Rebellion in Scotland.

With the great upward surge of trade in Norwich, riches gathered quickly everywhere. Merchant-squires rebuilt their manor houses, and city merchants, who had only recently made their fortunes, rented or bought estates, mostly within driving distance of their city warehouses. The new roads were solid enough to make it possible to live in the country, at any rate for most months of the year. Norfolk was already rich in ancient brick halls and manor houses, many of which were now being wholly or partially concealed by the new smart display of Palladianism.

An added incentive to living in the country was the great revolution in farming. The 2nd Viscount Townshend had earlier in the century brought the first turnip seeds over from Hanover and planted them at Raynham, and, 'wishing to watch them come up', had added many comforts to his already splendid country house in order to make this possible. Thanks to 'Turnip Townshend', as his lordship was nicknamed, and to his friend Thomas Coke of Holkham (later to become the 1st Earl of Leicester), together with the enthusiasm of the young landlords who studied commerce in the Netherlands and brought back modern Dutch methods, the county was soon ahead of all others in agricultural techniques. The Norfolk System was to become famous throughout England. Instead of leaving land to lie fallow for one year in three, wheat, turnips, barley and clover were planted in a four-year rotation, thus producing a much greater yield of human foodstuffs than before, with enough fodder to keep livestock alive throughout the winter and so to avoid the slaughtering of immature stock.

Coke was as keen on building his fine Palladian seat of Holkham Hall as he was in grazing sheep on the land around it. Sir Jacob Astley carried out vast improvements on his already magnificent Melton Constable Hall. William Woodhouse built and then enlarged an impressive Kimberley Hall near its ancient predecessor. But of all the great houses of Norfolk, whether adapted from medieval castles or unfortified manors or built as palaces or stately homes, the most magnificent of the fine palaces to be built or rebuilt in Norfolk during the middle of the eighteenth century was the Prime Minister's replacement of the Walpole family manor at Houghton. With its giant columns, its classical domes above its richly-carved pediment, its noble bays and Venetian windows set in angle pavilions, its splendour towered above all others. His descendants live there still. Inside, he dedicated the lower floor 'to hunters, hospitality, noise, dirt and business', rather as the merchants kept theirs for trade, 'and the *piano nobile* to taste, expense, state and parade'. He covered the walls with rich panelling and silk, the ceilings with painted cherubs and garlands, and surrounded the doors with sumptuous carvings. He then furnished the house with specially-designed pieces. Downstairs these were solid but of fine craftsmanship and upstairs elegant and stately enough for his more favoured political and commercial guests to lounge upon, lean against, sit at or lie in. With a fortune made from prudent speculation in the South Sea Company and advice from others well versed in commerce, he began to form a picture gallery of outstanding merit. He had married the daughter of the Lord Mayor of London and had three sons, one of whom had three illegitimate daughters, all of whom made spectacular marriages. Illegitimacy was not much of a stumbling-block among the rich, powerful and beautiful. But soon the Prime Minister of George I and II was no longer rich or powerful. He died in 1745, £40,000 in debt. Whatever advice he may have taken from the Gurneys on government spending, he can hardly have followed it in his private affairs. Extravagance, overspending and, above all, getting into debt were forbidden in the tenets of the Society of Friends. Thus the Quakers moved into the country with caution, often renting rather than buying houses, but not too far from the city to cause unnecessary expense. A walk of an hour or two to the city was not considered a waste of time. They kept horses and carriages adequate for their work, family attendance at meetings, and travel and sport, but not for show. The same applied to their estates. They were all maintained with enough produce from their farms and gardens to live on, give away and to enable their owners to entertain generously but not lavishly. Their indoor and outdoor staff was expected to be clean, sober and loyal, but not unduly subservient. Richard Kett's son, wishing to live all the year round in the country, sold the family estates at Roughton, near Cromer, and bought Seething House, nearer to Norwich, an early seventeenth-century gabled house with mullioned windows, which still stands, near Seething's round-towered Norman church.

It was in the same year, 1747, that Joseph Gurney bought Keswick Old Hall, four miles from Norwich. He and Hannah, their widowed daughter and the two younger, still unmarried, sons, Samuel and 'young' Joseph, moved there, leaving the living quarters of the court House, Magdalen Street, to Johnny and Bett and their increasing family.

The land at Keswick, with some kind of a house and outbuildings, with a dove-cot, orchard and hop ground, had originally belonged to the Elizabethan Sir Henry Hobart, who built Blickling Hall. It had only changed families twice since then. When Joseph bought Keswick Hall it was a simple rectangular house of no particular period, with one crow-stepped gabled porch, and a formal parterre garden behind. Attractive farm buildings across a lane still form an arched gateway suggesting an Italian farmyard. The rambling additions of large shady trees and summer-houses were yet to come. Keswick mill, with its jolly three-bay miller's house by the weir, on the River Wensum, was part of the deal. The Old Hall remained in the Gurney family till this decade and Keswick New Hall, built much later, has only just ceased to belong to the family and is now, like Earlham Hall, part of the University of East Anglia.

Joseph had only a short time to enjoy his new home. His last illness was one of great suffering, but he said cheerfully that it had been the business of his whole life to prepare for such a time. He died in 1750, leaving Hannah, the 'Fair Quaker', to preside over Keswick.

By the end of that year all four sons of John and Elizabeth Gurney of Charing Cross, Norwich, were dead. The eldest brother, the Weavers' friend, had died some time before, and his eldest son, known as 'John of Brooke', who had married his first cousin, the daughter of Edmund, clerk of the Meeting House, of Mile End, Norwich, now rented Brooke Old Hall, a house of extreme antiquity 'bought fairly' by an abbot of Bury St. Edmunds, to which community the property had been given by William the Conqueror. John of Brooke's younger but taller brother, Henry Gurney, (married to the daughter of an already well-known apothecary, Dr. Benjamin Bartlett of Bolton, York-shire) regarded Little Barningham Manor as his country house. Both brothers worked together as partners, living most of the year with their families over their place of business at 35 Tooley Street, now Pitt Street, Norwich, in which building they eventually opened the first Gurney's bank.

With Keswick to visit for country pursuits, Johnny now rarely went to north Norfolk with his cousins, who continued to shoot and fish over their own land and, to some extent, as they always had, over their various neighbours'. The alliance between the late Prime Minister's brother Horatio and the late Weavers' Friend's sons, now aged thirty-two and twenty-nine, was beginning to wear thin. Mr. Walpole's gardener reported that he had come upon the Gurneys and their party shooting pheasants on part of the one-time Potts's land, at Mannington, which had lately been bought by Horatio Walpole. Considering how he was satirised by his contemporaries 'for his brusque speech' he showed tolerable restraint in the letter he wrote to the Gurneys complaining of nothing more than 'a deliberate and unprovoked distruction' of his game by those whom he had always treated as his particular friends. He mentions that if they had only let him know they wanted 'a day's frolick' he would gladly have ordered his gamekeeper to attend to them and gratify them, in proper places, but certainly not in his pheasant nursery. Moreover, that the 'tall Mr. Gurney' (Henry) had been seen to kill a hen pheasant, and Mr. Walpole emphasised that the most notorious poachers were more discreet than that, unless they had a particular spite against a gentleman. 'I will not have so mean an opinion of you as to imagine that you take this licence because you give me your votes and interest to serve in parliament for Norwich, and I hope you have not so mean an opinion of me to imagine that I dare not presume on that account to mention it to you. I may by this time say that I am very vexed.'

The brothers replied individually, exercising an economy, much favoured later in the family, of using the same sheet of paper. They wrote respectfully but with what Walpole described as a 'sturdy attitude', combining peaceful words with their refusal to yield.

John of Brooke, who denied being with Henry's party at Barningham on the day in question, dropped a hint that much game was being killed in the area unbeknown to any of them, and both brothers suggested that Mr. Horatio Walpole's gamekeeper was probably in the habit of killing his master's game and selling it in Norwich. He writes that it was 'notorious that a number of pheasants and hares that had come to the city every week would not be so great if gentlemen's gamekeepers did their duty' – and this despite the law forbidding the selling of game. Henry confessed to shooting the hen pheasant, but John of Brooke said that his family's sole purpose in shooting over their Barningham estate was to get a little game for presents for merchant friends in Norwich. He would not admit that there was any pleasure in the sport.

The Gurneys later employed Smith, regularly gamekeeper to

the Bishop of Norwich, to shoot some more pheasants for
presents for their customers, on their own estate. Unfortunately
Smith also trespassed in the Walpole woods. This time Walpole
informed the Bishop, who sacked Smith. Walpole wrote again
with less restraint to John of Brooke, complaining of Smith's
behaviour 'in pretending to take upon himself to kill game three
days together in my grove under your authority'. He ends 'my
good friend I do not deserve this usage.' The correspondence
went on into several letters in which John of Brooke tried to
avoid further trouble, though, having never taken measures to
detain all the birds that came on to his land, as some landlords
would, he 'could hardly be regarded as a common poacher'.
Walpole emphasised that he was not 'of a peevish and revengeful
disposition', and he asked the Bishop to take Smith back. There
he hoped the matter would be 'forgot', and if ever the Gurneys
wanted a brace of pheasants or more he would be pleased to
arrange for his gamekeeper to deliver them.

The whole affair suggests a probably quite unconscious cock-
robin instinct over territorial rights. Towards the end of the
correspondence news came that the late Prime Minister's son had
died, and that his grandson, George Walpole, aged twenty-one,
had inherited the title of 3rd Earl of Orford, together with the
house and treasures at Houghton. George was described as a
charming figure with the easy, genuine air of a man of quality but
his uncle, Horace Walpole, the author, who was eventually to
succeed him, said that he had a stammer and made promises
everywhere which he never kept. 'Drinks without inclination;
has women, not without inclination, bragged as much as an old
man, was immeasurably obstinate and embarked upon preposterous wagers.' George made one of these in the form of a race
between five turkeys and five geese waddling between Norwich
and London. The winner of the stake of £500 was to be the owner
of whichever team reached the City of London with the smallest
losses. Although gambling was outside Quaker approval, the
race itself was considered quite sporting. Escapades such as that
of Lord Orford driving his team of four red deer in his phaeton
when they were unexpectedly hunted by a pack of hounds cross-

ing the road also caused mild amusement among the sporting Quakers, though George's uncle was deeply shocked. Grooms and outriders could not stop the stag, and the huntsmen were unable to call off their hounds. Just in time the stag turned in at the inn in Newmarket where the hounds were usually stabled, and ostlers closed the doors on the pack. Mr. Walpole was even more shocked when his nephew sold the Houghton treasures to Catherine, Empress of Russia, for £40,000 in order to pay off his grandfather's debts. In the eyes of the Gurneys this was a highly commendable act, though Mr. Walpole considered that he was 'stripping the temple of glory and of his affections'. Lord Orford never married his mistress, Patty, former housemaid at Houghton, but, under the name of Mrs. Turk she presided over his table in such a respectable way that clergymen, church organists, lawyers, bankers and other reputable businessmen now mingled with the horse-dealers and racing crowd from Newmarket who had replaced the politicians in Houghton's former glory. However, for the Gurneys, what really severed the friendship was Lord Orford raising, with his cousin, Lord Townshend, the Norfolk militia in preparation for what was to become the Seven Years War.

Through Quaker thrift and lack of the fashionable show of the times, the Gurneys were now very much better off than their titled neighbours. John and Henry Gurney, in Tooley Street, Norwich, were still general merchants; young Edmund dealt more with the Dutch projects, and Johnny, backed by Sam, had gained the entire monopoly of the import of material for all the Norwich weavers, which he sold to the manufacturers, on credit, at his own risk. It was a risk worth taking, for so greatly was he respected that he was always repaid. And he, in turn, writes in his journal that 'neither the temptation of prosperity nor the kindness of esteem of the great men of this world' would permit him to stray from what he believed to be true.

At Keswick, Hannah Springall had recovered sufficiently by 1752 to remarry. Once again she married a widower of one of the ten Barclay beauties, Timothy Bevan, which caused him to be referred to, rightly, as his 'wife's husband's wife's sister's widower.' Her only son was born the following year, and now her youngest brother, 'young' Joseph Gurney, married yet another of David Barclay's ten daughters, Christiana, the youngest, who was then sixteen.

In due course the first of half-Gurney, half-Barclay babies was born to Christiana at the great house in Cheapside, originally known as the Sign of the Bear. It had been built on three sites after the Great Fire between Milk Street and Honey Lane, with its extensive living apartments over its high warehouses and counting-houses.

Joseph and Christiana's second daughter was born two years later at Keswick, where all Hannah's (the 'Fair Quaker's') grandchildren met whenever possible. One of her nieces, a daughter of Henry Gurney, remembered her at this time; 'tall and, when I knew her, a remarkably fine, dignified old lady who survived her husband ten years'.

Only six months later, Joseph took his young wife Christiana with their two little girls, Prissy and Chrissy, aged four and two, and their nursery-maid for a row on the Broads; there was a slight mist over the water and, a few days later, Joseph, the children and the nursery-maid became seriously ill with a fever which was believed to be due to 'the miasma rising from the malarial swamps of Wroxham Broad' (though more likely it was some virus infection). The children recovered and so did the nursery-maid, but Joseph died, aged thirty-two, leaving his beautiful wife and two pretty, flaxen-haired, straight-backed little daughters to live on in Great Yarmouth. They retained the affectionate interest of the children's Gurney cousins in Norfolk, while paying frequent visits to their paternal grandfather, David Barclay of Cheapside, in London.

Like the Guerneys, the Barclays had for centuries been country land-owners who were not averse to taking up arms until turning Quaker in the seventeenth century.

Chapter Five

Robert and the Colonel
1639–1669

At the time when the Elizabethan Henry Gurney was restoring
his moated heritage in Norfolk, George Barclay was keeping his
ancestral fortress in order on the east coast of Scotland. The estate
of Mathers, in the Mearns, had been in the Barclay family for
well over two hundred and fifty years, as shown in its 'grant of
Mathers 1351'. A generation later, when Parson Edmund
Gurney was teasing the bishops of Norwich, the Barclays were
forced to sell their beloved home. In 1642, the eldest Barclay son,
David, aged fourteen, left Scotland to join the Swedish army as a
soldier of fortune. In a scarlet tunic, white-plumed hat, full
trunks, high black boots and gilt spurs, he fought for Gustavus
Adolphus, Protestant king of Sweden, against the Roman
Catholic forces of the Austrian Empire. Gustavus left a mark on
each man that is still recognisable in history in a sense of honour,
fearless courage, cheerful acceptance of adversity, clear-
headedness, and strong Christian principles. It was to him that
young Barclay undoubtedly owed a particular quality that he was
able to pass on through his later commitment to Quakerism at its
most perilous period. Just before Gustavus was killed in battle at
the age of thirty-eight, Barclay was recalled to Scotland to help to
suppress what was described as a local dispute. He and his fellow
Scots officers had not even landed off the coast of Yorkshire
when their ship was attacked by a hostile force who took their
'saidles and pistoles', and only when they found themselves
prisoners did they realise that England was on the brink of civil
war.

They appealed to King Charles I, and were released to take part in the violent rebellion that had broken out in the north.[1] Scotland was divided into three great parties. One was that of the uncompromising Royalists, led by the King, who wanted one religion for all his people, dictated by the bishops and as laid out in the new Service Book. Then there were the equally extreme Covenanters, who abjured bishops, condemned the Service Book, and fought to restore the Presbyterian Church in Scotland. Thirdly there were those of the moderate party, who maintained that, although they were against the King's policy, they still supported the monarchy. Barclay threw in his lot with the moderate party, together with many of his Keith, Forbes and Creighton cousins. The party was later led by another Gilbert, 11th Earl of Erroll, earl marshal, cousin and close friend of Barclay. Barclay's duty was to 'be a sufficient guard to the Prince of Wales' person if he should land', of which there was some hope at that time. He was raised to general, and was to have 500 horses – besides his own regiment of horse, 'Barclay's Dragouners' – but with these he had to 'cover all of Scotland benorth the water of Tay'. But soon the parties were breaking up and reforming. Men of conscience were swayed this way and that, and it was impossible to tell where each man's loyalty lay. Personal quarrels were settled in the name of religion, and leaders thought nothing of burning each other's houses down and setting light to each other's crops with heedless abandon.

This was not war as taught by Gustavus, the Lion of the North, with his skilful sieges and well-defined systems crowned with honour. Following the ruthless sack of Aberdeen, the Colonel's younger brother, James, a captain in his own regiment, was killed at Philliphaugh in 1644 'on the long grass meadow that lies beside Ettrick water'. In the midst of all this bloodshed and destruction, George Fox's exhortations to renounce both war and professional clergy with the religious doctrines that were its cause, and 'listen only to God's voice within', fell like longed-

---

[1] The National Covenant of 1638 was the Scottish Presbyterians' answer to the Book of Common Prayer being imposed on the Scottish church.

for summer rain on many anxious and confused minds. It was during the northern risings that Colonel Barclay first heard Fox preach, although he did not throw in his lot with the Quakers for nearly twenty years. He was said to have a strong religious spirit, but his individuality of character, tenacity and inflexibility of purpose could also be interpreted as stubbornness, unpredictability and illogicality, for at the height of the 'troubles', when the Colonel was military governor, he entered the enemy's camp to woo and soon to win the hand of the daughter of Sir Robert Gordon, a staunch Covenanter. On Christmas Day, 1647, a contract of marriage was concluded between Colonel David Barclay and Katherine Gordon, known as the White Rose of Scotland. Her mother was Lady Jean, daughter of the 4th Earl of Huntley. Colonel Barclay, tall, fair-haired and now thirty-six years old, must have made a tremendous impression on Katherine's parents to be accepted by them. Her father was the premier baronet of Nova Scotia, son of the 12th Earl of Sutherland, and a second cousin of King James VI of Scotland. Sir Robert Gordon was vice-chamberlain of Scotland, historian of the House of Sutherland, and had been privy councillor and gentleman of the bedchamber to both James I and Charles I. The marriage contract was signed by several of Barclay's fellow officers, even though they had recently devastated the Gordon country. The contract stated that the Colonel was obliged to bestow on his bride about £5,000, to be settled by the advice of both fathers. This sum was somehow produced by a complicated mortgage arrangement, made in the hope of securing from Barclay's cousin Gilbert, the earl marshal, the ruined castle and estate of Ury, near the old Barclay estate of Mathers. David Barclay had left Scotland as a lad with nothing and, although professional soldiers were well rewarded where booty was available to be shared, he could hardly have returned with enough to replace the ancient family estate of Mathers with this new one, and marry an aristocratic wife. Perhaps he had already begun to do 'a bit of Barclay's banking on the side', for among his papers are acknowledgments of loans referred to 'in friendly borrowing' and a list of names of creditors to whom he had advanced sums of varying amounts of gold. Ury had been much reduced in value by warfare. Farms, cottages and buildings had been levelled to the ground. Growing crops had been ruthlessly trampled on. Stores of hay and corn had been burnt in their granaries. Plantations had been felled, and rotten trunks and trees had fallen into the stream and damned it, so that it spread out into swamps. Any of the wretched peasantry who had escaped the savagery of the soldiers had crept back to their ruined homes with no spirit to replant the land beyond the few acres necessary for their own maintenance. But to Barclay's pioneering spirit the desolate rock-dotted moor was a challenge, and as a man of vision he could see a future home, as beloved as Mathers had been, on the gently undulating ground among the little hills and southern slopes that lay between the coast and the howe of Mearns. As a sportsman he spotted the game on the hill and the salmon and trout leaping in the Cowie that sparkled over the stones below. As a man of business, he recognised the value of the easy approach to the port of Stonehaven, only two miles away by a good road.

The purchase of Ury was officially completed over a year later on his wedding-day, 26th January, 1648, but there was still to be a long wait before obtaining possession, owing at first to Gilbert's involvement in the military attempt to rescue Charles I from custody, and later on to Cromwellian stringencies.

Meanwhile the Colonel remained in command of Strathbogey castle, half an hour's ride from his wife's home of Gordonstoun (today the public school where royal princes are educated), standing in its howe facing the blue ranges of the Grampian hills. It was then one great medieval stronghold with walls eight feet thick and a tangle of secret passages and hidden staircases. 'The Bog of Gight', as it had hitherto been known, was a gloomy enough building seen from the outside, with small windows, high-pitched roofs and pepper-pot turrets as a sign of an owner-occupancy. But it was a safe place for the White Rose to bear and raise her children.

The first child, Robert, was born on 23rd December, 1648, only a month before the execution of Charles I whose absent son was immediately declared King Charles II in Scotland and

Ireland. He soon made the hoped-for landing in Scotland, where he was kept in hiding until his coronation at Scone on New Year's Day 1651. Gilbert, Earl Marshal, officiated, but after Charles had fled to Normandy, he was imprisoned and heavily fined by Cromwell, much of his land being forfeited. Colonel Barclay did what he could for his cousin, including obtaining an excellent allowance for his wife.

Gilbert wrote to him in 1659, 'Cousin I have received so many favours from you, especially the late evidence ye have given of your kindness and respects to me at this time.' He goes on to say that he hopes in return to be able to strengthen the conveyance of Ury to him 'by all that's in my power, as ye shall desire the same, with jovial heartiness. And I do entreat, that when anything relating to me shall come before you, that you will own the same for my interest and good.' He ends his letter with his wife asking to be remembered to the Colonel 'and we both to your lady and little Robin'.

'Little Robin', Robert, spent his early years at Gordonstoun with two younger brothers, two sisters and eight first cousins who all lived there at the same time. When their fathers and grandfather were absent on military and political business, Sir Robert Gordon's second wife, daughter of the scholarly dean of Salisbury, was in command. They all adored her and called her 'Manmaa'.

The long stone corridors and vaulted chambers of Gordonstoun Castle rang with the voices and laughter of the children of the stepson and daughters. All were brought up on strictly Presbyterian principles but much of the bleakness of Calvinism was outweighed by the charm and intelligence of their grandmother, the beauty of the two mothers and the lively interest of their grandfather's many and varied friends.

It was Manmaa who noticed Robert's exceptionally alert mind, and when he was about eleven years old, Colonel Barclay's brother, rector of the Scottish college in Paris, persuaded his parents to let him educate the boy in France. Robert was younger than his fellow pupils, but he did well and enjoyed the colourful life, though afterwards it filled him with remorse to

remember that he had been taught fencing and other gentlemanly, but distinctly un-Quakerly, subjects. He studied classics
and learnt to read volumes in their original French, Latin, Greek
and Hebrew. His uncle enjoyed teaching him and made a great
favourite of him.

Meanwhile Robert's mother, whose health was failing, became worried about the dangers of Roman Catholic influences at
a college that was designed for preparing Roman Catholic mis-
sionaries. She longed to see the boy and begged her husband to
fetch him. He promised to do so, but she died in March 1663,
aged forty-three, before he was able to set out.

A letter survives from Lucy Gordon to the Colonel, answering
one in which he must have agreed to bring her grandson home
from Paris. It is headed 'Gordonstoun, July 17th, 1663:

Dear Son, I received yours from London the 13th of April. I was
exceedingly glad to hear that you were well, for I did long much to
hear from you, all the things that you have sent to Edinburgh, I shall
use the best means I can to bring them here. Both your little boys
have had the pox, but very favourably. Davie was not sick at all with
them, but John had three days of fever, but it has done him much
good, for he is now very lusty and begins to find his tongue.

I bless God for the resolution you have taken to fetch your son,
although your brother would not send him to you by the Rhine, yet I
cannot believe he will keep him against your will. You should do
well to walk wisely to get your son with the consent of his uncle, but
if he will not, then you had better want his kindness than buy it with
the loss of your son.

I am old, and although I praise God in health for the present, yet I
know not whenever I shall see you. I desire you to see your little ones
bred in the ways of God, and I shall pray the Lord to continue you to
them and that they may be comforts to you. This is the prayer of your
affectionate mother to serve you, Lucy Gordon.

It was typical of the dean's daughter that she should, within
two paragraphs of her letter, both ask her stepson-in-law to keep
the ten commandments and at the same time advise him, that if

his brother refused to give up his brilliant and attractive son he had better 'want his kindness' and kidnap him.

At last the Colonel was able to set out on the dangerous and uncomfortable journey from Gordonstoun to Paris. Here he found his son steeped in the doctrines of the Roman Church and his brother unwilling to part with his promising pupil, now nearly fifteen. But the Colonel stood firm against his brother, who now offered to make the boy his heir. It was agreed that Robert should decide for himself.

Robert was fond of his uncle and grateful for the lively argumentative teaching and intellectual opportunities in Paris, but he knew his duty. 'He is my father', he said 'and must be obeyed.' His uncle was so incensed that he bequeathed all his wealth to religious houses in France, with instructions for an inscription to go on his grave referring to his lineal descent from the sovereigns of every country in Europe that could be fitted on to the tablet, ending up with his 'warm attachment to the most holy Roman church was the more remarkable as it was opposed by most of his countrymen'.

For Robert it must have felt strange to be back at Gordonstoun. Not only had his mother died while he was away, but also his grandfather. Manmaa, his step-grandmother, welcomed him warmly and allowed him to work in his grandfather's great library.

On his return from Paris, the Colonel made a courageous move. Although he had not yet decided to adopt the tenets of the Quakers, a record states that he 'declined from doctrine and discipline of the kirk, denying it to be a kirk. The Synod orders him to be processed.'

Thus began a series of discussions and arguments in which the Colonel, as a member first of the Scottish Parliament and then of Cromwell's, preserved his independent outlook and finally severed his connections with the covenanting party.

Every day he found 'a fresh evidence of the world's instability in all conditions from the king on the throne to the beggar on the dung hill'. It was time, he felt, to spend the remainder of his days wholly in the service of God. He examined the credentials of all variations of Protestant religions and found the Quakers to be 'a plain, sober, self-denied religious people', that they 'neither taught nor exercised war, that they loved one another, their practice was agreeable to the standard accorded in the New Testament'.

When Robert was eighteen, his father was suddenly arrested and imprisoned in Edinburgh Castle at the instigation of the Royalist party, although he insisted that there had never been a time when he was not loyal to his sovereign. At first, punishment was more in the nature of heavy fines than actual long detention, and the Colonel was able to continue living at Gordonstoun much of the time, for Ury was still in a state of complete dilapidation.

It was during the year of the Fire of London, 1666, that the Colonel embraced the Quaker faith, and his son Robert also felt 'constrained to embrace the same doctrine'. Robert was soon in zealous dispute with eminent scholars of theology, not only verbally but also in writing. Joining the Quakers put him in direct opposition to the young men of his age and background, whose levity and extravagance led by the court, in manners, dress and customs, were almost universal. Such fashions as men swirling their hats from their heads on the approach of ladies or social superiors had only lately been introduced from France. Hitherto hats were worn everywhere, at court, indoors, at meals and in church, and were only doffed at the name of God. It was one of the stricter Quaker tenets that a man should raise his hat only at the name of God, and this Robert usually observed, much in the spirit of not going out of his way to acquire the latest court customs.

'Away with your long peaks behind in the skirts of your waistcoats,' George Fox was thundering, 'your skimming-dish hats, unnecessary buttons, short sleeves, short black aprons, vizzards, great flying scarves, like colours on your back.'

Although Quaker clothes were deliberately plain at a time when others were exceptionally elaborate, there were no hard and fast rules and no objections to their being excellently cut and made of superfine material. Robert never dreamt of discarding

his green silk coat nor his gold-headed cane simply as a quali-
fication of true Christianity, nor did he see it necessary to break
the tradition of his mother's family by keeping away from the
Court where, among other of his cousins, Robert Gordon, 'the
Warlock', was to become a gentleman of the household of their
cousin, the new King Charles II. Robert Barclay remained
friends with all his childhood companions and relations, particularly those with whom he had been brought up at Gordonstoun.

Another cousin at Court was Prince Rupert of the Rhine. His
mother, the King's sister, Elizabeth 'The Winter Queen of
Bohemia', who had married Frederick V, Elector of the Pala-
tinate, was 'cousin-german' (first cousin once removed) of
Robert Barclay's mother, and had died the same year as she had.
She had come to London to seek refuge with her nephew, King
Charles II, from her many troubles in Bohemia. As a 'martyr to
Protestantism' she was buried in Westminster Abbey. Prince
Rupert, her fascinating and cultured son, was another typical
product of the Swedish army, which he joined following the
deaths of his father and eldest brother, soon after Gustavus himself
was killed in action. Prince Rupert had since served with distinction in the Civil War, and now this court-martialled-and-
acquitted soldier-turned-sailor was about to become constable of
Windsor castle. He was highly enlightened in the arts and
sciences, witty, fascinating and delightful, with a streak of sheer
goodness concealed behind the levity that so entertained his
cousin the King.

It was in this bright, rich, debonair young Restoration set, led
by the King's brother, the Duke of York (later King James II),
that Robert Barclay met the particularly frivolous young dandy,
William Penn. Penn was a natural extrovert and showman, but
behind his bravado and quick repartee Robert detected not only a
genuine concern for the religious confusion of the age but an
almost mystical piety. This was after Penn had been sent down
from Oxford for 'plucking gowns from the wearers' backs'
during street rioting, and then had been sent to study instead in
Paris, returning, according to Samuel Pepys, who was an inferior

officer to Penn's father at the Admiralty, 'in a great deal, if not too much, variety of the French garb, and an affected manner of speech and gait'.

Penn was then sent to manage a family estate in Cork. Here, in Ireland, he began by cutting a dash at the brilliant but puritanical vice-regal court of James, Duke of Ormonde, who had recently brought from France memories of the opulent grandeur of Louis XIV, along with the happy effects in France of the toleration of Huguenots. So, while with one hand the Duke set out to make Dublin a splendid ceremonial capital, with the other he loosed the rein on all dissenters from the established Protestant Church, including such small minorities as the Quakers, as well as the huge Roman Catholic majority.

Dublin was until then just another British colonial settlement, hastily raised among the ruined fragments of the Anglo-Norman walled seaport, with only one bridge across the River Liffey. Ormonde gave it the Royal Hospital at Kilmannhan, whose magnificent interiors are still to be wondered at; he gave it Phoenix Park, with its deer whose descendants still dapple the long stretches of green, and he gave the initial boost to its rising up into the imposing and civilised residential city it was to become. The river was dredged, and spanned by finely proportioned bridges. Classical buildings began to rise like great country mansions among the airy squares and long streets.

Penn lingered within the orbit of the Court, where rich, political, intellectual and spiritual men continued the discussions he had already heard begun in France. But when a mutiny broke out, William volunteered for service and behaved with such bravery that he was offered a commission, which he declined. He attended a Quaker meeting where he was arrested for exceeding the permitted puritanical enthusiasm. After his release he returned to London, dressed in a drab coat with matching flapped waistcoat and knee-breeches, and hose of the same colour, with square-toed shoes and his own hair tied back with a black ribbon under a large, broad-brimmed black hat, which he refused to remove even to the king. His father, Admiral Sir William Penn, was furious. He was an inventive but conventional man, who in the Great Fire had saved All Hallows' church beside the Tower of London by ordering sailors to blow up houses near the church to make a fire-break. It was in this church that his son had earlier been baptised.

However, shortly after meeting Robert, young William Penn wholeheartedly became a Quaker. The organisation and discipline of the Society had hardly kept pace with its rapid development during the Civil War, and, by now, internal schisms began to threaten its stability. Penn's gift for controversial writing, backed by study at Lincoln's Inn, together with Robert Barclay's theological scholarship, did much to counteract the often wild and inaccurate rantings of the more obscurantist Quaker enthusiasts. Thus Fox found these two well-to-do highly-educated young men, with their lively wit and approach, invaluable allies. Their extensive learning and easy access to semi-royal society gave Quakerism new strength at a time when persecution was again on the increase.

Restraint on the Colonel was tightening again, and he was no longer able to visit his farms at Ury nor start rebuilding as he had intended. However, there was enough left of the old castle for him to patch up a temporary home for Robert to live there to start restoring the estate. Meanwhile the younger children remained at Gordonstoun with Manmaa.

Robert was much helped by Keith Falconer, another young Friend, who acted as factor when Robert was most involved in writing during William Penn's year in the Tower of London. Penn was committed for holding open-air meetings, preaching, and publishing an inflammatory pamphlet, *The Sandy Foundation Shaken*. While there he wrote his famous work *No Cross, No Crown*. He kept in touch with Robert who, through intercessions from his cousin the Duke of York, helped to bring about Penn's release.

By paying exorbitant fines, the Colonel was able to procure intermittent freedom, subject to such restrictions as confining himself to the town of Montrose, and not moving without licence. In his semi-imprisonment he must have been carrying on some kind of business to have been able to pay the enormous fines recorded. Most likely there was a continuation of the earlier-mentioned loans, backed by borrowing from substantial landowners. As a former Member of Parliament he would have known where the money lay and where it was most needed.

The magistrates were next recommended that 'they be careful no Quaikers frequented his company except his owne sonne'. From Montrose it was less than a couple of hours' ride to Ury, and so the Colonel was able, by licence, to meet Robert there to plan the making of a habitable mansion out of the old ruins. The main pile stood on a little plateau in the fork of the river Cowie to the south and a winding burn to the east. It faced the morning sun, with a fine view of the sea to the south-east. Already Robert and Falconer had planted young trees, mostly conifers, on the rising ground above, to shelter the site from the north winds. Above this belt were two natural lochs to which wild fowl came.

Robert's father was still greatly respected in the county as the Laird of Ury. Although, as a Quaker, he now disassociated himself from war and *honorary* titles, his retiring rank of colonel was still an acceptable title, as was that of Laird of Ury, which gave him, although he was himself still a part-time prisoner, jurisdiction over nearly all his extensive acreage. The charter of Ury, which had been temporarily suspended, included a long list of

> landes, maynes, manor-places, house-biggings, yairdes, orchyairds, dowcats [dovecotes], pairtes, pendicles, and pertinentes thereof, and salmond fishings belonging thereto, upon the waters of Cowie, as weel in salt as in fresh water . . . and all the haill the townes and lands of Maugray, Woodhead, Poubair, Balnageicht, Glechno and Cairnetoune, milne [mill] of Cowie, milne, pleugh, milne lands, multures, sequelles, and knaveship, thereof . . . the tounes and lands of Redclock, Finlaystoune, Easter and Wester Logies, Montquich called Twilles, Burnlauch, Rorthineck and Corslay, with all their pendicles and pertinents.

The list winds up with 'All and haill the lands and maynes of Dunnottar, all and haill the milne of Stonehyve, landes, multures'.

Dunnottar Castle, a mile and a half south of Stonehaven, is a spectacular fortress on a rock by the sea. It can still be reached by a path from the mainland, with breathtaking views from its embrasures. It had been built in the time of King Robert the Bruce, and had been in the hands of Gilbert, the Earl Marshal, until he sold it to the Colonel as part of the Ury estate. During the Civil War it was held by the Royalists, and the Scottish crown jewels were hidden there until they were smuggled out by a Dunnottar minister's wife. Although she and her husband were tortured, they kept their secret.

Despite a certain amount of opposition from the tenants, and the general unreceptiveness of Scotland, Robert was able to collect enough followers to occupy the first Quaker meeting at Ury. In Aberdeen he met other Friends, including the wife of a highly respected magistrate, Baillie Mollison. Robert's plain letter of proposal to the Mollisons' daughter, Christian, shows none of the easy warmth of expression of his published writings. Perhaps he was overcome with bashfulness. It begins,

> Dear Friend, Having for some time past had it several times upon my mind to have saluted thee in this manner of writing, and to enter into liberal correspondence with thee, so far as my freedom will allow, I am glad that this small occasion hath made way the beginning of it. For love of thy converse, the desire of thy friendship, the sympathy of thy way, and the meekness of thy spirit hath often, as thou mays't have observed occasioned me to make thee quick opportunity to have the benefit of thy company. [After a brief sermon he ends] in the present flowings thereof I have truly solicited thee, desiring and expecting that in the same thou mays't feel and judge. Robert Barclay.

To have accepted him on this formal phraseology, Christian must have already been bowled over by Robert's tall graceful figure and fair hair, if not by his green silk coat. Theirs, in 1669, was the first of many Quaker marriages in the family. Robert was twenty-one and Christian sixteen. The wedding took place in her father's house, beginning with the usual silence. Only by permit was the Colonel able to be present at his eldest son's wedding.

However, the peace inside the Mollison's house did not extend to the streets outside, where other magistrates, priests and the people about Aberdeen were already in an over-excited state over dissenters in general, 'which fury,' it is recorded, 'was somewhat increased by Robert Barclay's marriage which had been publickly performed that morning at her father's house . . . whereby the priests found their authority so slighted, and were exasperated thereat, that by the Bishop of Aberdeen's means, they procured letters to summons Robert Barclay before the Privy Council for ane unlawful marriage.' But the decision was over-ruled and the couple were able to settle, unmolested if still without much comfort, at Ury.

When the Colonel went out and about, courageous old soldier that he was, he made no attempt to forgo his conspicuous black cloak, severely plain black garments and flat broad-brimmed hat, although (incited by the clergy) people continued to hurl not only abuse but also garbage at anyone wearing the Quaker habit. Although the Colonel could no longer allow himself to fight, even in self-defence, his heart was high as ever, and he returned the floutings and jeerings with warnings of what was in store for those who failed to see the light in their own hearts.

When one of his relations lamented the common rudeness of the crowd to him and pointed out how differently he was now treated, he answered cheerfully that he found more satisfaction, as well as honour, in being insulted for his religious principles than when some years before it was the custom, when he entered the town, for the magistrates to meet him several miles out and conduct him to a public entertainment in their Town Hall and then escort him out again to gain his favour.

Robert, when he was in Stonehaven or Aberdeen, usually went his way without making himself particularly noticeable. On one occasion only in Aberdeen he felt compelled to make an exhibition of himself. It was soon after his marriage, some aspects of which may have shaken his puritanical nature into a show of public remorse – or perhaps he wanted to please his bride, who was always a 'plainer' Quaker than he was; anyway, be that as it may, dressed in sackcloth and strewn with ashes, he passed through the streets of Aberdeen, exhorting all to mend their ways and abandon extravagance. At the top of his Barclay voice he asked why they, who called themselves Christians, were so amazed at sackcloth and ashes which, according to their own acknowledgements, were so suitable to their own state. This was the only time he showed signs of the fanaticism frequently indulged in by many of the extremist followers of George Fox. Afterwards he admitted that the whole episode filled him with repugnance, if not regret. At all other times he went normally about among his friends in every walk of life. His cheerful spirits, charming manners and agreeable conversation made him a great favourite, and his ability to speak several languages helped to put foreign Friends in the picture.

Only one language he abhorred and that was foul language, despite his ability to communicate as easily with the 'b'Gadding and b'Godding' court wags as with the more fiercely swearing market folk and peasantry. Swearing, whether for effect or in anger or in courts of law was against all Quaker tenets. Refusal to take oaths frequently landed Quakers in prison.

It was because the Colonel refused to take oaths that his imprisonment became severe again. It was said that in Edinburgh Castle he occupied a small cell over the main entrance kept for Covenanting leaders. It could be partitioned in two through the raising of the portcullis. It was without light or air beyond that which filtered through the narrow slit in the wall. Exercise was only permitted on the ramparts. Whatever the exact details of his imprisonment were, it was not until the following year that the Colonel's full liberty was granted, and building could begin at Ury. The thick walls of the old castle-built L-shaped house had been made of great blocks of local granite, with small deep-set windows and a turret at each end. Although it was not to be restored as a fortified dwelling, it remained, if need arose, as capable of withstanding a siege as any of the other restored ancient castles in the district. In fact, the later building of the long, low meeting house, with its large airy windows, was to become the only likely cause of such a siege.

It may well be asked how it was possible to proceed with

meetings here. Professor Masson, in his *Life of Milton* explains something of the Quaker tenacity of the time:

> You may break in upon them, hoot at them, roar at them, drag them about; the Meeting, if it is of any size, ostensibly still goes on. Throw them out at the doors in twos and threes and they but re-enter at the windows and quietly resume their places. Pull their Meeting House down, and they re-assemble next day most punctually among the broken walls and rafters. Shovel sand or earth down upon them, and there they sit, a sight to see, musing immovably among the rubbish. This is no description from fancy, it was the actual practice of the Quakers all over the country. They held their meetings, regularly, perseveringly, and without the least concealment, keeping the doors of their Meeting Houses purposely open that all might enter, informers, constables, or soldiers and do whatever they chose.

At Ury, the first Quaker meetings of surly tenants and (at first) sceptical neighbours, grew to regular weekly meetings. An administrative structure was established with monthly meetings and two yearling meetings in Scotland, one at Edinburgh and one at Aberdeen.

Chapter Six

Robert and Christian
1670–1680

Now began a time of great sweetness and inspiration that made
the name of Ury bring a glow of love to all who knew it. Far and
wide it cast its rays and it was the prototype of this family's
christian homes all over the world, even after Quakerism had
given way, in later generations, to the Church of England.
Andrew Jaffray writes of the 'beauty, good order, and holiness,
that shined therein at Ury, I can say to my refreshment and many
others as in a quiet habitation. The high walled house, flanked by
two turrets stood then all by itself in the middle of a field, with a
small spinney above it, and the Cowie flowing away to Stonehaven and the sea.'

The Colonel lived here with Robert and his wife, and his other
children until they married and made homes of their own.
Christian, who managed the household, lived up to her name.
Her kindly and charitable outlook, even to those who most
harshly ill-treated the Friends, made the home singularly peaceful. There was a complete absence of violent language, rancour
or resentment. She believed in early rising, exquisite cleanliness
and every hour apportioned to its duty. Her book of household
recipes reveals that she was what would today be called a dedicated 'good-earther', with an ever-widening experience of how
wild food can be safely used in cooking and of how to make the
best of home-grown produce of all kinds. Fishing and farming
were the traditional industries of the Mearns coast.

As on the Norfolk coast, the east winds in spring and early

summer brought frequent sea mists known there as 'haars', but these gave way to more sunshine than was found almost anywhere else in Scotland, and so Christian was able to grow peaches and 'blew figs' against the southern walls round her kitchen garden. It was not unusual at this time to set a number of 'boles' or niches into such walls for the bees to nest in. Christian's many uses of honey, for cooking and mead, reveal that she must have had a great many hives. She used herbs extensively, explaining that, as the forty or so needed for one recipe 'cannot be had together, therefore they that come first must be put into one gallon of brandy, English, till the rest had to be had, and when they are all got, steep them 24 hours and then still them.'

As Christian needed no aids to disguise any lack of freshness, as inland townsfolk did, she gives few recipes for cooking meat which, like the game, salmon and trout recorded killed at Ury, must have been plainly spit-roasted, needing no additives.

George Fox expressed himself strongly against hunting and hawking, and the yearly Meeting renounced them clearly. In fact, at Ury hunting was looked upon as a necessity, both for filling the larder and training young horses, which Robert was known to have enjoyed; he also went shooting up on the hill with his father, and both enjoyed their skill as fishermen.

Most of Christian's draughts were based on quantities of wine and brandy made from foxgloves and sweet-smelling woods, or Canary wine in which herbs had been steeped. 'She laid herself out to assist and give advice to sick people and supplied their necessities, especially the poor, many of whom came 10, 20, 30 and even 40 miles and upwards receiving great benefit, for her success was wonderful. She was a well accomplished woman in every way and of singular virtues which she improved to the praise of the Lord.' How free of pain and misery must the poor have felt as they staggered away and sank on to the grass near the burn, comforted by Christian's potions and the godly love that went with them!

Besides their own household and (eventually) seven children, not to mention the poor, there was a constant stream of visitors, not necessarily Friends, to be refreshed. The Colonel went out to greet them, even if they had walked from Aberdeen to hurl abuse. A little of Christian's 'surfeit water' and some comfortable words from Robert always calmed them. Fashionably flounced, powdered and perfumed gentry were made as welcome at Ury as were the most rigid Puritans. The Countess of Erroll was an oft-noticed visitor. Christian received them all in her simple, clean, unadorned waisted frock, plain apron and fichu, with her uncurled hair covered with a cap of fine white cambric. Her babies appeared in tucked, but never lace-edged, gowns with rows of tiny stitches and embroidery that was never more worldly than herring-bone stitch. The table was always neatly. laid with a spotlessly white cloth; china was white or pale coloured to blend with the food; silver, if used at all, and glass were undecorated; forks were still by no means universal, and even visting lairds brought their own knives with which they cut up their food. There were none of the elaborate candelabra that lit some of their tables at home. Quaker candlesticks were invari-ably, as the name implies, merely iron spikes onto which the candles were stuck. Some Quakers had scruples against wearing dyed clothes, with the idea that the dye might hide dirt; in nearby Aberdeen they were ordered 'let no coloured plaids be worn anymore, but either mantles or low hoods.' But Christian tempered the advice with her own expert knowledge of dyeing, used local plants to produce the gentle greys and blues and yellows needed for materials worn by Friends. But her greatest expertise was as a physician. She devised several recipes for the 'dropsie', and used 'best Roman vitriolle as much as you please', mixed with honey 'for evil fistulas, cancers and ulcers'. She offered comforts for the 'tooth-ake', 'the gandis', (meaning jaundice) and 'reums' and 'a consumption, the gravell, rupter, and stone'. Her real speciality was eye troubles, and she was reported to have cured a cataract. Powders and 'plaisters' and 'elixirs' often depended upon their component herbs being gathered a certain number of days before or after the change of the moon, as did the actual taking of her draughts. Although superstitions were against Quaker beliefs, the influence of the moon in medicine was as acceptable and natural a phenomenon as high tide at Stonehaven. Even if Christian did show faith in Scottish folk-lore more than southerners would approve, the fact that any Friend was loved and respected gave him or her a right to sway a little 'off-centre', as indeed did Robert, Penn and many other great Quakers to come.

What a relief for Lady Erroll when she called, some of Christian's delicately flavoured pure unspiced sauces and custards must have been! At the time when the chatelaines of more worldly manor houses competed to have sent to the table elaborate, colourful and highly-spiced dishes, Christian's book of household recipes reveal that, though the food at Ury was necessarily 'plain', it was not only nourishing but also healthy and delicious. As in all true Quaker-cooked food, only the purest and best ingredients were used, with fruit and vegetables picked and stored at the moment of perfection, and meals prepared and cooked with the greatest care. The dishes were generally white throughout the meal – artichoke soup, chicken breasts in onion sauce, and apple snow. Except for fresh fruit, all food was dished up in subdued Quaker hues, and even plums and quinces were picked while still green to make white 'marmelett'; the white breed of elderberries was picked for wine rather than the black ones that produced red wine, and white raspberries and white currants were grown in preference to red.

Ury was almost self-supporting with its farms and sporting soils, its peat for fuel, its wild berries, mushrooms and herbs, and its extensive kitchen garden and orchards.

Sugar, 'French brandy', 'gascoin wine' and other imported commodities came by sea to nearby Stonehaven, Christian's shopping town. There were also two yearly fairs, one in June and one in October, held near the 'Great Road' that crossed the Ury estate. Besides cattle and country products, Christian could buy at the fairs stockings, linen, clothing, kitchen ladles, funnels, graters and choppers, frying-pans and skillets. Most of the heavy wooden kitchen furniture – the great table and benches, the long low troughs in which the bread was mixed, and the pestle and mortar stands – were made by the estate workers at the same time as they replaced and added panelling and other woodwork when restoring the house. Much of the furniture in other parts of the house would have been specially made in this way – hutch-like cupboards and box-like settles and chairs and tables.

In some places Friends were treated to advice from joiners, ships' carpenters, brass founders, saddlers and shoemakers, who told them that chests of drawers ought to be plain, 'all of one colour without any swelling works'. The overseers travelled about, inspecting houses, objecting to ornamental eaves, drawing-room curtains and other Babylonish adornings, including pewter and brass pots, pans and candlesticks evidently for ornament. Framed pictures on the walls were not permitted, but collections in books or portfolios were allowed for educational purpose, preferably only in black and white. Portraits, it was considered, tended to conceit, but the art of making silhouette portraits later became permissible as records.

Decorations on cradles were expected to contaminate the baby. However, more ornamental furniture from an earlier period, inherited by the Colonel and the White Rose of Scotland would not have offended Robert, who was referred to by a Gordon cousin as 'scholastic and metaphysical, living so truly above forms that they are nothing to him one way or another'.

His descendants' homes are to this day touched by the lasting effects of this era. They are never actually bleak and uncomfortable, for wood fires blaze in open fireplaces, but there is more home-made furniture to be found than in most British homes, intermingled with heirlooms, dogs and children. Up-to-date shop-bought pieces are still a rarity, as they were then.

Two young Barclay descendants wrote in their diaries of a visit they made to Ury 'of which we have heard so much. It was as I expected it would be except the drive up to it is longer. The approaches to the house are extremely pretty but the house itself with its white-washed walls want for beauty and regularity.' They would have preferred grey granite to the white that, Christian held, stood for purity. They wrote their diaries settled in 'one of the turrets opening by a narrow passage to the drawing-room', which was the only quiet room in the house. 'There are a great number of closets, some so curiously concealed that it is evident that they were intended for hiding-places. Windows and doors seem to have been superfluities in this house. Small slits gave light in ancient days' (meaning the days before Ury was rebuilt and became the Quaker Mecca), when 'the entrance to the house was at the top of the tower in which we now are. Inhabitants ascended by means of rope ladders which when safely housed they drew up after them. The ancient prison is now converted into the more peaceful purpose of a larder.' They went into Robert's 'library' where he worked, 'a little atom of a room cut into the thickness of the wall in the drawing-room, fitted up all round with book shelves except on one side where is the fireplace and a small dresser kind of table with a stool.' They noticed Robert's gold-headed canes and old Bible boxes, including one little box dated 1661, which had been the Colonel's. In fact this visit was paid by Robert's great-great-granddaughters 150 years after he wrote in his little room, but all that time it was kept locked up and left exactly as it was when he wrote in it.

His most important book, which took him seven years to write in Latin in this 'atom of a room', was his *Apologia*, from which he derived the nickname of 'The Apologist'. Later he translated it into English as *An Apology*. It was this translation that John Guerney was to read in Norwich jail five years later. The book caused bitter dispute and close discussion among men of all sorts and shades of religious opinion. Robert's insistence upon the doctrine of the inward light was contrary to accepted standards, and his condemnation of the sacraments shocked every sect. And yet the truly scholarly theologians could find no flaw in Barclay's arguments.

Fox and the Quakers generally rejoiced over *The Apology*[1] and basked in the world-respect for a sect which could produce such a masterpiece. The learned John Norris, Church of England clergyman, with an almost perpetual bone to pick with Quakerism, said he could easily forgive the general exultation

---

[1] Voltaire wrote that 'It was surprising how Robert Barclay's *Apology* written only by a private gentleman, should have an effect as to procure almost a general release to the whole sect from the suffering they then underwent.'

among the Quakers over Barclay's folio and 'knows not well how to blame', for he knew no religion so rich in reputation for great men that would not be glad of acquiring such a writer, particularly the Quakers who had been so barren in productions of this kind. Now scattered notions were reduced to order and appeared in a regular system. He added: 'Mr. Barclay is a very great man,[2] and were it not for the common prejudice that lies against him as a Quaker, he would be sure not to miss being preferred to the greatest wits the age has produced.'

The book went into six English editions and was also published in French, High Dutch, Low Dutch, Spanish, and in its original Latin. It became the standard book of Quaker theory, and years later Macaulay wrote 'it was a lucky chance for the Quakers that they got Robert Barclay and William Penn to make sense of the unintelligible jargon of George Fox and Nayler.'

The Apology was printed in Amsterdam and while Robert was in Holland, after seeing the printer he went on to Herwalden to visit his cousin Elizabeth, Princess Palatine, sister of Prince Rupert of the Rhine (whom Robert already knew). Their elder brother was now Elector Palatine. Princess Elizabeth was a brilliant scholar and Abbess of an ancient religious foundation which, as a Protestant institution, had been left undisturbed at the Reformation. Although a mother superior, she was not entirely removed from the world of luxury, and was in close touch with the English court. She took an immediate liking to Robert, who gave her a copy of his book and took a letter from her to Prince Rupert, begging him to mitigate the persecution of the Friends, in whom Robert had interested her so deeply. The visit was cut short by an urgent message from home, telling Robert of the re-arrest of his father in Aberdeen, with several other prominent

---

[2] A Scottish minister, singing of two former fighting Barclays 'ended his ballad with:

> But lo! a third appears, with serious air!
> His Prince's darling and his country's care.
> Seeking his religion, which so late before
> Was like a jumbled mass of dross and all,
> Refined by him, and burnished o'er with Art;
> Awakes the spirit and attracts the heart.

Friends at a meeting 'prohibited by law'. Robert returned at once to England and was met at Harwich with the news that his father had been asked to pay a fine which amounted to over a fourth of his annual income. Having refused to pay it, he was imprisoned in the Tolbooth of Aberdeen.

Robert went straight to London, where he received a reply to two letters of encouragement he had written to his father. Writing from The Tolbooth, Aberdeen, the Colonel begins: 'Dear Child, I had thine from London and likewise from Harwich which was 20 days coming.' He describes the conditions in prison and how one of the Friends preached out of the prison window to the people in the streets, whereupon the magistrates 'lead-nailed' all the prison windows so that the prisoners were barred from breathing free air, they even nailed up the very chinks that let the light in from the stairs.

Robert was determined to see King Charles himself, and lay the case before him in order to destroy the pretext that the Friends had infringed the Conventicle Act, which was the only legal ground for their prosecutions. While waiting for an appointment, he wrote the first of many letters to Princess Elizabeth that have been preserved. He begins, 'Dear Friend', and tells her that he had delivered her letter to her brother 'who was civile to me. I also took occasion from this to employ him to be assisting me in ane address I intend to make to the King, on behalf of my father and about 40 more of our Friends that are about some months ago imprisoned in Scotland for conscience sake, in which he promised his concurrence.' He sent messages of encouragement to her lady-in-waiting, who had resolved to learn English.

His letter reached the Princess five weeks later, and she replied in her own hand the same day, beginning 'My dear Friend in our Saviour Jesus Christ,' and told him that whatever she had studied and learnt, it was dirt in comparison to the true knowledge she had learnt from him. It seems likely that the Abbess-Princess was a sporting lady and Robert may well have hunted in Holland while staying with her, for she uses hunting analogies when telling Robert that she sometimes had a glimpse of the True Light: 'I do not attend it as I should, being drawn away by the works of my calling which must be done and, as your swift English hounds, I often over-run my scent, being called back when it is too late.' She asks him to pray for her, and says his letters will always be welcome and so will his friends, if any choose to visit. She hopes her brother will be successful 'having promised to do his best I know he will perform it. He has ever been true to his word, and you shall find me with the grace of the Lord, a true friend Elizabeth.' She adds a P.S. that her lady-in-waiting has been so busy nursing smallpox that she has had no time to learn English.

Robert had no difficulty in gaining access to the King, and he presented his petition. According to *A Life of Penn*, by George Sewell, Robert assumed the formal Quaker garb for this occasion, and kept his hat on. He approached the King with a roll of paper in his hand. Charles waved aside the officials who would have checked him, and, taking the roll, threw himself back in his chair of state to read it, while Robert stood, courteous but not subservient, awaiting his pleasure. The King is said to have read the appeal attentively and to observe to those around that it appeared a hard case adding, 'What shall we do for these people?' 'But some light-minded persons approached and engaged His Majesty in merry conversation.' The King was about to put the matter to one side when he saw the patient gaze of the young Quaker standing there and summoned the Duke of Lauderdale, ordering him to transmit the paper to the Council of Scotland for its consideration. Lauderdale, who was then Commissioner of Scotland, had no time for the Quakers, but was forced to despatch an order, and Robert was reassured that his father, 'whom,' he said, 'he loved with tender affection', was to be released with his companions.

Robert then presented the King with a copy of *The Apology*, and a letter explaining why he could not dedicate it to him. He also added, in the plain, if not actually tactless, manner of the Quakers, a warning against 'the flattery of court parasites', and begged the King 'to see the light in his own conscience'.

The King appeared to be more amused than resentful, and, back in Scotland, Robert continued to be well received at Court in Edinburgh. Meanwhile no action was taken on behalf of the prisoners. Robert wrote again to the Princess to tell her of his ill-success in spite of court promises. He stayed around hopefully, and many years later wrote, 'I am sure those who frequent the courts of princes find often more reason for wearying than pleasure, and so it proved often with me and nothing but to serve my friends obliged me to do so dangerous a drudgery, where people are much more capable to get hurt than good.'

In his next letter to the Princess, written on 6th September, 1676, he ends

> and thus are shut up together 42 men in one great room, who, not of self-will nor their own choice, but by the providence of God are placed for a time together in heavenly community. I this day take this journey towards them, not doubting that I shall be taken and shut up with them, and with all cheerfulness of spirit and prepared to partake with them their bonds, not doubting that I shall also share their joy. It will be very refreshing and comfortable to me in my prison, to hear of thee for thy prosperity and increase of the truth is desired by me, as that of my soul. Thy faithful friend R. Barclay.

Robert's anticipation was soon realised. He was arrested while attending a meeting in Aberdeen, and was imprisoned with his father and various cousins. The Princess wrote at once scolding him. 'It is a cross to me that you will not make use of the liberty that God miraculously gave you, but will return to Scotland to be clapt up again in prison.' She also wrote to her brother, Prince Rupert:

> Dear Brother I have written to you some months ago, by Robert Barclay, who passed this way, and hearing I was your sister, desired to speak with me. I knew him to be a Quaker by his hat, and took occasion to inform myself of all their opinions, and finding that they were to submit to magistrates in real things, omitting the ceremonial, I wished in my heart the King might have many such subjects: and since I have heard that notwithstanding his Majesty's most gracious letter on his behalf to the Council of Scotland, he has been clapt up in prison, with the rest of his friends, and they threaten to hang them

unless they subscribe to their own banishment; and this upon a law made against other sects, that appeared armed for the maintenance of their heresy, which goes direct against the principles of those which are ready to suffer all that can be inflicted and still love and pray for their enemies.

Therefore dear brother if you can do anything to prevent their destruction I doubt not but you will do an action acceptable to God Almighty and conducive to the service of your royal master, for the Presbyterians are their main enemies, to whom they are an eye-sore, as being witnesses against all their violent ways. I care not though his Majesty see my letter; it is written out of no less than humble affection for him than most sensible compassion for the innocent sufferers. You will act therein according to your own discretion, and I beseech you still consider me as yours Elizabeth.

A monsr leur Prince Rupert a londres.

While in prison, Robert kept up a warm and helpful correspondence with the Princess and he also wrote many other letters on behalf of the Quakers.

Now Robert saw for himself how every effort was made to make the confinement as uncomfortable as possible. They were next sent to a cold narrow building with a door opening on to 'the eastern ocean' where there was very little room and only one small window, so that the prisoners could not see to eat their food except by candle light or when the door was open. The room had a chimney, but it smoked so that they could not light a fire. Robert kept up the spirits of those around him with jokes as well as prayer.

During his seven months in prison, not only did Robert continue his lively correspondence with the Princess, but also he wrote many other letters. One was to the Archbishop of St. Andrews, who was known to be one of the most cruel and tyrannical oppressors of the Friends. It was addressed, again perhaps not too tactfully, to 'James Sharpe, Archbishop of St. Andrews (so called)'. He puts the case of the imprisoned Friends with moderation, giving the facts without comment: the injustice of the charges, the length the prisoners had illegally been kept in confinement, and how their goods had been miserably spoiled. He suggested that the Archbishop was not fully aware of these practices. He gave him a fairly stiff sermon, and then said that no persecution or rigour of the law could shake the faith of the Friends, and that they were prepared cheerfully to enjoy even death itself, doubting not that God would raise witnesses out of their ashes who would outlive all the violence and cruelty of man. He ended up with a chance prophesy which, had his letter been made public, might have endowed him with a place in Scottish mythology. He writes:

> albeit should thyself be most inexorable and violent towards us, thou may assure thyself not to receive any evil from us, therefore, to the God of truth, to whom vengeance belongs, we leave it, who will certainly in his own time and way revenge our Quarrel, whose dreadful Judgement shall be more terrible to thee and much more justly to be feared, than the violent assaults of secret assassinations of thy other antagonists. That thou may prevent both the one and the other by a Christian moderation suitable to the office thou layest claim to is the desire of thy soul's well-wisher. Signed R. Barclay.

It was written in the small room facing the eastern ocean on 6th April 1677, and the prisoners awaited a reply. It never came, but two years later the Archbishop, when travelling in his coach on the road to St. Andrews, was barbarously murdered for his treachery, not to the Quakers, but to the Presbyterian Church, which had entrusted its cause to him and been heartlessly betrayed. A body of Covenanters had taken the law into their own hands and avenged their wrongs. A few days before the murder of the Archbishop on 3rd May, 1679, Robert and his sister were passing the kirk which belonged to the Archbishop and they heard a most terrifying howling sound. They sent their servant to peer through the windows but he could see nothing; when he returned the noise began again and went on till they rode out of hearing. They both mentioned this immediately afterwards, before the Archbishop had been attacked.

Robert was now writing to the Princess as 'Dear and well-beloved Elizabeth', signing himself, 'Thy real and unfeined friend,' and she, to him, 'Your loving friend.'

Prince Rupert, who had been suffering, she said, 'from a sore legg', at last roused himself and either he or the Duke of York – or both – petitioned the King. Colonel Barclay and his son suddenly found themselves at large and were able to return to Ury. Princess Elizabeth wrote, 'I do love the Duke of York for it.'

A letter survives from the Duke of York to the Duke of Lauderdale, asking him to be as favourable to Robert and the Colonel as he could be 'as to the inconveniences which may happen to them by reason of their persuasion in point of religion', explaining that they were related to the King and so 'will deserve some favour, though they have the misfortune to be Quakers'.

In view of the Duke of York's lack of sympathy with Quakers and the many recorded occasions when he took the opportunity of consulting Robert, it seems that farming and writing books were not Robert's only source of income. With his clear head and ability to assess quickly, it seems likely that the Duke of York sought Barclay's advice as well as Penn's on financial matters and that Robert, like, possibly, his father and certainly some of his Quaker descendants, was not only a preacher but also a banker.

Soon after Robert's release, he was travelling again, this time to Bristol, and in the summer he set off from Harwich with George Fox, William Penn, George Keith and other Friends to organise yearly meetings in Amsterdam, and quarterly and monthly meetings in other continental countries, but their ship was becalmed within a league of the coast of Holland and they had to ride at anchor for the night. This was more than the impatient Penn could bear, and although Robert had borne his months in prison 'with evenness of spirit', a night's delay was too much for him, too. They persuaded two of the crew to let down a small boat and row them to the shore, but before they could reach it, the harbour gates were closed and they preferred to lie in a fisherman's boat all night rather than be rowed back to the ship when its boat returned. As soon as the gates were opened in the morning they were 'first in'. Fox described this in his journal. He was able to add later that, despite language difficulties, 'there was a mighty concourse and the mystery of iniquity and godliness were opened and declared in the demonstration.'

There were a large number of Friends in Holland and not only they came in force, but also, Penn writes, 'a great concourse of people of several opinions, as Baptist, Seekers, Socinians, Brownists and some of the Collegians. Robert Barclay, George Keith and I did severally declare the everlasting truth among them and the meeting ended sweetly and well.'

As soon as Princess Elizabeth heard they were there, she hastened to invite them to visit her, a four days' journey by boat and post-wagon. She gave them a great welcome, and, although Barclay and Penn were both under thirty, and she was sixty-two, she found 'she could speak to them as a scholar to scholar, as a thinker to thinker, without exaggeration or uninstructed enthusiasm.' She also found them 'both remarkable for personal dignity and beauty of face and carriage'. After supper they held a meeting with the Princess and various of their friends. When that was over, they were asked to hold yet another for the servants; from this the Princess, taking Robert's hand, said she would be absent herself 'so as not to cause an embarrassment'. The next day the Princess arranged a meeting for the whole town of Herwardine, and they stayed several days. When it was time to say goodbye the Princess wept. 'Come again, before you go to Germany,' she said, and Penn replied, 'We are in God's hands, Friend Elizabeth. We cannot dispose of ourselves but we will not forget thee nor those belonging to thee.' Robert felt, rightly, that they would never meet again. On his way home to Scotland, he stopped at Theobalds, once the fabulous hunting-palace of James I, built by the first Lord Burleigh for the entertainment of Queen Elizabeth I. Here his cousin, George Keith, was founding a Quaker school, with some financial help in the form of a loan from the Barclays.

Robert's next letter to the Princess, thanking her for her hospitality, admits that the persecution of the Quakers in Scotland had seemed to die down, but he now heard reports that things were not so good again. Back at Ury he found that the magistrates, 'vexed because they could not have further access to his person at that time', had procured a warrant to distrain the Colonel's goods. A man was sent to Ury to 'poynd' the Colonel, who pointed out that the warrant only applied to the shire of Mearns. However, this was ignored and ten of the Ury labouring oxen were taken; this, by Act of Parliament, was forbidden in the ploughing season, even in a case of just debt. Two cows and a young bull were also taken, and a quantity of corn. The beasts were driven to Stonehaven, but nobody would buy them. Their keeper found them so expensive in pasture that he had difficulty in keeping them from starving till the spring. They were finally disposed of in lieu of a debt owed to a group of students who had held a public dispute with the Quakers.

The Barclays were both arrested again at a meeting but, owing to the Duke of York's instructions to the Duke of Lauderdale, they were only detained for a few hours.

Robert's last letter to the Princess was written from Rotterdam, where he was 'on business'. He wished he could have gone to see her, but he was 'under great bodily weakness'. The Princess herself died a few months later.

Robert next tried to persuade the Duke of York to include Quakers in his 'liberty of conscience rights', designed, so far, only to cover Papists. But the Duke merely wrote disparagingly of the Quakers to his old friend the Duke of Lauderdale and persuaded a few more of his friends to join the Church of Rome, which they did eagerly, with a view to pleasing the future king 'for their own yield'.

In 1679 the reigning king, Charles II, ratified the Charter of Ury, giving the lands of free barony, with civil and criminal jurisdiction, to 'Colonel Barclay and his heirs'. This was the year in which the Duke of York became a member of the Scottish Privy Council and took up residence at Holyrood. Much magnificent building and elaborate decorating had been going on at the palace. Robert Barclay, who had seen like splendours arising in Paris, heartily wished for more restraint, with the money saved to be spent on the poor. But despite his admonitions, he was constantly summoned to conferences with James, as several surviving letters show.

The Duke of York, relenting of his former lack of interest, addressed a letter 'to Robert Barclay of Ury from Windsor', dated June 27th, 1680. 'I send you here enclosed a letter to the Lord Advocate, as you desired. I chuse to write to him because I had spoken to him of it, when in Scotland. You see I do my part, and I make no doubt that he will do his, and then you will have no further trouble in that affair. Signed JAMES Directed for Mr. Barclay.'

Robert received this letter when he was in Edinburgh, 'Carrying out some law business on his father's account'. The Duke was giving him an introduction to the legal authority most likely to be of use to his cause. A correspondence resulted between the Earl of Perth and Robert Barclay of Ury, the same year. Perth later became Lord Chancellor, somewhat detracting from his charm by adding the thumbscrew to instruments of torture for extorting evidence.

In his more humane days Lord Perth writes at length from Edinburgh on 12th October, 1680.

> I had one indeed from you two weeks ago but had so little leisure since, that I ventured upon your goodness, and took some moments to myself, which should have been yours, could I have written as easily, as my heart was full of the sense of your kindness.
>
> This goes by Mr. Falconer, an occasion I would not let go without telling you, that your friend here is still mindful of you and your concerns, nor wants he any solicitations to do you all the kindness I could prompt him to, for he was as zealous that way as I can be, but no occasion has offered since. I will resolve to be what God pleases, as ploughman or courtier, or what else may be most for his honour. I know this is much too long a letter: forgive me, and believe you have not a faithfuller friend than your affection friend, Perth.
>
> 12 at night.
>
> P.S. I have spoken to the Duke since I wrote my letter and he is well satisfied to have a rental, though my own opinion is that it should be exactly as given and all the proposed advantages of such purchase as evident as can be but this you shall do according to your pleasure.
>
> The Duke speaks wonderfully kind of you, adiu.'

The matter sounds much more like an investment in real estate to raise the much needed money for the King than any kind of political intrigue, which on Quaker grounds Robert would certainly be against. Straightforward business, however, was regarded by Robert and subsequent Quakers as thoroughly commendable.

Chapter Seven

Robert and George Fox
1680–1690

George Fox thoroughly approved of Penn and Barclay's friendship with the Duke of York. Not only did it provide influences to
lessen the sufferings of the Friends, but it was also of vital
importance to Fox's dream of forming a colony of Friends in
America. This had first come to him when he himself went to
America, fifty years after the Pilgrim fathers had landed from
the *Mayflower* near Cape Cod. Now the whole province lying
between the Hudson and Delaware estuaries had been made over
to the Duke of York by his brother, the King, to re-grant as he
thought fit. New Jersey, won from the Dutch, was treated by the
English as royal property to be used for the enrichment of
courtiers. The eastern part, already settled, was highly profitable, but the west, which was still occupied by Red Indians, was a
colonial possession of apparently little consequence.

Through the Duke of York's influence, Penn's enthusiasm,
and Barclay's perceptive ability to see how future transactions
could be legally and fairly achieved, Penn was able to draw up a
prospectus offering Quakers a chance to 'buy' tracts of this land
from the Indians in exchange for a long list of various articles
known to be irresistible to them. 230 Friends responded (mostly
from Yorkshire and London), and by the summer of 1677 had
already gone aboard the ship *Kent*, when by chance the King
happened to be aboard the royal barge as the *Kent* was about to
weigh anchor. On hearing that the passengers were Quakers, he
bade them farewell with his blessing, but observed to Penn, 'You
will soon be in the Indians' war kettle.' The Duke of York turned
to the King with a shrug and said, 'What are we to expect from

such noodles that they will have nothing to do with gin and gunpowder, and say that guns were invented not to kill men but hawks and wolves?'

King Charles, though sympathetic towards the dissenters, enjoyed a joke at their expense. On meeting Penn in the park, the monarch swept off his own hat.

'Why dost thou take off thy hat, Friend Charles?' enquired Penn.

'Because,' said the king, 'wherever I am it is customary for only one person to remain uncovered.'

Other ships followed the *Kent* to America and within eighteen months there were some 800 Friends in the colony. Unfortunately, on the list of such 'irresistibles' as kettles, garments, tools, looking-glasses and ornaments, was rum, which had such disastrous effects on the hitherto teetotal Indians that the more enlightened of their chiefs begged the colonists to take it back. The dissenters settled on the Delaware river and built the town of Burlington. Some miles away on the opposite bank rose Philadelphia, 'the city of brotherly love'. Early settlers (many of whom were weavers by trade) were compelled to dress plainly in their homespun clothes, but as successive shiploads of upper-class colonists arrived, and the object of starting a new life became blurred, the weavers made the most of the flamboyant fashions of Paris and London that began to creep in, and copied them to their great profit. In 1679, Penn, with the help of twelve Friends, including Robert Barclay, and eleven others, was able to buy outright the province of East New Jersey, which measured 300 miles by 160 'of extreme fertility, unusual wealth and richness of all kinds'.

Penn's contribution came largely from a considerable sum of money that his father left him, partly in the form of a loan made to King Charles by the late Admiral Penn. The King insisted on calling the new colony Pennsylvania, which Penn disliked, as appearing too much like personal vanity contradictory to his teaching. 'Sylvania' was suggested for the pretty wooded country, to which King Charles prefixed 'Penn', pointing out playfully that this stood for Penn's father, who had originally lent the Crown at any rate part of the cost. This was banking on a royal scale.

Penn called his new constitution 'the Holy Experiment'. It was to be a true democracy without any class or race distinction; no army or navy, no established church; no oaths to be taken nor common daily work done on Sundays. There was to be a humane penal code with reformative punishment, with work-shops where prisoners could re-find themselves. Capital punish-ment was to be reserved for wilful murder and treason. There was to be some regulation of restrictions on slavery[1] and pro-vision for education, with strict regulations against puritan sins such as swearing, lying, duels and card-playing etc.

The very virtues of the Quakers, their stubborn determination and consistency of purpose, made them a difficult people to govern. But peace remained for seventy years.

The system, though too idealistic to avoid many economic, legal and financial difficulties, worked considerably better than that in other settlements, in which the Englishman's first employment was to built forts, plant cannon, keep guard and practise arms.

In 1682 Penn crossed the Atlantic in the ship *Welcome*, to take possession, with only the principles of the Gospel, and 'neither cannon, sword nor musket'. He landed with 100 Friends among thousands of war-painted and feathered Indians, just as savage as any others 'but seeing he was incapable of injuring them, they immediately extended their friendship'. The celebrated meeting between the new Quaker owners of the province and the Indians, who had become their subjects, then took place.

Robert Barclay was offered the governorship of East Jersey, as New Jersey was then called, and accepted it on condition that he was not required to go to America himself. The post carried no salary, but he was allotted 5,000 acres above his proprietary share, which he might grant to others as he saw fit. Charles II confirmed the government's grant, and the Royal Commission

---

[1] In 1696, came the first official pronouncement of the Society of Friends advocating care of slaves and forbidding their importation, and in 1771, the Yearly Meeting made anti-slavery its first protest.

states that: 'such are his known fidelity and capacity, that he has the government during life; but that no other governor after him shall have it longer than 3 years.'

When an unexpected old debt, owed by Gilbert, the late Earl of Erroll, was repaid to the Colonel, he spent half on shipping provisions and servants from Aberdeen to East Jersey for his second son, John, to take up the 500 acres in his father's gift; this estate he called Plainfields. He made a home there and married and had a son also named John.

The rest of the Colonel's repayment was invested, or formed school fees, in George Keith's school at Theobalds, where Robert and Christian took their eldest son, Rob, then aged eleven. Rob's grandfather went with them as far as Edinburgh and then turned back. The others went on to London and settled the boy in at boarding school. Theobalds is about twelve miles from central London, where Robert and Christian spent most of the summer visiting Friends while Robert worked on his Quaker concerns.

They started the journey home with Christian's brother, and a great friend who had been an eminent merchant in Holland, another of the proprietors of East Jersey. Christian gave an account years later to her grandson of the misfortune they had in their journey to Stonegate Hole, between Huntingdon and Stilton, when they were attacked by highwaymen.

> One of them presented a pistol to Robert, he took him by the arm, very calmly asking him how he came to be so rude, for he knew his business; the fellow trembling dropped the pistol out of his hand on the ground, in great surprise, and did not so much as search or demand anything from him; his brother-in-law was rifled and rudely used, and the poor Dutchman it was thought more by accident than design, was shot in the thigh, who being with some difficulty brought to Stilton, died within a few days of the wound.

Christian added that she had observed her husband that morning more pensive than usual, and he told her it was his opinion, that some unusual trial or exercise was before them that day; but when the affair happened he enjoyed a remarkable serenity. After having seen their friend decently buried, they returned home after, as he calls it in his pocket book, 'a long and tedious journey'.

In 1687 Charles II died, after his last joke, when he asked to be excused for taking an unconscienable time in dying. His brother James, Duke of York, now the Roman Catholic king of Protestant England, continued to consult Robert whose 'business and acts of charity' kept him in London for some months. Robert's experienced knowledge of Roman Catholicism, derived from his school days in Paris, and his frequent consultations with the new King brought forth the suggestion from several in authority that Robert was himself a Roman Catholic. His numerous Roman Catholic friends knew otherwise.

The King received generous financial aid from Parliament, but can hardly have followed Robert's advice on how to invest it, for most of it was soon spent on raising a new army.

With James II's administration ceasing to molest Roman Catholics, Robert was able to persuade him to include *all* dissenters. 350 Friends had died in prison in the reign of Charles II. Now, except for Quaker debtors, most survivors were freed.

While Robert was away on one of these occasions, the Privy Council of Scotland made a general arrest of more than 100 Covenanters who had refused or delayed the signing of the oath of allegiance, together with many of their women and children. The captives were driven northwards, writes Sir Walter Scott in the introduction to *Old Mortality* 'like a flock of bullocks, but with less proportion to provide for their wants for they suffered not a little on the journey and the mocks, gibes, and contemptuous tunes played by the fiddlers and pipers who had come from every quarter as they passed, to triumph over the revilers of their calling.' Robert was appalled to hear that they had finally been penned up in the subterranean dungeon of Dunnottar Castle, which had a window opening on to the precipice which overhangs the German Ocean.

Although, technically, Dunnottar was included in the Ury estate, it was outside the limits of the Barclays' baronial jurisdiction, so that, despite attempts, the Colonel was powerless to interfere. Robert returned home to find that about fourteen prisoners had escaped through a hole, only to be dashed to pieces on the rocks. Their friends had gathered up their remains and buried them in Dunnottar churchyard.

The same young Barclay great-granddaughters who wrote of their pilgrimage to the Apologist's study, add that at the same time they

> scrambled down a hill and up a rock and came to the ruins of Dunnottar Castle, visiting the vault where Covenanters were confined [150 years before]. Here in the wall, hands and thumbs of the unfortunate people were firmly wedged down; guards made them pay even for water, and when they complained, the water was emptied on the floor and they were told that the guards were not obliged to bring them bowls or pitchers without pay. Here was a hole through which some tried to escape.

Many others died and thirty-seven, unable to endure the miseries and tortures of imprisonment, took the oath of allegiance. All Robert Barclay was able to do was to use his colonial powers to help the victims of the new persecution to find homes in New Jersey, but so many were weakened by privation and suffering that they died on the voyage out.

The Colonel's last year at Ury began happily with his youngest son, Davie (once nursed through chickenpox by Manmaa at Gordonstoun) at home with Robert and Christian and six grandchildren. Rob, the eldest, now thirteen, said that his grandfather's

> humility and sincerity in his religion was most remarkable and exemplary in his whole conduct particularly in the time of public prayer. He was as proper, tall, personage of a man as could be seen among many thousands; his hair, white as the flax, but quite bald upon the top of his head, which obliged him to wear, commonly, a black satin cap under his hat. It was observable, that he always kneeled in time of public prayer, pulled off his hat with one hand, and his cap with the other, and so continued during the whole time of prayers; I have often seen it.

The Colonel was now seventy-six. Robert wrote of him, 'There be hardly to be found one of a thousand like him for natural vigor of his age.'

Robert was much at Ury that year. To counteract his long hours of writing at his desk, he took a great deal of exercise on the estate. When he was not training young horses at Ury, he was striding about the hill with his gun, while Christian and the children gathered mushrooms to dry and preserve. Robert not only thoroughly enjoyed fishing in the River Cowie but he had also acquired salmon-fishing on the waters of Don. In the *Apology* he wrote, 'There are innocent divertisements which may sufficiently serve for relaxation . . . for man can't always be in the same intentiveness of mind . . . such is for Friends to visit one another, to hear or read history, to speak soberly of the present or past transactions; to follow after gardening; to use geometrical and mathematical experiments, and such other things of this nature.' The 'fast English hounds', referred to by Princess Elizabeth of Bavaria, would certainly have been found at Ury, with sentimental old retrievers, well-trained young gun dogs, and nests of puppies in the hay above the horses.

Robert's youngest brother, Davie, was now twenty-four and a 'young man of high hopes'. Their father gave him enough money to follow his brother John to East Jersey to set up as a merchant. The Colonel bought a property for him in the Quaker province and goods to the value of £150, all of which Cargoe, together with eight servants, he put aboard the ship *America* in August 1685 when he set sail for East New Jersey.

Robert attended his sister's wedding in Edinburgh to Sir Euen Cameron, Laird of Lochiell, and then went on to York, continuing by post horse to London, where he had frequent access to the King. But he was anxious to get home to Ury as soon as possible now that there was no other young man to support his ageing father. On his return, he reached Edinburgh only to be called back to London on affairs of the King. When at last he got away, he arrived home at Ury to learn the tragic news of David's death on his voyage to East Jersey, a great blow to all his family but especially to his old father, whose vigour began to decline from that moment.

Robert was reluctant to leave Ury again at such a time, particularly as Christian was pregnant and 'carrying uneasily'. But Fox was depending on him to present an address to the King, asking that the King's Declaration of Indulgence (made on his accession) should now be remade for posterity. Although the main persecution of the Quakers had been checked, Friends were now being harried by legal prosecutions and ruinous fines for non-payment of tithes and other smaller offences.

A message came that the King could see Robert, and off he went to London again. He had barely concluded his business with the King, and had not even had a chance to see Fox, when the call came to return at once to Christian, who was dangerously ill, as was his father, of a virulent fever. Normally a message took at least a week to deliver and an ordinary traveller, even without stops to preach and do business, as most Quakers made, much longer. But messages are recorded as being delivered between London and Edinburgh within three days. Even riding hard, on hired horses, it would have taken Robert considerably longer to cover the 500 miles to Ury. He ended the journey just in time to be, as the Colonel told him, 'my witness in the presence of God, that the Lord is nigh'. Presently he breathed a final sentence: 'The truth is over all.' Christian's seventh and last baby had already arrived – a daughter – after a terrible confinement.

They buried the Colonel in a little burying-place he had prepared on the hillside, when, at the height of the persecutions, Friends' burial grounds were condemned and the dead removed from them and re-interred in churchyards. The Colonel had said they should build a great wall round this new place, with a gate with a strong lock on it. Robert was now the Laird of Ury with much to be done on the estate of this nature.

An urgent appeal now arrived from George Fox, written just before the Colonel's death in October of which Fox had not then heard.

Edmonton, 5th Mo 1686. Dear Friend Robert Barclay, With my love to thee, and thy wife and father, and the rest . . . The occasion of

133

writing to thee at this time is that the Friends are very sensible of the great service thou hast concerning the Truth with the King and all the court and that thou hast their ear more than any Friend, and Liberty on Friends and Truth's behalf. And now dear Robert, we understanding that the occasion of sudden return, concerning the condition thy wife was now in, being now over by her being delivered, I desire thee and it is the desire of several friends, that whilst the door is open and the way so plain, thou wouldst be pleased to come to London with speed as soon as maybe. There is great service in thy coming on several accounts, more than I shall mention at this time; and so I hope the Lord will incline thy heart to weigh and consider thy service in it (Signed) George Fox.

But for Robert the door was by now anything but open nor the way plain for him to return to London at once. Not only were there his father's affairs to wind up but also the usually capable Christian had been brought low by nursing her old father-in-law so soon after her own illness and confinement. This was followed by the death of Robert's unmarried sister in Aberdeenshire, and it was not until the following spring of 1686 that he was able to return to London. King James by this time was in Chester, and Robert, having concluded his own business in London concerning Pennsylvania, prisons, and the interest of the Quakers generally, journeyed on to Chester, where he laid the statement of the grievances of the Friends before the King, proffering advice (that was not to be taken) to moderate his 'papist' policies. William Penn was there and, despite his complaining of some depression of spirit and bad health due to the strenuous life he led, together they held a large meeting in the Tennis Court at Chester. Afterwards, on the rough cobbled streets, Robert's horse stumbled and he had a serious fall. However, he continued his journey home through Lancashire in order to visit George Fox at his home at Swarthmore. He then rode on to Edinburgh and, calling on the Earl of Perth at Drummond Castle, he reached Ury, with relief, to be treated for his fall by Christian with her finest herbal ointments and her best liquid restoratives.

In April King James published his *Declaration for Liberty of Conscience* for the second time, but it met with much opposition as being the thin end of the wedge of re-establishing the Roman Church. The Archbishop of Canterbury and six bishops declared it to be illegal. King James tactlessly gave a splendid reception to the Pope's nuncio at Windsor, receiving him in a state usually accorded only to a foreign monarch. Bishops refused to read the *Declaration for Liberty of Conscience* from their pulpits, and seven more bishops were imprisoned, this time in the Tower of London.

By now, except for the minority of Roman Catholics, King James had few friends left except among the Quakers, whom he was still ready to meet more than halfway. Robert Barclay was much distressed over the differences between James II and his Parliament, but although he had many serious discussions with the King, and both he and Penn had frequently suggested his modifying his policy, it was against their Quaker tenet to interfere with politics, and Robert wrote at the time, 'I considered it not my business to make a judgement of these things.'

King James must have known that his chances of retaining the throne were growing slighter, for he repaid Robert £300 owing to his late father.

In the Tower of London, that summer, the bishops denied that they had been responsible for the death of innocent men during the religious persecutions. They demanded proofs, and Robert Barclay was deputed to visit them. He was able to show them undeniable evidence of some persons who, by order of bishops, had been kept in prison till death, even against the advice of physicians who were not Quakers. The bishops were unable to deny this. Robert, reassuring them that the Quakers had no intention of publishing such matters, begged them to moderate their views when they were free, and to look more favourably on liberty of conscience. It must have gone hard with those bishops being literally a captive audience to a sermon delivered by one of the sect they most despised.

The Quakers now turned to presenting another address to King James II, assuring him of their loyalty and affection, but begging for a complete clearance from all the jails of Friends who were still being detained for refusing to take oaths and on other smaller accounts. The King accepted the address with good humour, but Penn and Barclay must have known as well as anyone that his reign was nearing its end.

It is recorded in the family that, 'at their final parting, Robert was standing alone with the King at a window whence they could see a weather-vane, which showed in the parlance of the court "whether the wind set from the Papist or Protestant quarter", and James looking out, said, doubtless with some bitterness, "The wind is now fair for the Prince of Orange, his coming over." Robert Barclay said regretfully, "It seems hard that no expedient could be found to satisfy the people." To which the King replied, "I would do anything becoming a gentleman, except to part with the liberty of conscience which I never will while I live."'

Soon afterwards the King's second wife, Queen Mary of Modena, gave birth to the son who was declared to be the invention of a papist plot, and brought into the palace in a warming-pan in order to produce a male heir who could quickly be christened as a Roman Catholic.

The seven bishops were acquitted and were drawn in triumph through the streets of London, while a secret message went off to the King's daughter, Mary, married to Charles I's grandson, William of Orange, with the invitation to take over the throne at once.

When William of Orange landed at Torbay on November 5th, 1688, James concentrated his forces at Salisbury. The west flocked to the standard of the Prince of Orange, and was soon followed by the rest of England. James fled and was captured. Escape to France was made easy for him. Here he eventually joined the Queen and his baby son. William and Mary became joint sovereigns. One of the first measures William was to take was the passing of the Toleration Act[2] which the Friends regarded as proof that they had not suffered in vain. The Protestant Church remained, but the minority sect could worship as it

---

[2] The Toleration Act of 1689, allowing Nonconformists to worship more freely, brought an end to meetings being raided, but legalised for over a century certain civil disabilities for all Dissenters, notably excluding them from university education and positions of public responsibility.

wished. The 'glorious revolution' was over and Robert Barclay never returned to London.

At Ury there were now seven children. One of their many guests, John Gratton, writing of his visit to Ury, observed that when the children were up and dressed in the morning Christian 'sate down with them before breakfast and in religious manner waited upon the Lord.' A variation of this form of family prayers, accompanied by the tantalising smell of breakfast toast and eggs and bacon, continued in the homes of many of Christian's descendants to the middle of the present century.

Although Christian herself later received a summons for disturbing the peace in church by getting up and replying at length to the minister, she was in definite favour of considerably less noise at home. It was hardly surprising that, with her seven rumbustious children Christian desired 'that we may all travel more and more into silence'. And how understandable to any mother that, as Christian passed round her 'white and green marmaletts', she should have cause to advocate the avoidance of 'superfluous words and jesting, yea, needless words from both young and old'.

Robert, the eldest, aged sixteen, had now left Theobalds and was able to do a great deal to help his father with the farm and the estate generally. He had all the natural inclinations to become a keen forester, landscape gardener and a naturalist-sportsman. Together he and his father planned and planted and laid out extensions to the garden to make it 'not only a productive place but one of great beauty and in every way of innocent delight'. In both aims they succeeded, as can be found in the accounts of the many children who continued to enjoy the garden for 200 years.

'A cherry garden and delightful avenues,' are described, 'of 25 different sorts of trees with the many colirs of the leaves so nicely intermixed', with 'nearly a thousand trees, thought to be a most considerable planting so very near the East sea.'

A quarter of a mile north of the house, in a hollow surrounded with rising ground upon all sides but one, is a very beautiful pond with two islands in it, planted with trees, in which the wild ducks breed yearly of their own accord. The pond is well stored with fishes, several very fine springs being brought into it, and the rising ground round it planted with trees of various sorts, as elms, birch, and willows near the water, and having a boat in it to go to the islands makes it a very pleasant place.

He hath also, about half a mile from his house to the North East, a natural pond or loch, in which are very good perch and very large; and much frequented by wild ducks.

Young Rob did much of the actual work himself as well as acting as a kind of unofficial gamekeeper, taking his duties as the son of a landed proprietor and feudal baron more seriously than his father did. Records survive of the baron court at which, later, young Rob held forth on the questions of destruction of 'wodis and docattis (dovecotes) and the killing of haires, doves, partridges, moore foullis (moor fowls) duke and drake and the poaching thereof.'

Robert Barclay, like his father the Colonel before him, was a man of such farsighted imagination that the plans made and begun to be carried out during the next two years with his son may well have given him as much satisfaction as if they had been completed in his lifetime. Alterations were also to be made to the house; a new front door was planned, with a sheltering porch. Wooden shutters were to be added to some of the windows to keep out the prevailing wind. The workmen started to hack away the stone to make the new entrance, but the wall was so hard and strong that they were only able to carry away enough stone chippings to fill their aprons. Robert himself cannot have given much in the way of physical help by now, for his health was already troubling him. He wrote to a Friend saying that he was so indisposed he could not meet him but would send his man with 'the raw project, which thou may see, it being the first and only coppy I have, to receive the amendments of thy mature judgement which, when thou *hast perused them corrected*'. He told him to send it on, but 'I shall expect my coppy back, next week and the weather being tollerable, iff in health, upon advertisement, will meet thee where thou wilt point.'

A series of meetings had been arranged in Aberdeen in the

autumn of 1690, and though Robert, still only forty-two, felt worn and wearied out, he undertook to attend them and to arrange for Friends to visit the scattered Quakers in wild outlying districts who could not easily reach the towns. He rode up to Kingswells, the house of the Jaffrays whose son was eventually to marry his daughter, little Christian, and he and some other preachers visiting the Jaffrays sat up late, discussing and arguing. One who watched him observed 'his exalted look, as if he was holding communing with God, and had lost recollection of the place and the company, and when he roused to take food he barely tasted it, and bade saddle the horses at once, as he would fein be at home.'

He went back to Ury, though clearly unfit to travel, and was at once struck down with a violent fever, but only for a few days in which he gave his whole mind to comforting the family and telling Christian and their eldest boy how they should continue without him, until he had barely strength to lay his hands on the head of each of his children. He died on the 3rd October 1690, 'passing peacefully at sunset, with messages of love to all on his lips'.

He was buried beside his father, on the summit of the hill which the Colonel had chosen, looking over their beloved countryside with its stretches of purple heather, belts of dark pine trees and clumps of golden gorse. Among the many letters written to Christian was one from George Fox beginning, 'Now dear Friend, though the Lord hath taken thy dear husband from thee his wife and his children, the Lord will be a husband to thee and a father to thy children . . . much more might be written concerning this faithful brother in the Lord, and pillar in the church of Christ, who was a man I very much loved for his labour and the truth, but I will leave the rest to his countrymen.' George Fox died himself just over three months later, leaving William Penn to lament over the passing 'of the bright stars almost together, and of the first magnitude'. Penn lived on nearly another thirty years, and Christian even longer, so that she saw the Colonel's and Robert's and their eldest son's dreams for Ury fully realised.

Rob was eighteen when his father died but, owing to a long gap while Robert was travelling, the rest of Christian's children were still small. John, who later settled and married in Dublin, was only three. Two of his sisters were not much older. Both married Forbes brothers and also settled in Dublin. Two elder sisters married and remained in Scotland. David was eight when his father died. Like his grandfather and namesake, the Colonel, David had an easy understanding of figures and found no difficulty in working out complicated money arrangements that baffled his more literary-minded and country-oriented brother.

From the merchants of Stonehaven and from noticing what merchandise left their quays, David Barclay picked up enough to decide, when still a young man, to become an export merchant. With his portion from his father of about £500 he became a London apprentice to James Taylor, citizen and glover and, like all wise apprentices, married his master's daughter. He worked in association with his father-in-law and joined the Drapers' Company but, as a Quaker, had to be asked to be excused from serving as its Master, for which he was fined £20. By then he had opened up trade abroad on a tremendous scale, and had become one of the most respected export merchants in London, living in the finest house in Cheapside, a main thoroughfare for centuries and seat of important linen drapers and goldsmiths.

David Barclay's fine mansion, known as the Sign of the Bear, had been built on a double site after the Great Fire by Sir Edward Waldo, who had entertained Charles II and his suite by 'setting themselves on the balcony, under a canopy of state' to get the best view available of the Lord Mayor's Show. The Sign of the Bear stood between Milk Street and Honey Lane, looking across the busy cobbled thoroughfare to the high door in the tower of St. Mary le Bow, whose proudest of all Wren's steeples was a constant reminder to the Quaker Barclays of the Established Church of England. David had six children by his first wife, Anne Taylor, and after she died in 1721, another eight by his second wife, Priscilla Freame, his banker's daughter.

Chapter Eight

David of Cheapside
1761–1770

By the summer of 1761, when David Gurney's young widow,
Christiana, returned, after a day on the Norfolk broads with her
two little girls, to the house of her father, David Barclay of
Cheapside, the Sign of the Bear had disappeared. The heavy
wooden signs and their rusting frames had become dangerous:
indeed, one had brought down a whole wall into the street,
killing a passer-by. Now David Barclay just as proudly displayed
the new street number 108 above the main entrance and office,
which was bow-fronted not unlike a shop. Beyond it was 'a great
warehouse, counting-houses, parlour and kitchen', with extensions built out behind over the coach-house and loose boxes
round the stable yard. From the dark central hall a broad staircase
led in two stages up to the first floor, where the long dining-room
stretched out behind the sparsely furnished drawing-room, with
its balcony overlooking Cheapside. The stairs led on up to two
more bedroom floors with, here and there, a curiously placed
little door shaped to fit additional steps leading to the nurseries
built on for the original fourteen children. Now the nurseries
were in use again for the grandchildren.

Christiana's uncle, Rob Barclay, Laird of Ury, wrote of his
father, the Apologist, '50 years to the day after Robert died, his
three sons and four daughters were still alive and there were
already over fifty grandchildren and great-grandchildren living.'
And now another twenty years had passed, and Christiana was
leading her little Prissy and Chrissy to a top front window to
point out the dragon wind-vane she had known as a child on the

steeple of St. Mary-le-Bow, across the street. The next day they declared it had flown away, and indeed it was not until they were a couple of elderly Quaker spinsters living in Bath that the dragon vane was restored.

There were two 'only child' grandchildren of about the same ages as Chrissy and Prissy – Lucy, daughter of another of the ten beauties, who married her first cousin, the current laird of Ury; and Agatha, daughter of Christiana's brother and a Bradford heiress who had died after Agatha's birth. Then there were the children of another brother, at least one of whom was born in the house in Cheapside. There were also the children, who were yet to be seen, of her eldest brother who had emigrated to America and married there. But her favourites were the children of her dearest sister Catherine, the one 'Barclay Beauty' of the ten said to have 'married entirely for love'. Catherine was 'small, like several of her sisters, fair complexioned with dark eyes, a profusion of flaxen hair, her mind elastic, influencing her body, for she was all lightness and activity and native cheerfulness flowed from engaging features. Her manners were gentle and her talk merry, but, although she was a Friend in spirit, she never closely followed Quaker habits.' She loved the theatre and she loved her family, but most of all she loved Daniel Bell, 'a medium-sized, sinewy, ruddy complexioned agricultural student without so much as a square rood of his own to farm'. Since Catherine was determined to marry him, her father bought him seventy acres, and, when that failed, set him up as a coal merchant with 'a pleasant convenient house' at Stamford Hill with seventy more acres of Hackney marsh behind it and a wharf and a warehouse on the River Lea for the coal.

But Daniel Bell appears to have had little heart for coal, preferring fox-hunting. He was kind, easy-tempered, affectionate and contented – too contented, perhaps. Today he would have been called an ecologist, for he was a keen naturalist and ardent sportsman, 'expressing himself with satisfaction in both the bountiful and disastrous in nature'. All weather was for the best, as were shipwrecks, earthquakes, and a continual flow of little Bells.

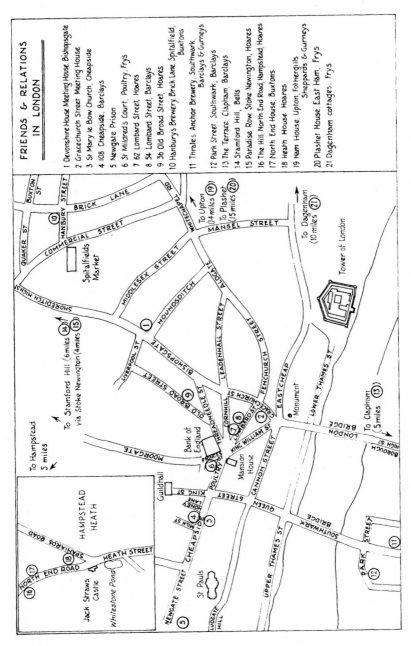

FRIENDS & RELATIONS
IN LONDON

1 Devonshire House Meeting House, Bishopsgate
2 Gracechurch Street Meeting House
3 St Mary le Bow Church. Cheapside
4 108 Cheapside. Barclays
5 Newgate Prison
6 St Mildred's Court, Poultry. Frys
7 62 Lombard Street, Hoares
8 54 Lombard Street, Barclays
9 36 Old Broad Street, Hoares
10 Hanbury's Brewery, Brick Lane, Spitalfield.
   Buxtons
11 Thrales Anchor Brewery, Southwark.
   Barclays & Gurneys
12 Park Street. Southwark, Barclays
13 The Terrace. Clapham. Barclays
14 Stamford Hill. Bells
15 Paradise Row, Stoke Newington, Hoares
16 The Hill, North End Road, Hampstead, Hoares
17 North End House, Buxtons
18 Heath House Hoares
19 Ham House, Upton, Fothergills
20 Plashet House. East Ham. Frys
   Sheppards & Gurneys
21 Dagenham cottages. Frys

Nothing can have been more delightful, disorganising and noisy than a visit from Stamford Hill by Catherine and her brood, Prixy, Dan Bell, Kitty, Becky and six more to come. The squeaks and tumbles on the stairs, the hisses to try to keep them all quiet – and, it was said, old David, their grandfather, trying to enjoy his family while avoiding Daniel's attempts to borrow five pounds.

It was lovely for Christiana and her little girls to see them all, but with her husband so lately dead, although Quakers did not go into mourning, it was hard for her to enjoy anything that was too much of a party.

When it was learnt in the family that enquiries had been made on behalf of the new King, George III, whether he might bring his bride, Queen Charlotte, whom he had only just married, to David Barclay's house to watch her first Lord Mayor's Show from his balcony. He had gladly extended an invitation, but Christiana felt that she could not face the hurry and fatigue beforehand, let alone meet the royal guests.

Lord Bruce, who was in waiting, informed her brother that the King 'sensible of the trouble which he should give', asked to inquire whether the honour of knighthood would be acceptable. Old David was 'astonished at their condescension' but answered politely if plainly that he 'desired no other compensation than the satisfaction he should receive by accommodating the royal family'.

Christiana returned to Norfolk with Prissy, Chrissy and their faithful nanny, leaving her sister, who had hurried down from Scotland with little Lucy, now aged five, to tell her all about it.

Their father spared no expense in repairing the house both inside and out, as well as decorating it and the balcony with a quantity of plainly scolloped, rather than frilled, valances and curtains of finest cloth. Lord Bruce came several times to teach them their duty and direct the arrangements of the furniture 'but the head of the house was firm on the matter of their costume, and insisted that the family should be dressed as plain Friends.' This caused a certain amount of excitement among several of them, but they had to comply, and when the brothers were

144

dressed in plain cloth and the sisters in plain silks with dressed
black hoods, their father admitted drily that 'on the whole they
made a genteel appearance, and acted their part in the mas-
querade very well.' The testimony of *The Apology* appeared to be
maintained.

'About one o'clock on 13th November 1761, papa and mama
took their stands at the street door where our two brothers had
been waiting a long time to receive the nobility, about 100 of
whom were waiting in the warehouse, from which every appearance of merchandise was removed and it was properly decorated
for the purpose.' In fact they waited several hours, for according to
the Annual Register of 1761, the royal cavalcade set out from the
palace about twelve o'clock, but 'by mismanagement of those
who should have cleared the way of hackney coaches and ob-
structions', not to mention the crush and press of ambling chair-
men, galloping butchers' boys and the hooped skirts of the ladies
of a certain class who should not be allowed, it was said at the
time, to stroll the streets at noonday, 'it was nearly four hours
before the royal family got to Friend Barclay's house opposite
Bow Church.'

When the royal family arrived, they were conducted into one
of the counting-houses which was transformed into 'a very
pretty parlour'. The brothers then spread a carpet on the platform
that had been extended on to the street. The Queen came up,
handed by her chamberlain; the King followed with the rest of
the royal family according to their rank. As they went up the first
flight of solid stairs in the house the King and Queen were faced
by the sombre sight of no less than forty of the family ranged on
the next flight, silent and immobile in their orthodox habits, all
heads covered. The royal family hastened to the balcony to show
themselves to the populace 'roaring, hurrahing, hiccuping,
waving and pointing below'. Though afterwards both their
Majesties 'considered their visit to the honest Quaker as devoid
of etiquette, yet his family contrived to maintain an elegant
decorum without infringing upon their own primitive simplicity . . . the King's example of kissing all the fawn-coloured
ladies was followed by the princes, his brothers and his royal

145

uncle.' Little Lucy, however, refused to be kissed by a stranger and would not go with the Duke of York to be introduced to the King until her mother had assured her that he was no less than a prince; then she gave him her hand most willingly and frolicked along beside him. Whereupon her mother, who was most anxious about her behaviour, writes that her

> little darling Lucy unexpectedly remembered all instruction and kissed the Queen's hand with such grace that I thought the princess dowager would smother her with kisses. On the return to the drawing-room such a report was made that 'little miss' was sent for again while she greatly amused the King by telling him she loved the King though she must not love fine things and that her grandpapa would not allow her to make a curtsy. The simplicity of her dress and manner seemed to give the King great pleasure and she was dismissed with applause.

Prixy Bell, being a little older, apologised to the King for not making a curtsy, as her grandpapa would not permit it. She was reassured that the objection of Friends 'to bend the knee to Baal', was met by the King by absolving them from the law of kneeling in his presence.

> The great repast had been laid out in the back parlour and the kitchen, which was elegantly set off for the occasion, [and while the Queen and others were refreshing themselves with it, Lucy was, she writes,] 'in raptures, not only from the brilliancy of her appearance, [but by] that inexpressible something that is beyond a set of features . . . [the Queen] is vastly genteel, with an air truly majestic. Her hair, which is of light colour, being in what is called Coronation ringlets, has a circle of diamonds. Her clothes, which were as rich as gold and silver and silk could make them, were a suit from which fell a train supported by a little page in scarlet and silver. The lustre of her stomacher was inconceivable, on which was represented, by the vast profusion of diamonds placed on it, the magnificence attending so great a prince – who, I must tell you, I think a fine personable man. I doubt not that the novelty of our appearance aroused her curiosity, from amidst such a profusion of glitter, we must look like a parcel of nuns.

The leave taken by the royal family was 'such as we might expect from our equals, full of apologies for the trouble they had given us and returning thanks for the entertainment. My brothers attended them to the coach in the same manner as they had received them, only with the additional honour of assisting the Queen to get in.' The old Quaker prayed that God would be pleased to bless the King and all his family, and this was received in the spirit in which it was intended.

A story then circulating declared that the King and Queen were one day driving down Cheapside when the horses took fright and were stopped by David Barclay, who said 'Friend George, wilt thou bring thy wife Charlotte into my house to recover from her alarm?' But whether this was started by friends of the Friends in defence of David Barclay's involvement with such glamour, or whether by the duchess (of Richmond) who expressed disappointment at not being invited to Mr. Barclay's and rather grudgingly accepted the Lord Mayor's offer of a seat nearly opposite the Sign of the Bear, will never be known.

Back in Norfolk. Christiana's 'brothers' and 'sisters', as families always referred affectionately to in-laws and blood-siblings alike, were as intrigued as she was to hear 'how matters were concluded at Cheapside on the late important day'.

When Christiana's brother-in-law, Johnny, moved to Keswick on his mother's death, he and his wife Bett made her eleven grandchildren feel as much at home there as they had done in her day, a tendency that uncles inheriting well-loved grandparental homes have continued to show in the family to this day. Not only Christiana's two little girls were as welcome as ever, but also such of her little Bell nephews and nieces as happened to be sent to stay with her for the sea air of Yarmouth, where she lived. John of Keswick, as Johnny was now known, not wishing to be separated from his delicate brother, Sam, who was also now married, built a second house close to his own old Hall for Sammy and his family, with a front door without steps so that his brother could now wheel himself in a chair in and out of the house. Gradually sixteen rustic summer-houses grew up, almost like bushes, in the garden they shared, each with a space left between the seats for Sam's chair.

John and Bett had twelve children, all born in the Court House, Magdalen Street, but alas eight died between the ages of one and thirteen. A son of four and daughter of thirteen died a few years after they moved to Keswick, leaving four to supply the enormous crop of Keswick descendants. Hardly surprisingly, Bett's little Johnny, known when his father became John of Keswick as 'Johnny-for-short', was pampered by his mother and kept at home from school at the slightest cough. When he went to school it was in the family carriage, which gave rise to considerable teasing, not only from his fellow scholars, but also from the urchins of the town. His bright red hair brought forth jibes of 'Have ye got a bonfire on yer head?' He was fair-skinned and slight and exceptionally lively, despite his mother's fears. His brother Richard, seven years older, had brown hair, a rather florid complexion and prominent nose, which was thought to be responsible for his curiously nasal voice. 'Little Johnny was merry and kind, and Richard was bluff and generous.' Their only sister, Rachel, was fair and full of fun, and the younger brother, Joseph, was solemn and grave. So close were these brothers and their sister that they were known in the family as the 'Devoted Four'.

When Johnny-for-short was fourteen, he made his first real friend who was not a relation. Sam Hoare was the youngest son of a staid Stoke Newington Quaker, originally from Cork. He was apprenticed, aged fourteen, to John and Henry Gurney, and lived with their family in what is now Pitt Street. John, the shorter brother, was by then a widower with only one teenage daughter, and so it was from the Yorkshire wife of the 'tall Mr. Gurney' that Sam took his domestic orders. Her son, Bartlett, was only nine when Sam arrived. She also had six daughters, so for Sam Hoare the discovery of a boy cousin his own age must have been something of a relief, although he did not show it. He was a quiet reserved boy with a far better education behind him than Johnny-for-short had picked up on his spasmodic sorties to school in the carriage. Sam had been sent to boarding-school at Penketh in Lancashire at the age of five, of which experience he only remembered pocketing an apple pie and putting another on his plate to make quite sure of a second helping, and hearing a voice, that seemed to come from heaven, calling out, 'Sam, eat that which thou hast got in thy pocket first.' He then went to the then well-known Riveaux school when it was first established at Highbury.

Sam was always short of money and when he went out on 'excursions of pleasure with the Gurneys', writes his daughter, 'they, who had more money at command, payed his expenses.' Sam was fond of animals and birds, and kept tame pigeons, an innocent enough pursuit. Johnny-for-short loved him for his almost morose shyness and lack of grace, which were both so opposite to his own nature. The young apprentice, completely ignoring his masters' six daughters, remained dolefully in love with a girl years older than himself, who hardly seemed to notice his existence. Sam was always quietly, if not actually shabbily, dressed, as befitted a young Friend, in 'a suit of one colour', if drab could be called a colour. The one occasion that he appeared looking at all smart was when he returned from Stoke Newington in a blue coat, wearing a powdered bob wig. Within hours he had fallen into the mill pool at Hempstead when shooting with his master and came out covered in duck weed. He wrote to his father entreating him to help him to replace his coat, causing his father to write to Henry Gurney enquiring if the extravagant demands of his son were 'the result of dissipation and bad company'.

John of Keswick was also at this time expressing a fear lest his increasing opulence should lead his children away from those religious habits in which they had been educated. He expressed this anxiety, not in a letter, but in a combined journal and memorandum, considerably smaller than the sixteenth-century John Gurney's manuscript books, but serving much the same purpose. Each page, now turning brown like autumn leaves, is interleaved with pale mulberry-coloured blotting paper. Much of the writing consists of religious reflection in which he regrets that his children had not altogether fallen in with the peculiarities of Quakerism, for, he says, nothing else would have led him to dissent from the established church of England. In fact his family had not strayed very far. There were times when they missed attending meeting, when their speech as well as their behaviour had not always the uplifting nature demanded by the Quakers, though they had no difficulty in using the 'single language' – the biblical *thees* and *thous* which they had learnt to speak at their mother's knee, nor in referring to the month of the year and days of the week by numbers rather than the 'heathen names used by the worldly'. In so many instances Quakerism had become a cult rather than a Christian cause, with Friends adhering to the outward and visible signs, the archaic uniform and language, rather than the simplicity of faith.

His second son, Johnny-for-short, in particular, was not in all respects strictly maintaining the habits of a Friend, though this was probably due to the over-indulgence of his mother, whose 'grand darling' he had always been. However, he was 'generous, ardent, warm-hearted and abounding in kindness'.

John of Keswick's book shows intermittent surprise at his 'remarkable prosperity'. His property had been £11,000 just before the birth of his second son, but had increased towards the end of his life, through prodigiously hard work, utterly honest dealings, and spending only about one third of his income, by ninefold. 'Despite wool failure due to death among sheep a few years since' and 'dearer wool in Ireland with English yarn much cheaper', despite 'big losses', it appeared on his inspection, he writes, that he calculates the year before 'I was worth £100,000 including my household goods. This year I gained £1900 of which I spent and paid out about £500.' This was his private account and not that of the firm or of his brother and partner, Sam. It gives some idea of the savings that could be made by a 'manufacturer country squire' who avoided all show. John of Keswick travelled a great deal, kept open house to almost all comers, gave generously to charity, and was extremely open-handed with his own family.

Quaker merchants' coaches were without the brilliant decoration of other rich men's. John Gurney only allowed his sombre coach to be finished with plain green wheels. There were no springs and even on the new turnpikes the coach could give a bumpy ride. He mentions 'a journey to Bath, myself, wife and attendants. Crown Inn, Maidenhead. Nothing particular occurred more than rolling over the roads eating drinking and sleeping.'

'Nothing particular occurred' was something worth recording in days when even the soundest harness was liable to snap, a wheeler go lame or another horse to stumble, or there be no cock-horse at the bottom of a hill to help them up. This journey was not entirely on behalf of the Society nor, for once, the woollen industry, but John had not been well and the healthful waters of Bath and its doctors was so highly recommended that even a Quaker considered them worth trying.

Sometimes John of Keswick filled the coach with his family, and it was with their uncle and aunt that Prissy and Chrissy were first introduced to their beloved Bath, where they later lived together for many years.

Johnny-for-short and his friend Sam Hoare compared notes over those family outings. A Keswick journey of twenty-five miles, starting after an early breakfast, and refreshing the horses twice on the road, brought them to their destination late in the evening. Time usually passed quickly on these journeys with 'stories and anecdotes and quaint observations'. Sam's sister refers, however, to the Hoare family journeys as 'insupportably tedious'. Their father used his own carriage and horses with post leaders, taking a week to reach his favourite destination of Scarborough. Sam was happier fishing and occasionally shooting with the Gurneys than being forced to join the stately trundle. Indeed, although he was not particularly partial to poetry, he preferred to read *Paradise Lost* in one of the Keswick summerhouses with 'lame Sam Gurney', whose two little daughters played about under the ancient trees close by the lake. The east side of the old Hall was covered by an extraordinary large vine, and there was a heronry near at hand by the river, and a rookery and the remains of Keswick church at no great distance. He spoke of the old walled gardens and plantations of much beauty, and of the walks by the riverside. There was at Keswick something that combined calm and liveliness.

Johnny-for-short's mother, born 'Bett' Kett, had all the spirit of her rebellious forebears, mixed with an abounding generosity and her own particular kind of Quakerism, which was not exactly dominated by economy. Her family teased her good-naturedly over her indecision over plans both great and small. She was celebrated for changing her mind over meals: she would order a good plain plum duff for dinner, and then be tempted 'because she was so eminently indulgent to her children and grandchildren', by the thought of almond frummery or delicious whipped syllabubs, and then go back to changing a breast of mutton for a sausage pie. During the course of the morning, the cook became so confused by her changing her orders that on one occasion she 'prepared everything fixed and sent them all up so that a most enormous repast of many dishes appeared on the table'.

When Johnny-for-short went to stay with Sam's family in a pleasant, unassuming house in Paradise Row, Stoke Newington, he had to admit that the atmosphere was set at 'a more consistent pitch'.

Sam Hoare's father had agreed to change his mode of dress once only in his lifetime to please his bride, but 'would alter it no more.' Thus, in the plain surroundings of the meeting house he had stood out as being ornate, dressed, as in the former reign, in a large white wig with rows of curls, and a mulberry coloured suit, the coat with wide sleeves opening very high from the wrists with sugar loaf buttons, black worsted stockings and shirt front, instead of a frill, so elaborately plaited that only the housekeeper was equal to putting finishing touches to her master's costume. Sam's mother, however, never went out without her black bonnet and 'duffield' (or duffle) cloak, whose coarse wool from Antwerp was favoured by very 'plain' Friends.

When visiting Sam Hoare's family in London, Johnny-for-short would certainly have called on his aunt Christiana's parents, the David Barclays, at 108 Cheapside. David was by now an old man, with a wife twenty years younger than himself.

In 1766, when Johnny-for-short was sixteen, the David Barclays were faced with a totally unexpected blow by the deaths, within a week, of first Mrs. David Barclay's brother, a senior partner of Freames Bank of 54 Lombard Street, and then his partner, James Barclay, who was both her brother-in-law and her stepson.

However, the bank was saved through Christiana, mother of Chrissy and Prissy, recovering from the death of her young husband four years before this, and becoming the wife of the late banker James Freame's only son, John Freame, aged thirty-one. The David Barclays had a way of producing the most complicated relationships by not only bridging generation gaps but by marrying back into their own family. David Barclay of Cheapside and his eldest son had made themselves brothers-in-law by marrying two sisters, the two daughters of the late John Freame of Freame's Bank. The amalgamation between the two successful houses of 108 Cheapside and 54 Lombard Street was triply insured. David's daughter marrying her mother's co-heir of Freame's Bank tied the matter neatly up. Christiana moved from Yarmouth to 54 Lombard Street where also lived, under the rigid discipline of young John Freame's widowed mother, John Barclay, his five children and his pretty would-be fashionable wife. These great rambling business houses had plenty of living-room for several families as well as the firm's apprentices, all of whom dined together, unless a young wife could think of an excuse to dine alone in her room or with her children.

David Barclay went to great lengths to make openings and offer business opportunities to all his sons, sons-in-law, nephews, grandsons and great-nephews. Some, carrying out the jobs honestly and diligently, believed themselves to be specially favoured by the influential David, although it might have been clear to all that in his father's eyes, the only rightful heir to the Cheapside build-up was David's own eldest son. It was curious how in a community in which there was said to be 'no first and no last but all equality,' the eldest son, as in the case of hereditary titles, was considered to be a man's indisputable heir. If there were no sons, then the eldest daughter took precedence.

However this eldest son had no intention of returning to take his place as heir from Philadelphia, where he had settled and built up his own merchant company. But he did allow his own only son, Robert, whose mother had died when he was two, to be brought to England when he was twelve, the year after the royal visit to Cheapside. Robert, or Black Bob as he called himself when he first met his many flaxen and apricot-haired cousins, was sent to live in the country with his eldest strictly Quaker uncle and the little Hudson heiress, Agatha, and her step-mother. Bob said later that he had no idea what a Quaker was, but as soon as he arrived in England his uncle divested him of the gold lace on his coat and declared him to be a Quaker. He was sent to school at Wandsworth where he was good enough at French, or anyway worked hard enough, to win a prize inscribed with his name. He was later taken into his grandfather's business at 108 Cheapside, in which house he also lived. Bob settled down at his grandfather's right hand and just had time to learn the essentials of the great export house before David Barclay of Cheapside died, in his eighty-eighth year.

For six months 108 Cheapside went on in memory of its founder as it had done before, with David's widow, twenty years younger than himself, still in command of the great place. By then Christiana had a son by John Freame junior, whom she took to Keswick with Prissy and Chrissy to visit their uncle and aunt. Almost at once two more important partners died within a month of each other. Delicate Sam Gurney could hardly have been expected to live to be more than forty-seven. What came as a really great shock, only a month later, in March 1770, was the sudden death of his brother John of Keswick, on whom Sam had always relied. His sons Richard and Johnny-for-short were twenty-seven and twenty. Rachel was fifteen on the day of her father's burial at the Gildencroft, and grave little Joseph was thirteen.

John Gurney of Keswick was just fifty-five, and building up a great reputation. His shrewd opinion was considered a heavy loss to Norwich commerce and his kindness was much missed by the city's poor. 'Grace was his form and in that form enshrined,' eloquently writes 'Crito' in a long poem on his death, published in the *Gentleman's Magazine*. 'As in its temple, dwelt a purer mind.'

John left £100,000, a great deal of money at that time, and partnerships to his two sons, with the instruction to change the name of the firm to R. and J. Gurney. David Barclay of Cheapside, a year before, had left £100,000 with partnerships to his most likely descendants, of whom Robert Barclay, 'Bob', was to be the most important.

Hardly surprisingly, three out of four of the late John Gurney of Keswick's children eventually married three of the late David Barclay of Cheapside's grandchildren.

The deaths, within one year, of four immensely rich Quakers led to the funnelling of all their resources into what was to become the greatest commercial enterprise in the country, known today as Barclay's Bank.

But first the newly named firm of R. and J. Gurney had to find its feet, placed as it was on the rim of this great commercial vortex.

Chapter Nine

Johnny-for-short
1770–1775

'Do not forget to take a cloak and have plenty of gruel made to take with thee in case thou art sick,' Bett wrote to her 'grand-darling', before he set out from London on his first excursion on behalf of the newly-named firm of R. and J. Gurney. He was just twenty-one, and Richard, who was with him and already a seasoned traveller and established man of business, was twenty-six. Whether Johnny-for-short followed his mother's advice or not, he must have treasured her letter, for the envelope, formed by folding the double sheet of paper, is endorsed in his own hand 'mother's letter'. He could only have thought tenderly of his dear over-solicitous mother – the once rebellious Bett Kett – at home at Keswick, with young Rachel and grave Joseph and the other newly-widowed mother and her two little girls next door. The quiet fawn coats and matching breeches and boots may well have been concealed by warm cloaks, but there can have been no mistaking the significance of the brothers' black, broadbrimmed hats, uncocked with the braid or cockades that formed the normal tricorne of the period. The Quaker hat was as much a badge of religion as is a clergyman's collar today: in business it was the sure sign of security and honest dealing; in the customs house it was a reminder of the Quaker testimony against defrauding the King of any of his duties and excise.

The young Gurneys were on their way from Norwich, six months after the deaths of their father and uncle, to buy home-spun yarn from Southern Ireland.

Gruel or no gruel, the chances of being sea-sick were great, for during the last week in November 1770, their ship tossed for four days off Dublin 'in the most heavy gales I was ever in', writes its captain. 'There was damage to the main boom and several shrouds broken. I was obliged to carry sail to keep off the shore.'

Although the ship was badly damaged, the Gurneys were eventually reported 'safe at Strangford', which harbour, the captain calculated, somewhat inaccurately, as being about 'half-way between Dublin and Belfast – fourteen leagues from each'. A league being a variable measure, usually about three miles, the travellers might have expected to make the journey to Dublin in not much more than a day, if good horses could be found. But, as Johnny pointed out later, the captain's leagues were 'more variable than most', and although the Gurneys could have reached Belfast in a day, they found on landing that they had three days' travel before they could hope to reach Dublin. It was a hungry journey, for they carried little money for fear of roadside robbers whose attacks it was against their religious scruples to counter. The superstition that striking a Quaker was inevitably followed by ill luck and damnation was beginning to wear thin even in Ireland. However, the hats served as letters of introduction among traders, and once they reached Dublin a meal and a bed with congenial opportunities to exchange business and family news could be expected in any of the houses of the Friends, many of whom were related in some near or far-flung manner. There were still, in Dublin, several direct descendants of Robert Barclay, the Apologist, including the particularly agreeable Experience Barclay, daughter of an earlier Experience, the Apologist's daughter-in-law.

The broad streets, squares and crescents, the subtle variety of porticoes, fanlights and balcony railings can still give an idea of the elegance of the fair city when they were new enough to be bright and fresh, and yet had been laid out long enough for the trees in between them to unfold. Most of the great merchants' houses were in these elite new neighbourhoods. Others were interspersed, as a few still are, among the smaller buildings on the quays. A few Dutch houses with their crow-stepped gables still remain, dating back, as in Norwich, to the early introduction of Flemish weavers.

Ladies and the elderly were still carried in sedan chairs over distances too short to be worth their getting into their carriages. This was as much in the interest of safety as in order to keep their finery unblemished, for the riotous young Dublin bucks had unpleasant bouts of riding about, not only deliberately splashing mud but also slashing and mugging to watch the effect. 'Gentle-man-hoodlums' rushed about burgling and setting fire to even their own families' houses for the same reason.

The mocking of Quakers for their own sakes had now died down to no more than was to be expected from cheeky bare-footed urchins, who ran beside almost anyone dressed differently from themselves, calling out such jibes as 'Be me sowl, I like the joltin' of yer jaunty cap.'

However, hospitality was generous, spectacular and con-vivial. Even in Quaker houses, food and wine were lavish, although the scientific and literary conversation advocated by George Fox as a suitable form of recreation was sometimes replaced in Dublin by dancing, for which Johnny-for-short found he had a natural bent. He was described then as being about five feet ten inches high and very good looking without being regularly handsome, with 'a bright complexion and great animation of countenance as well as manner'.

When intellectual conversation led, as it invariably did, to business enquiries, Johnny-for-short's scanty education was off-set by an ability to assess points quickly, always with an eye to the humanities. He noticed that Irish spinners worked in their damp thatched-roof cottages in far worse conditions than any he had seen in and around Norwich. On their behalf he was anxious to buy yarn quickly and not to wait for the price to drop as it was expected to do.

The often-financially-embarrassed Sam Hoare, who was still apprenticed to the son of the Weavers' Friend in Norwich, had tentatively suggested that 'R. and J. Gurney' might call on his family business in Cork – 'if it were still operating'. It took four days to ride from Dublin to Cork, stopping at inns on the way.

The brothers found Hoare Lane, leading to a small banking establishment in the ruined city walls, with a 'lenny', or long shed, abutting on one of the old defence towers converted into a store. A gateway through the wall led to the long quay where merchants discharged their cargo from ships arriving on the tidal stream which is now Gratton Street. The Hoares themselves had long ago moved into a fine house about four miles east of Cork. The house was – and still is – called Factory Hill from the ruins of an Elizabethan factory in the grounds, 'resembling an ancient castle ruin, picturesquely clothed in ivy'.

The military atmosphere of Factory Hill showed few signs of this branch of the family ever having been Quakers. The master of the house, Edward Hoare, Sam's second cousin and exactly his age, was a cornet in the Thirteenth Light Dragoons. In only four months in the army he had already acquired a sufficiently extravagant outlook to lead him later into considerable debts. He spent money on all the trimmings that Friends were brought up to despise, such as a heavily embroidered satin mess-coat and a delicately-stitched waistcoat and velvet breeches; he trailed an elegantly embossed dress-sword, and, in the stables, his horse's harness was studded with elaborate brasses. The Gurneys weighed up whether a war with France, to which Edward Hoare was not unnaturally eagerly looking forward, was an ethical necessity for the well-being of mankind, and Richard decided, in a letter home, that it was not. He also noted that as a member of the Society of Friends he himself would have been as unacceptable to the army as the army was to the Quakers. But he could see Edward's point: that riding into battle must be as exhilarating as fox-hunting. It would never have occurred to either Richard or Johnny-for-short that the pleasure they themselves derived from field sport was anything but wholesome and unworldly. Impromptu hunting, shooting (often from the saddle), and coursing hares were sports to which most of the Anglo-Irish devoted their time in the appropriate seasons.

Richard found more in common with their host than their mutual enthusiasm for horses. Edward Hoare was also the master of an estate about the same size as Richard's own, situated about the same distance from Cork as Keswick is from Norwich. Edward's mother had managed Factory Hill since her husband's death six years before, which may have partially accounted for Edward's lack of interest in keeping the estate in order during his army career.

It was a cheerful household, kept noisy by younger brothers and sisters, and by the open hospitality extended to Edward's brother officers and their equally dashing young lady friends. Meals were sumptuous, and Sam Hoare's modest expenses in Norfolk were more than repaid. It must have come as something of a surprise to the Gurneys to find that the rest of parsimonious old 'Friend Hoare's' family were all extremely wealthy and well-connected members of County Cork society. Young Sam's and Edward's common great-grandfather had made his fortune from land granted by Cromwell after serving in his army in Ireland; he then invested his rents in the provision trade while at the same time borrowing and lending money over the wine counter, and, so, with his brother, founding what amounted to the first bank in Cork. Meanwhile another Hoare, claimed as a cousin, had set up in Cheapside under the goldsmith's sign of The Golden Bottle and became banker to Cromwell. Bankers were then termed 'Goldsmiths who keepe running cashes'. In that generation cashes were kept running under the sign of The Golden Bottle through the buying and selling of horses in Smithfield's Friday horse market (which had been flourishing since Norman times, with, at one time, horse-racing to go with it). The firm, together with its bottle, was moved in about 1700 to Fleet Street, where it is now the last of the private deposit banks to remain in the realm. The Golden-Bottle Hoares produced a succession of lord mayors of London, the latest of whom, when the Gurneys were at Factory Hill, had bought Lord Stourton's castle in Dorset. Here he built a fabulous Palladian-style house surrounded by pleasure gardens, lakes and woodlands, which he renamed Stourhead, now National Trust property.

In the Cork bank, young Sam's grandfather had taken a considerably plainer course by becoming a Quaker. The third of his four wives, all buried in a row in the Friends' burial ground in Cork, was a Quaker minister, who roamed the roads of Ireland and England preaching her faith while enduring persecution with

Great Ellingham Hall, Norfolk. Still little changed since its restoration by Henry Gournay in the 1570s.

The House of John Gurney (b. 1655) at Charing Cross, Norwich. It was replaced in 1878 by a wedge of red brick shops, which surviving building is also on two levels.

John Gurney's eldest son, 'The Weaver's Friend' (b. 1688) and his grandson, Bartlett Gurney, of Northrepps Cottage (b. 1756), the first of this branch to leave the Society of Friends, hence the turned down collar not worn by Quakers.

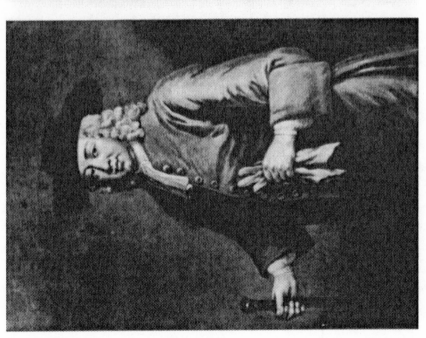

Joseph Gurney (b. 1692), brother of 'The Weaver's Friend' and his wife, Hannah Middleton, 'The Fair Quaker'.

Ury, restored by Colonel Barclay (b. 1610) in the 1660s, showing the
Meeting House founded by his son, 'The Apologist' (b. 1648).

The house in Cheapside, London, of 'The Apologist's' son, David
Barclay (b. 1682) during a visit from King George III and Queen
Charlotte in 1761.

Top left and right Grandfather and grandson; 'Sam' Hoare (b. 1751) and his namesake (b. 1807), aged twelve. *Bottom left and right* Mother and daughter; Lucy Barclay of Ury (b. 1753) who, as a little girl 'would not curtsy to the King' and later married Samuel Galton, scientific industrialist. Her daughter was the 'interesting and bewitching' Mary Anne Galton, who became Mrs Schimmelpenninck, author and preacher.

'Johnny-for-short' Gurney (b. 1749) and his wife, 'Kitty' Bell, aged
nineteen, painted a year before they were married.

Earlham Hall, near Norwich, where the couple pictured above lived
and their eleven children were raised. The Gurneys rented Earlham
for six generations.

Above: Rachel, sister of 'Johnny-for-short' Gurney and wife of 'Bob' Barclay (b. 1751) of Clapham and Northrepps, with two of their fifteen children. Lucy (in arms) became Mrs R. W. Fox of Falmouth. *Below:* New Mills, Norwich, where 'Betsy' Gurney (later Elizabeth Fry) saw her father saving a child from drowning. Painting by John Crome (b. 1768), who taught her to draw.

Hudson of Keswick (b. 1775) and his wife, 'Mag' Barclay. Hudson's ambition was to write one good poem. Instead, he inadvertently became a multi-millionaire. *Below:* Hanbury and Buxton's brewery, Brick Lane, London, where Fowell Buxton (b. 1786) worked and lived with his wife, Hannah Gurney. At least three of their children were born here.

the quiet determination that her grandson, Sam Hoare, inherited. At Factory Hill the Gurneys were entertained by stories of aristocratic Quakers who 'enjoyed more servants to wash and iron, starch, tack and fold their delicate caps and handkerchiefs than were needed to keep lace and ordinary frills in order'. Irish Quakers of high eminence, lofty descent, wealth and education were always offered (and took) the best and foremost seats in meetings, despite George Fox's objection even to the use of an index in putting one name before another.

Richard next writes home from Waterford, which small town he likens to the family's well-known Cromer on the Norfolk coast. 'The worst weather for years, this is the 19th successive day of rain.' The brothers returned home from Waterford via Milford Haven.

In London they passed through the deep gorge of Cheapside houses to break their journey at 108. Here the master of the house, Robert Barclay from Philadelphia, was not yet twenty, with an unmarried aunt as chatelaine. As an important partner in his late grandfather's export firm, he sat at the head of the table whenever his uncle – guardian, David Barclay of Youngsbury resided, as he mostly did, in the country. Judging from the letters that passed between Bob Barclay and Johnny-for-short, as they soon addressed each other, they appear to have seen little, if anything, of each other until this visit. Now Bob found someone of his own age and outlook with whom he could consult and share confidences and jokes. Both were anxious to work out the priorities of the life before them rather than let their early control of inherited wealth either drive them into an excessive desire to make more money or cause them to drift into unnecessary extravagance. 'People who have been in affluent circumstances and sink low into poverty need great fortitude to keep calm,' Bob writes, 'and contrary, a sudden increase of riches to a poor person could probably have some disagreeable effect. These are examples in the extreme to relate to either of us but yet in a degree show the need for sense and discretion. I am persuaded that the happiness of life consists not in riches but contentment.' By way of apology for so long a sermon, Bob adds, as the page ends,

'N.B. Don't be alarmed at my turning over the other side, be patient and thou will presently find the end.'

Quite early in the correspondence that was to continue throughout their lives, Bob writes that 'a principal wish of mine is that our friendship may extend to the *end* and I hope never to do anything whereby I may forfeit thy good opinion which I exceedingly prize.' Both found female company delightful, particularly when it was accompanied by beauty. But even so, among the many references to beauties, Bob observes, 'it is in mental charm I give the preference, as being the most desirable and most durable addition to man's felicity.' He had been greatly attracted by his little 'half-cousin' Agatha, 'the Hudson heiress' whose father had taken Bob into his home at Youngsbury when he first arrived from America. Agatha was not only beautiful but also wise and all that a strictly-brought-up young Quakeress should be. Her stepmother, daughter of the Birmingham steel merchant, Sampson Lloyd, encouraged the light flirtation between Agatha and Bob, no doubt partly to keep the fortune from straying out of controllable reach, as much as to save the tender Agatha the pain of falling – inevitably unproductively – in love outside the Society of Friends. She and Bob were not full cousins, for their fathers were half-brothers: Agatha's father, David of Youngsbury, was the eldest son of old David of Cheapside's second marriage to Priscilla Freame.

Although Johnny-for-short writes of the usefulness of the Irish journey and his fears for the consequences of possible wars in America, France, Spain and the Netherlands (possibilities all fulfilled within the next decade), Bob's next letter, delivered by the London coach to Magdalen Street, is more playful.

'R. & J. Gurney' had despatched pheasants from the Keswick estate (unpoached, this generation, from the Walpoles) to the chatelaine of 108 in gratitude for hospitality.

Dear Johnny-for-short, thy epistle I received a few days since advising that a brace of pheasants intended for my aunt Priscilla Barclay were to make their corporal appearance here. This is to certify to thee and all others concerned that since the receipt of your letter there is

162

not a single pheasant appeared here with such directions. Whether
they deserted their guardians on their way hither or whether it was
only a hypothesis of thy fertile brain, that's not my business to find
out. It's sufficient for me that I can prove my assertions to be true by
the testimony of a crowd of witnesses, as great a crowd as this whole
house can muster. I have the happiness of assuring thee that at any
time I shall be perfectly ready to vindicate my conduct in this important transaction to any person of good understanding thou mayest, in
thy own wisdom, to approve to search into the matter.

Among the apprentices living at the great house in Cheapside
was another half-first-cousin of Bob's, Dan Bell, with whom
there were great jokes about the young buying wigs. Johnny-for-
short was for leaving his flaming red hair uncovered. Bob's
nickname of 'Black Bob' with which he signed himself now
became more apt than ever.
  Bob writes

Cousin Dan Benn received thy letter yesterday circumstances that
appeared to give him much pleasure, the like favour when thou canst
for a few minutes spare time from thy yarn to talk to thy distant
friends, thou may'st find its meeting with a most gracious reception
from black Bob, but though I cannot reasonably expect that punctuality in thy future correspondence without, as my venerable Dan has
a right to expect from the length of years that have past since your
first intimacy (and I cannot promise myself that mine will afford
equal pleasure or profit) I must be content to come in the second heat.
However nothing on my part shall be wanting to render our correspondence as acceptable as may be.

Dan Bell's claim to 'many years of intimacy' probably referred
to his aunt Christiana's taking him to stay at Keswick as a child.
His lively mother, Catherine Bell, was a younger half-sister of
Bob's Philadelphian father. Dan had known the grand-parental
home since he had first been able to stumble up its stark stairs. His
father, the would-be coal-merchant-ecologist, had, perhaps, led
his son to believe that he would be picked as his grandfather's

only heir, for Dan's much younger brother writes, years later, of the disappointment that the debonaire Dan does not appear to have been worried by at the time.

> Dan Bell, as he was always called [writes his brother] was a striking person, particularly engaging, a good deal like our father, most gentlemanly in manners, his mind light and refined, *and he gained admirers*. His personal friends and acquaintances were numerous, and his admirers of the other sex were not confined to a few – *and he had a susceptible heart*. He had a fine temper, affectionate disposition and winning ways; but there was a latent love of satire in the composition, marked as it were, on the forehead of real Barclay blood. Alas his life was marked by vicissitudes. He had hopeful expectations from his uncle who rendered his *influential power* to raising another, Robert Barclay, so Dan Bell had to make a scramble of it.

Whatever was inferred by 'making a scramble of it', Dan Bell certainly seemed determined to make a success of the hospitality of the house. Laughter was no longer suppressed on the stairs; jokes were no longer left unmade. Dan Bell used his 'gentlemanly manners and winning ways' to make himself particularly engaging to all. As a man about town, through being brought up nearer to London than either Bob or Johnny-for-short, he was anxious to introduce them to the fashionable delights west of the city. But Black Bob merely dismissed his suggestions for 'passing the time delightfully' as wasting time boringly. Dan Bell was more hopeful of Johnny-for-short, coming, as he did, from the depths of the country with his admitted lack of formal education. Dan Bell hoped to find him more intrigued by Mayfair, with its dancing-places and gambling-booths, boxing-matches and fire-eaters. Surely such a sportsman would want to visit Ducking Pond Yard, near Park Lane, where ducks were released to be scurried by spaniels in a pond boarded round to prevent the dogs from losing interest and scrambling out? There were tea-gardens to help to sustain the sporting nobility, and, Dan offered as a final temptation, 'those who brought their dogs were charged half price.' However, the most Dan Bell was able to achieve was to persuade Johnny to buy a lottery ticket. Prices were high, Dan

Bell pointed out, and the tickets were 'only £10'. Johnny-for-short could see for himself the royal arms of the state lottery office across the street in Cheapside. The state lotteries drew vast sums of money to the Treasury. 'Enough to cover the cost of one of the many wars abroad?' Bob reminded them that Quakers were supposed to be pacifists. But Dan Bell continued to stress the innocence of the whole affair. The numbers were picked from the wheel at the Guildhall by two small boys from Christ's Hospital School, but he refrained from mentioning that the procession of the wheel from Somerset House to the Guildhall was escorted by a troop of Lifeguards. Johnny-for-short made his first and probably last foolish investment, and some months later heard the results.

> Dear Cousin, [writes Dan Bell]
> It would have given me much pleasure to have had it in my power to have given thee a favourable account of the ticket I purchased for thee, but on examination I find it was drawn a blank. As the lottery is a mere chance and everyone that is concerned in it must undoubtedly be acquainted therewith, I hope it will be no great disappointment. If thou should be tempted to try thy fortune in the next lottery I will execute any commission with the best manner in my power and hope my endeavours may be crowned with better success than the present. I had wrote part of a letter to inform thee of this circumstance at Stamford Hill but a very agreeable lady who was present attracted my attention so much that I did not finish it, this I doubt will be a sufficient excuse for my not making thee acquainted with it before but I fancy there was no need of my apologising for my delay as bad news always comes soon enough.

Bob writes companionably from Cheapside, 'Dear Johnny (for short) The House of David is, at this juncture, separated and does not support 'young' today.' He mentions that Agatha is away. 'Dr. Fothergill and I and my usual confederates remain the stable pillars of Cheapside mansion. Chance or opportunity in concert, plus will, have of late led me frequently into the company of a fair friend in London Street where, of a truth, I am declared having much pleased with the rational and improving conversation of the aforesaid maid. Common fame once included thee in the list of her admirers.'

There is no indication who had replaced Agatha in Bob's heart. Dr. John Fothergill[1] was the well-known physician, philanthropist and naturalist, who kept up one of the finest botanical gardens in Europe at Ham House, Upton, now owned by the City of London and used as municipal nurseries to raise plants for the City's parks and window-boxes. Ham House itself, was later to become a dearly-loved home of the Gurney family. Dr. Fothergill became rich through 'Boulton's Buttons & Buckles' with which, for a while, he travelled the road from Birmingham preaching the Quaker word as he went. Encouraged by Fothergill's philanthropic ideas, Boulton built the first great model workshops in which the workers as well as the products were considered. The result was a rapid expansion into making much larger candelabra, clocks and ornamental boxes. These the Doctor found, together with Boulton's own over-enthusiasm, so awkward to deal with that he returned to his earlier interests. As a boy, he had been taught chemistry in Bradford by Dr. Benjamin Bartlett, apothecary father-in-law of Henry Gurney, to whom Sam Hoare was still, in 1771, apprenticed in Norwich.

The learned doctor had long before awakened a desire on the part of fellow Quakers to improve existing educational facilities. From early days the Yearly Meeting had been much concerned that no children should be deprived of education on account of poverty. Dr. Fothergill was a leader in the view that provision of schools must be undertaken by the central authority, with the hope that, he writes, 'step by step a foundation may be laid, giving the youth of our society as good an education as many think fit to give their dogs and horses'. A committee urged the raising of a fund to increase the salaries of teachers, since 'whilst no employment is in more consequence to the rising generation than that of a teacher, there is none that appears to be worse paid, or their labours more under-valued.' Dr. Fothergill believed that a central school would have a unifying effect on the Society,

[1] Dr. Hingston Fawkes, *John Fothergill and his Friends.*

letting its young people know each other and giving opportunities for friendship and marriage. Although sexes were usually
segregated at Ackworth, cousins were allowed to walk together –
though 'cousins' became a slightly elastic term.

Dr. Fothergill gave inspiration to the social worker at a time
when it was badly needed. He showed a fine love of humanity in
all he undertook. He constantly gave free professional help, and
even sometimes slipped a bank note into the hand of a needy
patient while taking a pulse.

Dr. Fothergill visualised what a fine city London could have
been had it been rebuilt after the Great Fire with wider streets to
allow for the increasing population. He suggested a tax on
wheels, pleaded for improved sanitation, public bathing-places,
and cemeteries outside the town. He studied the effect of weather
on certain diseases, and worked towards a general registration of
births and deaths, as kept by the Society of Friends. He tried to
replace poor, ignorant 'searchers', who reported their own idea
of the causes of death, by trained doctors, but without success. In
fact a great deal of Dr. Fothergill's magnificent work was pushed
aside until long after his death, and even Ackworth school was
only finally to be opened during the last year of his life.

Sam Hoare was among Dr. Fothergill's patients, and Sam's
parents among the generous contributors to the fund which the
Yearly Meeting was raising to found the Quaker School at
Ackworth, Yorkshire. As a trustee, Bob's uncle David, of
Youngsbury, was giving the project substantial financial backing
and it was for meetings connected with the school that Dr.
Fothergill was staying at 108 Cheapside. From his experience in
starting a 'House of Industry' at Youngsbury, Bob's uncle David
introduced the idea of including resident tailors and shoemakers
in the new school, and from Dr. Fothergill introduced the idea of
planting part of the five acres of land as an orchard and keeping
twenty-four cows for the 300 or so children they intended to
board there.

Another subject that the Doctor wanted to discuss in the
Cheapside mansion was the American colonies. He was later able
to assist Benjamin Franklin in drawing up a scheme of recon-

ciliation with them. Bob had some first-hand information from having been born in Pennyslvania, while David of Youngsbury had an estate in Jamaica and had owned a great number of slaves whom he emancipated (at considerable expense) by training them in new trades and handicrafts before settling them in America.

The 'usual confederates' whom Bob mentions in his letter first introducing Dr. Fothergill, included the various Barclays, Bevans and Freams who moved freely between Lombard Street and Cheapside on business or social rounds. Joseph Gurney Bevan was one of these. 'Joe' Bevan, as he was called, was the only son of the Hannah Gurney 'who could not get ready in time' and who had married one Barclay beauty's widower after another. Her present husband had been placed in the Lombard Street Bank in which he and Hannah and their only son, Joe Bevan, lived in the great community there. It was here that Richard and Johnny-for-short often stayed when they were in London with their aunt Hannah. When in Norfolk Joe Bevan always stayed at Keswick. He was now seventeen, and Richard and Johnny's only sister was nearly sixteen, and so, hardly surprisingly, when the brothers were in London, Rachel kept up the holiday banter with much provocative crossing out, no doubt intended for Joe Bevan. 'I have sent a large parcel of Duty and Love,' she writes to Johnny-for-short, 'some of which please present to uncle Bevan's family and take the rest thyself.' She writes mock languidly that she *will* write to cousin Agatha sometime, and tells Johnny not to leave London without enjoying some of her agreeable conversation. In another letter to him she writes that she is 'not in the mind as sometimes, having just finished my supper I am more inclined to take a nap than employ my pen'. However use it she does, with 'riding to be the chief subject of my epistle. I employed my horse 12 miles without fatigue.' She writes of windy heaths and hat blowing off and kindly young men coming to her rescue, one of whom sends 'respects to my brother and myself and it would give him much pleasure to see you bring each of you a wife down at least he hopes you will by that time have made a choice of some agreeable young woman among so large a collection. Love to cousin Agatha and uncle Bevan's family.' Rachel tried to sound grown-up and much in demand, yet she still revealed some teenage insecurity, signing herself 'thy insignificant sister'.

She writes of a journey on the first stage of which they reached Cambridge by twelve o'clock, 'leaving the town which I did without any reluctance, a place that makes me feel very stupid'. They went back in the chaise to Newmarket, composing a poem on the way to Joe Bevan about his adventures, in the style of the escapades of 'Master F.I.' (the Elizabethan series of spoof letters telling of a love affair conducted on a journey, which were believed to have been a leg-pull for Sir Christopher Hatton). At Attleborough, Richard was admitted into the chaise and they reached Keswick by dinner-time.

Joe Bevan kept up a playful correspondence with Johnny-for-short in the same vein, no doubt hoping the letters would be shared with Rachel. He suggested that Johnny should sell his horse to pay for the greatcoat he had lost. Dan Bell joins in with a P.S. to Johnny-for-short that 'common report has almost married Bob to one of the Friends of Bartholomew Close' (these were the James Sheppards, two of whom were to marry Gurneys). The correspondence was now being shared by more of the young in light-hearted mood. It was not long before Black Bob was sufficiently intrigued to go to Norfolk to see for himself what sounded, from all accounts, like a combination of the beauty and mental charm that he so admired.

Johnny-for-short was staying in Amsterdam with his friend Jan Wanderwerf, discussing yarn, Italian silk and other cargoes for the ship *Gurney* when his sister Rachel wrote to him from Keswick: 'While we were sitting at dinner we were surprised by the sudden appearance of Friend Bob. My horse has not stood in the stable since thy departure.' She tells of a particularly pleasant ride, turning left at the turnpike, and later compares the view with the country round Lord Buckingham's Blickling, ten miles away.

It was Dan Bell who observed that Bob had much enjoyed staying in Norfolk. 'I am sure it must be very difficult to steer clear of all the agreeable ladies that Norfolk produces, especially those which he unavoidably must have been in company with.' Dan Bell regrets that Johnny stayed too short a time in London to come to Stamford Hill.

Stamford Hill, between Stoke Newington and Tottenham, meant to the family the home of the Daniel Bells, in its seventy acres of land and wharf on the River Lea, with its ten children all living together in harmonious affection, with as much talent among them as, but considerably less income than, the rest of their relations. Now 'Prixie' (Priscilla) – the eldest, whom the king had excused from curtsying at the royal reception at Cheapside, was about to marry Edward Wakefield, city merchant and descendant of the City of London Wakefields, into which family some of the original Golden Bottle Hoares had married. This may have had some influence on her later establishing an early savings-bank system for the poor. She wrote books about insects, domecticity, and all kinds of travel, ranging from perambulations in London to excursions in America and Africa depending, as most travelogues had to then, largely upon hearsay. She loved the theatre and never allowed her or her husband's Quaker upbringing to interfere with first nights of Mrs. Siddons's performances. Somehow she managed to avoid the disapproval of the Elders of the Society of Friends in which her mother had been reared.

At Prixie's wedding, Johnny-for-short met all the eight Bell sisters together. Kitty, then eighteen, was next in age to the bride. She was taller, with a pile of shining chestnut hair, well-defined eyebrows and a fair complexion. She had brilliant dark eyes and an ever-questing expression.

In the autumn, Johnny-for-short, as true to his old friend as to his new, went on a long tour of England and Scotland with Sam Hoare. They travelled on horseback, wearing Quaker garb, their hats serving as meal tickets from one Friend's house to another. Lucy Barclay, who had refused to kiss the King on the royal visit to Cheapside, and who was now nearly grown-up, was on their route. Her father, the 5th Laird of Ury, was known by the family as 'The Great Master', who claimed to have visited every county in Scotland and England in order to compare methods of husbandry in different places. He made his outward journeys on horseback, but always returned on foot in order to be closer to the earth, 'A tired man will struggle hard to reach home.' A servant followed him on horseback with his portmanteau. When he became a Member of Parliament for Kincardineshire, he walked the 510 miles from Ury to the House of Commons, on one occasion in only ten days. He claimed to be the first man who ever sowed a turnip in a field north of the Firth of Forth, having picked up the idea in Norfolk. He took not only new implements from what he called the 'Great Agricultural School of Norfolk' but also a number of Norfolk ploughmen to use them. He cultivated enormous tracts of moor at Ury, and planted acres of forest trees.

In the year following Prixie's marriage the other young cousins continued to talk, laugh and ride together, and to write letters directed more from one house to another than from the individual who set them on paper. Dan Bell offered his sisters and cousins, and other young ladies he had scrutinised coming out of meetings, as wives almost as readily as he offered lottery tickets. Sisters wrote cheekily of their conquests to their brothers. All was playful and harmless until Richard and Johnny-for-short's sister, Rachel of Keswick, realised that what she called 'my unhappy levity that is too apt sometimes to lead me into error' was mistaken by a serious alderman of Norwich for a genuine advance. Rachel was sufficiently upset to get up early after an exceedingly worried night to write to her brothers in London, enclosing a letter from Alderman Ives with whom her brothers had done some not very satisfactory business a year to two before. The letter from Alderman Ives had been delivered the evening before by his servant. Ives was evidently making some kind of proposal to Rachel which deeply shocked her.

> Imagine my surprise, since it is impossible for me to express it, or the distressing apprehensions with which I was for some time surrounded, caused by your absence, without one to consult upon the occasion. I first thought of acquainting my dear mother with it, but

considering the uneasiness it would cause her and thinking it would
be better to know your sentiments first I have not, unless you think it
proper for me to do otherwise in regard to the notice I should take of
it you are the best judges. For your advice I impatiently wait since I
am sensible that I should avoid the snare into which from this
circumstance I have been unhappily betrayed. Hasten therefore my
dearest brothers to relieve my great anxiety and if possible write by
return of coach whether you think it's necessary for me to answer it.
If so I would wish you to say what would be best for me to write for
great is my weakness without your assistance. On that I am happy to
depend and hope it will be so. I am fearful this letter will cause you
some uneasiness but do not if possible let it lessen your enjoyment
since that would greatly add to my distress. Your unmixed goodness
to me continually excites my wishes that you may always be surrounded with them uninterruptedly but I think I should neither have
done justice to you or myself by concealing it and therefore I hastily
engage the first moment in acquainting you with this extraordinary
affair which I cannot account for having never been in his company
above five minutes except one afternoon about a year since, and
when we rode on horseback together the winter before that. In each
of these short interludes I hope I need not strive to convince you I
have endeavoured a propriety of behaviour rather reserved than with
freedom therefore I hope you will not think he have been led to it
from any liberty I have given him for my conduct be assured. Such a
circumstance as the above was the most distant from my thought,
therefore I entreat you by the tenderest affection, if possible, not to
blame me since I can plead ignorance of it in every respect. I know
that what I think I may call 'my unhappy levity' is too apt sometimes
to lead me into error, but in this case it has had no share.

Rachel did not want to abridge Richard's pleasures which, she
was sensible, must be great. She had not a little enjoyed his
account of them, but she did not wish so much for their return. 'I
have wrote this to both that it may be received immediately by
one or the other, I hope you will not feel so much on the receipt of
it as was expressed last night, by your agitated ever your constantly affectionate sister R. Gurney.'
Rachel tells her brothers she expects to accompany her
'amiable Cousin' whom she 'hoped to see next day' if a cold and

hoarseness which now attend her are better. 'We have been particularly happy together and I hope that harmony will always exist between us with its present warmth.' With the all-embracing claim of cousinship, brotherhood and sisterhood in these Quaker families, Black Bob might, through stretching some of the step-connections, have qualified as this 'amiable cousin'.

How the delicate question of Alderman Ives was dealt with is not recorded, though he appears again as a guest of the Gurneys in a later generation. Next time Richard went to Cheapside, he took Rachel with him, either to help him in proposing, with her father's consent, to Agatha, or to help Black Bob to ask for Rachel's hand. Agatha accepted Richard but news came of the death of Black Bob's father in Philadelphia and he had to go off for two years to settle up his estate.

Provisions from all of his well-wishers were packed up for him to take with him on his voyage. Johnny-for-short attempted to send, via Dan Bell, Norfolk pheasants for the hamper. Dan Bell's explanation for his failure to comply was entirely in character.

London 23rd February 1773. Dear Johnny, No doubt thou art much surprised at my not having sent the pheasants agreeable to the directions received this long since, but I could not find the captain thy letter mentioned, which circumstances I informed thy brother Richard of, when here, and he desired me not to forward it till he returned home, and promised then to mention it to thee and that I should hear from thee respecting it which not being the case I thought I would remind thee of it should it have slipped thy memory. I am thine affectionately, D. Bell Jnr. P.S. R. Barclay set sail from Gravesend on Sunday on his intended expedition to America in pretty good spirits.

Bob may have set off cheerfully enough, but for Rachel it was a week of extreme gloom, ending in a long-drawn-out funeral, at the Gildencroft, of her father's cousin, Benjamin Gurney. This Benjamin, son of the first Benjamin Gurney who was more interested in weaving techniques than in making money, remained sufficiently in touch with his cousins for some of them to be executors and witnesses of his will. When it came to the reading of the will, there was little left for his wife and children after paying his debts. His executors weighed in. One of Ben's outstanding bills was for one year's shaving, up to 25 October, 1772, £1 1s. and 'to ortring two wiggs £1 1s'. A tailor's bill included fustian breeches costing 3/6d.

Among Johnny-for-short's acts of charity that year (including subscribing to founding the Norfolk and Norwich hospital) was paying for schooling and firing for several children, including a ward called B. Read, whom he must have inherited from his father, if not from cousin Benjamin himself.

Bob wrote from Pennsylvania after the wedding of Richard and Agatha, enlarging upon the virtues of married life, his fatigue in America, what new Englanders were like, and how unsuitable he found bachelorhood. But the letter was addressed to Johnny-for-short, not to his sister Rachel.

Johnny-for-short was also by now in love, as everybody knew, including the object of his affection, Kitty Bell, the chestnut-haired lass of Stamford Hill. But alas, such an alliance as Johnny anticipated was not in the calculations of the more commercially-minded members of the Gurney-Barclay family. Even Richard tried to dissuade his brother from allowing his heart to overrule his head. Johnny-for-short became wretched in his dilemma. He had no wish to impede the realisation of the families' great commercial dream, but by bringing Kitty Bell into the family he believed a more worthwhile dream could be realised. Dan Bell, ever the matchmaker, pressed him to proceed, while Sam Hoare, now working in London and totally uninvolved in the case, advised caution. Black Bob was too far away to consult, and his sister Rachel, usually so valuable on the subject of love, could not bear to speak of it. Bett's only concern was for the unidentified illness that teased her son for nearly a year. Many causes of Johnny-for-short's malady are suggested in letters. They include business worries, fatigue, over-amusement, thunder, and an ill-fitting saddle. Even more suggestions for cures are made for the hapless youth. His mother constantly changed her views on both causes and cures. Aunt Hannah suggested his taking advice from Dr. Fothergill, who had just published his treatise on 'the Sore Throat'. His own Norwich

Doctor, Dr. Jemmy Alderson, prescribed rhubarb and soda mixture. Henry Gurney, son of the Weavers' Friend, suggested Johnny's joining him to take the waters at Bath. Dr. Gilbert Thompson advised sea-bathing at Brighthelmston (now Brighton). On writing again next day he added a prescription to the treatment.

Lodgings were immediately booked, and Johnny-for-short went off to bathe in sea-water – indoors, it is hoped, rather than out, in mid-November. His cousin Joe Bevan not only supplied him twice a week with titbits of gossip to keep up his spirits but also went in person for a few days to visit him. It was Joe Bevan who effected the cure. He began by begging Johnny-for-short to make up his mind and act in the definite way he always had done in business. But what finally seems to have dispersed the malaise was Joe Bevan's advice to buy himself a new bob wig to cover his flaming red hair. The wig was bought in Tunbridge Wells and Joe Bevan assesses the effects in a letter as making Johnny-for-short 'resemble sixteen string Jack, the highwayman'.

Kitty, who must have known throughout of the whole position, behaved with admirable detachment, and, presumably, when she saw the wig, gave way to uncontrollable gales of adoring laughter. One of the many congratulatory letters on the engagement enclosed a map of the 'Land of Matrimony'. Joe Bevan summed the whole thing up in verse. He composed an 'epithalamium' on John and Catherine's marriage which took place at the Friends' Meeting House at Tottenham on the 26th May, 1775.

Come all ye lads and lassies fair
And listen to my ditty.
I sing of a youth beyond compare
Who came from Norwich City.

His name if right I reach my song
Is called the handsome Johnny
His parts are far above the throng
He's proper, straight and bonny.

And fortune on his birth has smiled,
For wealth in store has he!
But with the gift of wealth alone
He could not happy be.

In the neighbourhood of London Town
As I've heard many say
There dwelt a charming damsel brown
Who stole his heart away.

The nut brown maid who caused his smart
Y'cleped the lovely Kitty,
Who reigning in his captive heart
Beheld the youth with pity.

But though it in modesty forbade
Her pity she should show
So handsome Johnny pining sad
Acquainted was with woe.

When mother's care and doctor's skill
The dire disease had chased
He straight resolved to come to the hill
Which his dear Kitty graced.

Then swift to Stamford Hill he came
Which was the maid's abode,
And there to her revealed the flame
That in his bosum glowed.

The lovely damsel heard his prayer
And mutual love confessed
So in one hour the happy pair
Found all their woes redressed.

And soon in Hymen's happy band
United they will be,
And may their future hours be passed
From pain and anguish free.

Chapter Ten

The Marriage Business
1775–1780

Robert Barclay returned from America, and little time was wasted in finding true love, allied to a fortune equal to his own, in Rachel of the Devoted Four. After their marriage they lived at 108 Cheapside for a few more years while Bob continued with the export business founded by his grandfather, old David Barclay of Cheapside. With clouds of war with America threatening, the export business was gradually wound up. The Anchor Brewery, Southwark, came up for sale on the death of Henry Thrale, lifelong friend of Dr. Johnson, who was his principal executor. Bob Barclay, with his Uncle David and two cousins, made a bid for it in joint partnership. Dr. Johnson was present at the sale, with his ink horn and pen hanging by a piece of string from his button-hole. He took a keen interest in the business, observing, 'We are not here to sell a parcel of boilers and vats, but the potentiality of growing rich beyond the dreams of avarice.' The price paid was £30,000, and afterwards Dr. Johnson remarked affably to Bob that he had heard he devoted time to reading, and advised him to persevere for 'no character is more to be esteemed than one where literature and commerce went hand in hand.'

At the same time, in Birmingham, David of Youngsbury's father-in-law, Sampson Lloyd, was turning over from manufacturing his own wares to backing other people's. Thus was founded the great present-day Lloyd's Bank. Sampson Lloyd had originally invented a machine for slitting steel into rods which had led on to his making guns. For these bellicose tendencies he was censured by his fellow Quakers, although the scientific approach greatly intrigued them.

Sampson Lloyd was among the founder-members of the Lunar Society, which met for a meal in each others' houses at full moon in the hopes of being well lit on their homeward journey. The Lunar Society kept no minutes, but out of their unplanned discussions came ideas, technical and political, and above all, religious. The Lunar Society was tolerant of all religions and even of none. Among those who attended the first meeting were Dr. Erasmus Darwin (grandfather of Charles Darwin, author of *The Origin of Species*) and Josiah Wedgewood, who had recently invented and perfected Queensware china in his potteries and was now busily experimenting with road and canal improvements. There was also Richard Edgeworth, whose daughter Maria became better known than himself through her children's stories, after publishing, jointly with her father, *Practical Education*. Matthew Boulton, whose button and buckle factory Dr. Fothergill had 'socially reformed', was another who was present, as was Dr. Withering of Edgbaston Hall, co-founder of Birmingham General Hospital and of its botanical garden in which he grew foxgloves in order to experiment in the hospital with their derivative drug, digitalis. Dr. Joseph Priestley, scientist and writer, and inflammatory pastor of the Dissenters' Meeting House in Birmingham, was there, and Samuel Galton, Quaker industrialist who treated such gatherings as extensions to George Fox's suggestions for using leisure-time when not visiting the sick.

All Quakers were encouraged to be naturalists, which led them in different ways to botany, farming, medicine, and experimenting with minerals. Inevitably, Quakers became leaders in industry because they could not use their influence and experience in politics or the Services and would not spend their fortunes, as other men did at the time, on building and furnishing palatial houses, on follies and carriages, on clothes and amusements and fast women. Instead, Friends spent their money on building telescopes, observatories and botanical gardens, and in taking time off to discuss science at leisure, more and more often in scientific societies.

As a founder member of the Lunar Society, Samuel Galton

invited the Society to meet in his house to view some of his inventions and to try out some of his experiments. His butler was heard to ask afterwards where the lunatics would be meeting next.

Sam Galton later married Lucy Barclay, daughter of the 'Great Master' of Ury. Thus with two marriage connections between the 'house of David' and Birmingham tycoons, Sampson Lloyd and Samuel Galton, and two more with Richard Gurney and his sister Rachel of Norwich, there was not much that one family firm did not know about the others. Thanks to this family grapevine the now mature sons of the Weavers' Friend, John and Henry Gurney, knew before most that the heyday of wool industry had reached its peak and its decline was in sight. With the newly-invented mechanical devices for spinning, driven by water-wheels and steam, flat, marshy Norfolk could not hope to compete with the fast-flowing streams and coal-producing areas of the north and midlands. It was time for changes. The explanation given to the burghers of Norwich by the sons of the Weavers' Friend was that Bartlett, their sole male heir, was not interested in the manufactory. In fact, so far, he had shown no interest in anything but hunting and shooting. On his behalf it was decided to turn, like Sampson Lloyd in Birmingham, fully over to banking.

Bartlett had come of age the day after the marriage of Bob Barclay and Rachel. No birthday celebrations were permitted among Friends. Instead the year of Bartlett's majority, 1775, was marked by the founding of Gurney's Bank in Pitt Street.

Bartlett began his business career with a clear rap from Johnny-for-short who, as Joe Bevan had already suggested, was far more definite in business than in love. Most of the family had shares in each other's companies, and Bartlett was told that he would have to propose any plan formally, and ask their views before he could consider disposing of their shares. He must learn that the Quakers were expected not to employ lawyers but to submit to Quaker arbitration. 'Such vagueness at the start of any new business is typical of failed houses.' The letter ends with a reminder that friendship between the families was essential.

Johnny-for-short was then only twenty-five, but it was said of him that 'Anyone engaged with him in arbitrations, executer-ship, or bancruptcy can bear witness to his quick mind which enabled him to see the case at once. Seeing him unravel the intricies of entangled accounts and so saving many a family from ruinous litigation was enlightening.'

Bartlett slightly resented Johnny's continuing to receive money on deposit at Magdalen Street after the new bank had been established, but Johnny assured him that there was nothing to worry about – in fact in the last twelve months he had re-peatedly refused offers of money, and, except for a few trifling amounts borrowed or lent among a few old friends, the firm had stuck to its main purpose. As Richard and Joseph were also in the Magdalen Street firm, Johnny-for-short pointed out that great delicacy should be observed by them all.

Johnny-for-short now made his home with Kitty in one wing of the Court House in Magdalen Street, where his mother, Bett, was using another wing as her winter quarters. Richard and Agatha were living in the main wing, in which their first child, Hudson, had been born. It was in this Court House that Bett had lost her first baby, and her sister-in-law had lost hers two days before the birth of Bett's next, Richard, now a young father himself.

Two more first cousins were born, again within the same week, in the Old Court House, both as healthy as each other. Agatha's second baby was born on Saturday 23rd March, 1776 and Kitty's first baby five days later. Agatha's own mother had died after her birth, twenty-three years before, and now history repeated itself: a week after the birth of her daughter, Agatha was dead.

'Mother and child doing well,' was something that could only be said with caution, even in the most protected homes. Kitty lost her next baby when he was six months old. She was still looking after Agatha's Hudson and his baby sister Gatty (named Agatha, after her mother) whom Kitty reared as a twin with her own Catherine. Hudson and Gatty were also 'overlooked' and certainly over-indulged by their grandmother, Bett. Bett was never in complete agreement with their more austerely Quaker maternal grandfather, David of Youngsbury, particularly when he sent his wife's niece, a granddaughter of Sampson Lloyd of Birmingham, to help to instil some sterner Quaker spirit into them.

This Rachel Hanbury was 'a good and loving Quaker in its dearest sense', but of far too gentle a nature to affect any child except by long-standing example. Her father was Osgood Hanbury of Hollfield Grange, Essex, son of John Hanbury, 'well known throughout Europe as the greatest tobacco merchant of his day, perhaps in the world'. Her great-grandfather, an adherent of George Fox, had written on his behalf to Robert Barclay, the Apologist, a century earlier, to beg for further help for Friends in prison. This was what qualified Rachel for her task. She was sixteen when she came, and barely seventeen when she agreed to marry her charges' father (but was warned not to add to his family till she was older). Richard moved with his new wife and two children out of Magdalen Street into 5 Surrey Street, ten minutes' walk away on the other side of the castle, the Brazendoors Gate end of Surrey Street. For country pursuits they stayed more than ever at Keswick, where grandmother Bett always summered.

· When his father, Henry Gurney, died in 1777, Bartlett moved the bank to 3 Redwell Plain, which stood on part of what is now the great Barclay's Bank on Bank Plain. The fine Georgian house, in which Bartlett, still a bachelor, lived had been a wine-merchant's in whose cellars bins of port and East and West Indian madeiras were exchanged for safes, bags of bullion and chests of plate. Gurney's Bank was now established as such, where bills on any part of Great Britain or Ireland could be exchanged for drafts on London, 'or discounted for cash on reasonable terms, and where money could be safely and privately deposited or borrowed, with an agreed interest paid either way. Deeds and treasures could be deposited, and useful information could be given concerning transfers of money abroad, investments and settlements'.

Two years later the Weavers' Friend's other son, Henry, died, and two of the Devoted Four joined Bartlett in his bank. The title of the firm was now Richard, Bartlett and Joseph Gurney. Gurney's bank cheques were printed as Messrs. R., B. and J. Gurney. Johnny-for-short preferred to concentrate on the yarn business at Magdalen Street, with the same small-scale banking there as before.

Business alliances triggered off marriages. The Friends still expected their members to marry within their own comparatively small circle. First-cousin marriages were taboo, but curiously attractive to both parties. Marriages between one generation and another were quite acceptable. Marriages between rich and poor Friends were not encouraged. Young, healthy, pure and preferably rich girls made the best wives; pretty, entertaining, lively ones, as in other walks of life, were in greatest demand.

Marriage partnerships were as closely looked into in advance as business and professional partnerships, with the knot being tied in all cases with as little ceremony and as few pieces of paper as possible. The couple were required to declare their intentions on two occasions to the monthly meeting which made enquiries about clearness from other engagements. They were then liberated to make their mutual promises in a meeting for worship and to sign a certificate which was later witnessed by others present. The large number of witnesses dated back to the days when Nonconformist marriages were illegal, and therefore the more people who could testify, if asked, that they had seen the couple being married, albeit in their own way, the less likelihood there would be of accusations of illegitimacy among the offspring.

The quality of the witnesses varied between regular members of the local society and an imposing list of worldly dignitaries, and the solid food eaten afterwards could be anything from beef and beer to a five-course banquet. When Susannah Barclay, one of old David's granddaughters, married Osgood Hanbury, brother of Richard Gurney's new bride, in Gracechurch Street in 1785, among those who signed the parchment were the French Ambassador, the Duke de Montmorency, with the Duke of Luxembourg, several French marchionesses, and various late governors of the West Indian islands and colonies in America. There was a suite of between thirty and forty carriages of the near relations of the newly-married party. At an earlier Fry marriage, the bill of fare included salmon, chickens, pigeon pie, goose, asparagus, pheasants, fricassee of rabbits, ragout, sweetbreads, ducks and hens, lamb and spinach, creamed gooseberry pie, and a stand of jellies and syllabubs. The bride's plain bonnet and stomacher were treasured together with the bill of fare.

Most of Johnny's and Kitty's contemporaries married, and such children as they had continued the network from one generation to another, uniting again in marriage, business, philanthropy, sport and, on eventually leaving the Society of Friends, in Parliament, the fighting services, university, the arts, and, above all, the Church. Until then, any association with the Established Church was frowned upon. But Anna Hanbury, sister of Richard Gurney's new bride, and brought up just as strictly, was threatened with expulsion from the Society of Friends when, according to the minutes of the Devonshire House Monthly Meeting, she was 'married by a priest to a person not of our Society'. Friends were appointed to make enquiries, but her Quaker tenacity, (evidently backed by tobacco influences, for her father, Osgood Hanbury Snr., had consented to the marriage) effected the retention of her membership, although she resigned of her own free will very much later.

The man who was not a Friend was Thomas Fowell Buxton, of Coggeshall, Essex. He had been christened by a dissenting minister, but later formally joined the Church of England. He was the son of Isaac Buxton and Sarah Fowell. The Buxtons, city 'oylemen' had formerly owned and lived in, for five generations, Paycocks, Coggeshall, which beautifully and heavily carved 'town house' is now a National Trust property. The Fowells had owned property in St. Petersburgh, and traded, as members of the Drapers' Company, with the Russian Empire.

Thomas Fowell Buxton's eldest son, named after him when he was baptised at Castle Hedingham church (in 1786) was to become the son-in-law of Johnny-for-short and Kitty, and later

M.P. for Weymouth and a leading prison reformer and slave-trade abolitionist. The 'man not of our Society's' daughter, Sarah Buxton, was to become companion and founder-partner of the Belfry School, Overstrand, Norfolk which celebrated its 150th anniversary in 1980, while his eldest grandson, William Forster, was to become a Liberal statesman and marry a daughter of the great Dr. Arnold, headmaster of Rugby, thus linking the family with the Darwins and the Huxleys.

Into the web in the 1780s were woven two more Hanbury cousins, through Dan Bell's introducing them to his sisters. What his sisters may have lacked in pecuniary endowment they made up for in beauty and wit. With their Barclay vivacity and energy, they made stimulating wives for progressive Quaker businessmen, and steadying mothers for their even more progressive sons. The Bell sisters were described as 'a very clever knot of women'. The two who married Hanbury brothers were both writers. Charlotte Bell, author of *The Good Nurse*, married Capel Hanbury, Plough Lane chemist, and this combination of pharmaceutical knowledge and practical attention to the sick led to them producing sons who built up, with William Allen, the father-in-law of one of them, what is now the vast company of Allen & Hanbury. Bell & Croydon was founded soon afterwards by another Bell cousin, who married Sarah Sheppard whose influential brother was to marry a Norfolk Gurney. Cornelius Bell began by employing a boy in his Oxford Street pharmacy to keep pounding away all day at an empty mortar to give an impression of flourishing trade.

Another of Dan's sisters married Abel Chapman (named after his father, the ship's victualler), and so became brother-in-law of both Bartlett and his cousin partner, 'grave' Joseph.

As for Dan Bell himself, 'his susceptible heart opened to an early attachment of such a nature as *never never* to be eradicated' writes his younger brother many years later. 'I know this weakness well. Eliza Scriven, of Dublin, gained this ardent love which met with reciprocity in the extremest degree and they both bewailed the bitter disappointment they experienced.' Eliza was daughter of the first Experience, and sister of the second, whom

Richard and Johnny-for-short had met on their Dublin visit in 1770. 'Every possible effort was made to prevent the match by her father, and, to end her sad story, he got her married, in a private way, to Sir John Macartney in a *fainting fit*. Driven to despair, he looked for beauty of person only and found it in Elinor Turner. But the souls of the *true* lovers were too closely knit ever to be disunited.' Nevertheless, the beautiful Elinor forgivingly gave Dan nine children, and Dan Bell forgivingly became a close friend of the John Macartneys.

Joe Bevan married young, had no children. As a pharmacist he built up the great establishment at Plough Court, which was later to achieve greater fame as Allen & Hanbury's. Joe Bevan's wife, Mary Plumstead, consoled herself with a cheerful ministry to the Society.

In due course, both Bartlett and his young partner-cousin, 'grave' Joseph, married daughters of Abel Chapman of Whitby, Yorkshire, whose Quakerly hospitality had long been enjoyed by the Barclays when they travelled from Ury to London. Abel Chapman was by now a ship's victualler on a gargantuan scale. Both daughters were forthright, of upright carriage and sound Quaker faith which they confessed in the clipped northern accents which they proudly retained among the longer drawn out 'ar's of East Anglian speech.

Bartlett was the first of his generation of Gurneys to leave the Society of Friends. Johnny-for-short did the best he could to prevent it, and Bartlett replied in 1786 with a letter addressed to 'Mr. John Gurney himself'.

Dear Coz., I read yours of the 20th inst. as a mark of that friendship and regard which has long subsisted twixt us on all occasions but as to the purpose for which it was wrote attending to the request I made some months ago to the Society of Quakers that they would no longer consider me a member of that body. I cannot find one argument that ought to make any alteration. I have no desire to alter the opinions of others or disturb the faith of those who concede themselves fixed on their religious principles, yet I must put in the plea that *love and charity*, which you attribute to your Society in a larger proportion than possessed by other religions, is very fallacious and it might have been urged with more propriety by any other religion, sects etc. *I have done what I thought was right.* You have spoken truly of the character of my amiable Hannah [his wife, and daughter of the ship's victualler] and I trust that her good sense is sufficient to disregard the impertinence of any mistaken bigoted zealot who might glance at our difference of opinion on this subject, as I fear not our happiness diminishing whilst we both do what we conceive our duties. My opinion must alter much before I can believe that your friendship would diminish on such an occasion. I value too highly your judgement and understanding for such a suspicion. Your affection cos.

Two of Bartlett's six sisters married Friends at a double wedding at Llammas Meeting House. Martha Gurney married John Birkbeck from Settle, Yorkshire, who took charge of a branch of Gurney's Bank in Lynn, in which bank-house the young couple lived and produced a daughter, Jane, who was to become Johnny-for-short's and Kitty's daughter-in-law. Sarah Gurney married James Sheppard who was known as 'the hunting Quaker' for being the first Friend to hunt in a scarlet coat, 'not,' he explained it away, 'as a gesture to fashion', but so that he could be as safely seen as any of the rest of the field when jumping out of a covert. Dr. Fothergill died that year and James Sheppard bought his delightful Ham House, Upton, which was to remain a well-loved Sheppard-Gurney home for several generations. This couple produced another daughter-in-law for Johnny-for-short and Kitty.

There were marriages, too, among the widowed mothers of the network. Christiana's second husband only lived long enough to ensure an heir to John Freame to take his place in the bank at 54 Lombard Street, which was now heavily supporting Thrale's Brewery. Christiana next married the Bath physician, Sir William Watson, friend and relation by marriage of Dr. Fothergill. Prissie and Chrissie Gurney moved with their mother to Bath, but refused all offers of marriage there as elsewhere. Chrissie, adored by all, became a minister. She was 'small in person, beautiful in countenance, elegant in manner, most fastidious in habits, delicate in health and refined in everything'. It was no fault of hers that she made others 'feel coarse'. A short biography of Prissie was written, and she herself edited *Gurney's Hymns*. She was equally lovable, good and sincere, but what seemed odd to others ('as it was believed it must do to herself') was that she was not a Quaker. Prissie herself said that she sometimes felt that, had the life of Richard Gurney's young wife, who died in childbirth in Magdalen Street, been spared she 'could not have resolved to leave the Society in which Agatha was such a conscientious and consistent member'. In the eyes of later generations of the family, the only sin Prissie and Chrissie ever committed was to allow a duplicate of the ancient family pedigree to become lost after their deaths.

At Keswick, the re-marriage of lame Sam Gurney's widow was the subject of much lively speculation before she finally agreed to accept Thomas Bland of the Magdalen Street countinghouse despite warnings of 'his passionate disposition and furious rages'.

Lame Sam Gurney's other daughter, Sarah, married Sam Hoare, who had seen her playing so delightfully in the garden at Keswick when he was an apprentice. After turning his back on all his master's six daughters he had fallen despairingly in love with a succession of ladies who would have nothing to do with him. Only two had been really kind to him, both nieces of Dr. Fothergill, but they were married already. Now the gentle Sarah Gurney, remembering the poetry-reading with her father in the Keswick summer-houses, accepted Sam. They started married life at 36 Old Broad Street, opposite what is now Liverpool Street station, where they grew roses in their garden and kept two maid-servants, a footman and a nurse. Nurse distinguished herself by falling into a violent fit when the house was besieged during the Gordon riots. 'The King's Bench and Fleet prisons were burning with great fury, and, outside, the mob were attacking houses and stripping them of everything they could lay hands on.' But it was the large party of Horse Guards, attended by a company of volunteers, halting exactly opposite the nursery window that was the last straw for poor Nurse. In a frantic

spindly hand Sarah writes to her mother a day-by-day account of
June 1780:

> The last three nights have presented scenes which my heart is ready to
> tremble at the remembrance of. We have each night seen dreadful
> fires burning – but the last far exceeded the others. Newgate was
> then destroyed, and every prisoner confined therein, was set at
> liberty, Lord Mansfield's house was also burnt to the ground; and the
> guards opposing, seven of the mob were killed . . . whilst I write I
> am continually interrupted by small parties passing through the street,
> and the cry of "no popery" is heard from every corner.

Sam ends one letter triumphantly 'Ld. Gordon was carried to the
tower last night. Our babes are well, as is the family in Lombard
Street.'

Babes were appearing everywhere but nowhere were they
surviving more lustily now than in the nurseries of Johnny-for-
short and Kitty. Discounting their second baby, who died aged
six months, the average age to which the other eleven lived was
sixty-three, a very high average indeed at that time, suggesting
that physical health was a strong factor in their many achieve-
ments. Such illness as they had naturally provided as much
anxiety as anybody else's, but time and again they made unexpected recoveries.

Of these eleven much has been published and their letters,
journals and other possessions have been treasured by their
numerous adherents and descendants. Only three of the Gurneys
of Earlham remained unmarried. Of these, Catherine, as the
eldest and mistress of Earlham, and Priscilla, as the youngest
and almost mystical Quaker preacher, have been generously
described and quoted. But Rachel, the second of the eleven to
reach maturity and the second to die, left not even a will behind
her, only the memory of her youthful beauty and the deeply
affecting love affair that was to demolish it. For me, she is the
one, of all the late-eighteenth-century arrivals, who peeps, if
illusively, most endearingly out of the letters and journals,
memories and sketches – laughing, singing, whispering, danc-

188

ing and weeping, all with such a balanced sense of what is right and what is not.

Rachel would have dearly loved to marry, but this completion of a life devoted to other people was denied her.

Chapter Eleven

Rachel and Kitty
1778–1792

Rachel Gurney 'of Earlham' was born on Saturday, 21st November, 1778 in the room in the Court House in Magdalen Street in which her parents' second baby had died that spring. Rachel was a pretty and delightful consolation. Two-and-a-half-year-old sister Catherine and her 'twin'-cousin, Gatty, and Gatty's brother, Hudson, were still in the nursery.

Dr. Alderson was treating the family with purges, rose water, endless mixtures and ointments, rhubarb pills, extract of lead, and all kinds of juleps, emulsions, linaments and decoctions. There was a mixture for the nurse and powders for the butler – hardly a week passed without medical attention, and throughout January he called every day. His total bill for the year was £15. 2s., which included attending Rachel's birth. Later, there was a bill for the inoculation of the children of her aunt, Rachel Barclay. There was much exchange of babies in every generation.

Betsy, the future Elizabeth Fry, was born eighteen months after Rachel. For the next six years, Kitty's winter babies were born in Magdalen Street, and her summer babies at the country home at Bramerton, four miles from Norwich on foot, horse-back or carriage, and six by boat along the winding river.

For Kitty, brought up among the breezy fields of Stamford Hill, the city of Norwich seemed in summer like a hot, dusty bowl. The rented home at Bramerton provided a halcyon retreat from the bustle of business premises in a main street. The children later remembered it as a simple house, opening straight on to

190

the rough, long grass and wild flowers of the common with its little hills and spinnies of oak and walnut trees. The common sloped down to the river winding through the meadows and farmsteads between Norwich and Yarmouth, with tall red and white sails seeming to slide through the hayfields, as they still do.

The garden was full of all kinds of summer fruits, and was what Betsy imagined the Garden of Eden to be like when she first heard about Adam and Eve. The song of birds, mingled with the bees and sounds of the children's voices, was Rachel's loveliest memory of it. The cuckoo seemed to call all day. The cherry blossom in the orchard was like a 'standing of brides'.

The house itself was made only barely comfortable, with beds and tables and chairs hired from a Norwich furniture-dealer. Stables were rented in Bramerton for the carriage and horses, which were shod and physicked there, as bills to 'Mr. Johnny Gurney' confirm.

Kitty worked out a daily programme, which leaves a series of delicious pictures of Catherine's, Rachel's and Betsy's summers up to the ages of ten, eight and seven and John's, Richenda's, Hannah's, Louisa's and Priscilla's up to six, five, four, three and two.

On waking, Kitty writes, she must 'pray in the manner of Friends, bringing the mind into a state of silent waiting and worship, preparatory to the active employment of the day'. When up, she must visit the children's various rooms and read the Bible before or after breakfast, and not forget 'the kindest attentions to my dearest companion before parting for the day'. After walking with the little ones and endeavouring to enjoy each individually, she set Catherine and Rachel to their lessons. Some of them she herself taught, but Hemlin, master of the village school, came to teach writing and ciphering, while Kitty visited the kitchen and turned her attention to the poor. There was a break from lessons for oft-mentioned 'nooning': dinner was not until three in the afternoon and so a snack of bread and butter, cake or fruit, was taken into the garden and eaten under a tree with one or two picked companions.

Kitty visited the nurseries again before her husband returned from the city for the main meal, after which all the children joined their parents. Although this was unusual among their contemporaries, Kitty felt it was all-important, as was her taking particular and individual leave of each child. She would spend the rest of the afternoon with her husband, or writing letters, reading or teaching the children, but callers frequently arrived and all was thrown aside for them.

After tea, 'amusements were supposed to be blended with instruction', though the impression is that they usually turned into noisy romps, invariably set off by Johnny-for-short himself. When the time of rest came, Kitty hoped 'to be quiet and uninterrupted with my best friend but not unmindful of the religious duties of life'. In her journal she set out the priorities of her duties. 'First to my maker, secondly to my husband and children, relations, servants and poor neighbours'.

The poor neighbours were of particular interest to the children, specially one with only one arm, and another, who had strawberry beds round a small pond, was specially favoured by the waddling Richenda, who developed an early taste for delicacies. The gardener's cottage was also popular, near which he caught them fish.

Good food was ample at Bramerton and, although the 'plainer' Friends tended to be teetotal, Johnny-for-short was not. Wines and rum and brandy-shrub appear in reasonable quantities in the Bramerton accounts.

As soon as they were old enough, Hudson, Gatty and Catherine and later Rachel, Betsy and the younger children were taken to First Day meeting in Goat Lane.

The explanation Kitty gave each child for attending a place of worship was that

it is necessary to retire with our friends and neighbours from hurry and business that we may think of Him who will consider us, his children, if we love him as a heavenly father. Do not, then, my dear child, suffer thy thoughts to wander or to dwell on trifles when thou art immediately before Him who thou must strive to love with all thy heart and soul.

It was uphill work preventing those little minds from wandering, and the relief of returning to the waiting carriage was great.

Another carriage was sometimes hired for Kitty from John Everett's livery stables when her husband was away travelling; he usually walked or rode into Magdalen Street from Bramerton. There were calls which Kitty felt she must return, often with a scrambling collection of little ones on the sole of the carriage and one or two upright on the seat. There were Friends to 'sit with in unity' and relations to visit, and secular gatherings and lectures to attend; to these Kitty later took her elder children.

She loved many of the plain Friends for their kindnesses and good works, but she had little sympathy with their joyless view that condemned as wrong the beautiful and happy things of life. Her Bell upbringing saw no harm in pictures, music and dancing. She also loved intellectual discussions and was a welcome addition to the Norwich scientific and literary circles, with her background of original thought and her own open, questing mind. Her annually increasing family inevitably made education of greater interest to her than mechanical inventions and chemical experiments or politics. She listened intelligently to the literary and scientific personages who made a habit of congregating in Norwich, even though their religions were widely different from her own. She talked to them and even led on those who openly admitted to atheism, and then drew her own conclusions, which she discussed later with her husband. He had never been bigoted in his religion, and their joint decision was that the simple Christian faith they instilled in their children would in no way be swayed by their being brought up to read serious books on any subjects, nor by their being taught something of the arts.

When Catherine was seven and Rachel five, Kitty wrote to her cousin Prissy Gurney in Bath admitting that 'I am so poor an economist of time that I scarcely make any progress in the education of my elder girls.' However, at least she tried to keep their minds free from injury. Meanwhile, she could not resist describing them to Prissy:

Kitty's good propensities increase. My lively Rachel has an ardent desire to do well, yet cannot always resist a powerful inclination to the contrary, but my dove-like Betsy scarcely ever offends, and is, in every sense of the word, truly engaging. Our charming boy has a violent inclination to be master, but his extraordinary attachment to me gives me a tolerable share of power: (which be assured, I by no means mean to resign.) If my sweet Richenda were not so much teased by her eyes should be in my opinion as lovely an infant as I have yet reared.

Perhaps Kitty had set her sights too high. In the rules she drew up for her children's education she states that they were to be well informed in their own language and in Latin, as being the most permanent, and in French, as most in general request. They must understand the simple beauties of mathematics and have a competent knowledge of ancient and modern history, geography and chronology, to which might be added the approved branches of natural history and a capacity for drawing from nature. The girls were to do plain work neatly, themselves, and to understand the cutting out of linen. They must not be ignorant of the common proprieties of the table, or deficient in the economy of any of the affairs of a family.

She consulted Dr. Fothergill when he was staying in Norfolk to lay out yet another botanical garden, this time for Anthony Hamond at High House, West Acre. He recommended Kitty to bring wild plants in from the common and plant them in the garden, to teach the children some basic botany and perhaps a little Latin. She accordingly laid out beds of wild flowers, which the children vigorously helped her to tend while, sometimes, learning their names and seasons of fruiting.

In Magdalen Street she taught them natural history on the same lines through a collection of shells which she had made and which she kept in a cabinet. She bought another cabinet for Rachel and Betsy; in this she encouraged them to keep (and name) curiosities picked up on trips to the country and sea-shore.

The two elder girls were physically and emotionally up to long days out shooting in the woods but Betsy would never get into the carriage if she saw a gun in it, it so terrified her. Catherine and

Rachel splashed and squealed in the icy surf at Cromer or Yarmouth, while Betsy howled with horror when invited to bathe. Nightmares of rising tides followed her throughout her childhood. On both kinds of family outings she gladly settled down at a safe distance from guns or ocean, sorting out fir-cones or shells whose names she later never mastered. But the cabinet that she shared with Rachel gave both of them great pleasure. There they kept their doll's tea-set, off which they often took their noonings together. It would never have occurred to Rachel to look down on Betsy for preferring play requiring less exertion of both body and mind than she and Catherine could so much more easily muster.

Back in Magdalen Street for the winter, the family heard again the rattle of coaches and broad-wheeled waggons and clipperty-clop of hooves on the cobbled street, and the clack of looms coming from the great weavers' windows in almost every street and alley. The Norwich School of painters gives an idea of the tumbledown but picturesque slums and riverside dwellings of the time. On Sundays the children were woken by the clanging of bells from many of the ancient churches that still stand inside the city boundaries. A short walk across Fie Bridge took them, on their way to Goat Lane, within sight of Johnny-for-short's great-grandparents' corner house at Charing Cross.

Dr. Alderson lived in Colegate Street, a turning off Magdalen Street on the opposite side to the Court House. They could see the poor people waiting for free treatment on the steps of the doctor's house.

Kitty made great friends with Mrs. Alderson and her bright, showy auburn-haired only child, Amelia, who had been sent to the French school, and was also taught dancing, singing and music, since her parents were not Quakers. The Aldersons did not belong to the Established Church, but attended the Octagon Chapel in their own street. The edifice, still elegant to this day, was built on the site of the old Presbyterian meeting house for the use of any dissenting sects. It was designed, as were the theatre, assembly house and many other splendid buildings in Dr. Alderson's time, by his friend and patient, the Norwich architect, Thomas Ivory.

Inevitably Kitty joined in discussions at the Aldersons' concerning the arts. She could see for herself that Amelia's natural exuberance was being channelled into arts and subjects at no risk to her soul, and she revised her plans for her own children's education. The elder girls greatly admired Amelia, and 'teased her to sing to them and tell them stories'.

When Amelia was fifteen and Catherine and Rachel were eight and six, Mrs. Alderson died. The idea of anybody's mother dying was almost more than the little girls could bear. They begged to be allowed to try to comfort Amelia, and from then on she was more often at Magdalen Street and Bramerton than ever. She taught the children to play charades and acting games, and to dance in the garden to her rhythmic songs. She soon recovered from her bereavement and cast aside her deep mourning, which was so alien to children surrounded by 'plain' Quakers who never wore mourning. She took over the running of her father's house and, it was said, 'to while away the time while he was on his rounds', she began to write novels and plays. In fact, she was a born fiction writer, and saw everything in the most dazzling colours. She rarely missed a production at the theatre and soon found her way back stage where she later made close enough friends with Mrs. Siddons to stay with her in London.

It was through Amelia that Rachel learnt that she and her brother and sisters were to leave both Norwich and Bramerton to move to a fine country mansion where they were to live all the year round. Amelia had ridden three miles out of the city with their father to see Earlham Hall, and brought back news of its tree-lined drive, imposing entrance and front hall as big as their own courtyard. The staircase was wide enough to drive a carriage up. In the garden there was a tree as tall as a ship, whose trunk had the girth of ten men. When the children seemed too overawed by such vastness, Amelia told them of the wonderful possibilities the house had for hide-and-seek. There were short flights of steps hidden behind doors; there were nooks and crannies, and more cupboards than she had time to count. The kitchen garden had even more fruit than had Bramerton garden. There was yet another tree under whose spreading branches they could act plays and pretend they had their own theatre. And in the park was a much smaller part of their own Bramerton river, so shallow that they could paddle in it.

Though not essentially a grand house, Earlham Hall was described at that time as 'one of the most ancient seats in the Norfolk suburbs, full of sylvan magnificence'. A heronry proved the antiquity of its trees. One English oak had 'a trunk 24 feet in girth, though divided in two large limbs a few feet from the ground. The branches of another oak were 19 inches in circumference, and an overspread of 152 yards.'

At the time when a much earlier Gurney than Johnny-for-short, Henry of Great Ellingham, was restoring his Hall there, a like manor house was being constructed at Earlham. To this were added further projections in 1642, as recorded on a wall in the west wing. By the middle of the eighteenth century, more wings and gables and windows of different periods and heights were embracing each other with seemingly affectionate abandon on the southern side, behind the still formal front courtyard with symmetrical, though some blind, windows to the north.

The estate at that time was owned by the Bacon family, descendants of Sir Francis Bacon's brother, Nicholas. A letter of 1761 reveals that the current Squire Bacon was 'very busy at Earlham, for he is doing a great deal to his house and building a katchend (kitchen).' Indeed, the garden front will be very handsome for other bay windows were to be brought out 'as that in ye white room' and a new building the same as this new room, 'so both wings will be alike.' In 1786, Mr. Bacon's grandson, Bacon Frank, died, and his widow leased the estate to Johnny-for-short. It is quoted that Quakers prefer to rent rather than buy property because 'it was thought the heart would be more firmly fixed on things eternal if living between hired walls, and be less likely to glory in earthly possessions.' There is also a suggestion that Johnny-for-short had already taken a lease on Earlham when he came of age, fourteen years before. If so, it may well have been part of one of his typical arrangements to avert bankruptcy, which he abhorred. The owners of Earlham had certainly over-spent themselves in the final rebuilding. Again, bills paid in 1779 for dyeing seventy curtains, and others for carpenters and build-ers, may have suggested an earlier connection with Earlham rather than with the firm in Magdalen Street. Be that as it may, Johnny-for-short certainly moved into Earlham the year that Bacon Frank died. Without, apparently, any anxiety about glorying in earthly possessions, he later bought some land near Earlham church, and so qualified to be known hereafter by the dignified name of John Gurney of Earlham. As for the house itself, he made no more alterations, and even the Bacon family portraits, set in some of the panelling, remained throughout the Gurney tenancy of well over a century. The drive came up from the turnpike through an avenue of limes, passing the sixteenth-century dove-house, which still stands. To the right, beyond the river, was the heronry. The bridge over it was then narrow and hump-backed, but with the same pebbly pool beside it where children still splash. Except for some stately Dutch gabling and ornately plastered ceilings added by the last of the Gurney in-habitants in the twentieth century, the house, now owned by the city of Norwich and forming part of the University of East Anglia, is not very different from what it was on the day Rachel and her brother and six sisters first climbed the six semicircular steps, and passed through the front door, which still opens, as it did for Rachel in 1786, into a large, but then low-ceilinged hall, whose broad boards were bare of carpets and almost of furniture throughout Rachel's life. The whole house was con-siderably barer than most houses of that calibre. There were few carpets, curtains or soft chairs. The furniture from Magdalen Street was distributed about the thirty or so rooms of the new home, and was only later added to by benches and chests, beds and tables, cradles and hutches made by the estate carpenter. Tearing round, the children identified some of the old pieces from their more compact previous home, though the red leather chairs and a giant sofa in the main living-rooms were strangers to them.

It was impossible to pass from the west end of the house, where the dining-room and great solid-panelled ante-room lay, to the east end where the kitchen quarters straggled out into the yard, without either crossing the front hall or going up by a series of irregular staircases over the top of it and down the other side. For these over-energetic children the latter route was preferred, but they could scamper by their mother's bedroom and their father's dressing-room and then on into the nursery quarters and up to the attic floor, above which nearly all the rooms ran into each other with unexpected steps and double doors, and an infinite variety of powder-closets and cupboards in between.

At first they kept the names of the rooms used by the owners of the house, no doubt through some of the old retainers remained in it. But gradually, as their uses changed, the 'white room, built to balance the other', with its five doors, became the day nursery, and the room above it, an eleven-sided room, reached by its own twisting staircase, became the night nursery. The south bedroom became Mrs. Gurney's room, and as the children grew up to occupy their own rooms, these took on their names, which still mark the row of bells by the servants' hall. Others took new names from their decorations. The 'chintz room', 'red room', 'bow room' and other favourite Earlham haunts were reproduced in the children's own homes later. In some, even the building, window-frames and fireplaces were reproduced as nearly as possible as well as their names.

Earlham rooms were well suited to changing their uses. Upstairs, there was no hard line between bedroom and living-room. Bedrooms were used at this time much more as bed-sitting-rooms. There are frequent references to the family and friends sitting round the fire in one bedroom or another. It was not considered improper for ladies to receive men by day in their bedrooms, even in a Puritan home. John of Earlham's dressing-room was also used as a sitting-room. The 'great parlour', a one-storeyed pavilion, Bacon-built and used for political meetings, retained its purpose as an occasional reception room. The room most written about over the years, the ante-room was, and still is, halfway up the shallow staircase from the hall. Here

Bacon portraits were let into the panelling, and here, on a platform raised about a foot in the canted bow of the windows, the
children rushed to look out at 'their river', that is sometimes
referred to in relation to Earlham as the Wensum and sometimes
the Yare. In fact, it is a tributary of the Wensum, which forms
part of the city boundaries of Norwich and flows out to sea via
Bramerton and the Broads under its present-day name of the
Yare.

Through the Ante-room, at right angles to it, is the drawing-
room, used for over ten years by the Gurneys as the schoolroom.
At the other end of the ante-room, a little staircase led up to the
Ante-room Chamber, a small, particularly cosy sitting-room,
much loved throughout the generations for its intimate character.

All windows looked out then on to unspoilt views. To the
north-west was Earlham church; to the west the osiers and
heronry by the river, with a small mossy dell just below. To the
south-west, Colney church could be seen beyond the great old
trees guarding the garden, and to the south the grass came right up
to the house in a rolling lawn, only divided from the grazing cows
by a ha-ha, or sunken wall, and some rustic farm fencing. There
was little of a formal garden between the shrubbery and the
kitchen garden where, when the Gurneys arrived, pear trees and
peaches stretched out long heavily-cropped branches on a high
wall. Gooseberries were fattening on well-kept bushes planted in
straight rows; strawberries were nestling under the leaves on the
ground. Plums and figs had already formed on their sumptuous
old trees.

Rachel said later that the house looked 'a different date from
every side, and wears a different expression, formidable on the
northern front, quizzical to the west, serene to the south and the
eastern household end, when seen from the kitchen garden,
mellow as a medieval town'.

In summer the family treated Earlham like Bramerton, merg-
ing the house into the garden; the windows were open from
dawn till dusk, the children climbing in and out of them at
ground level, although the garden door into the hall was always

open, too, in summer. This was exactly opposite the front door; when winter came, the hall must have been uncomfortably draughty, if not cold, despite one great chimney-piece beside the stairs. There were fireplaces in almost every room, however small, with coal fires burning in them. There were plenty of hands to fuel them. There seem to have been about fifteen indoor servants and an indeterminate number outdoors. Names mentioned include Mrs. Judd (the 'Mrs.' was a courtesy title used even by some Quaker families for a housekeeper); Scarnell, the butler; Williman; the 'old nurse', and nursery-maids Becky and Jemima, who became personal maids to the daughters as they grew up. William, the coachman, was on 'like terms' with his master. Christopher and Peter Burton were footmengrooms. In a plain Quaker family, it was expected that all the employees should be Quakers, too, but John of Earlham and Kitty were not insistent, although much of their attitude to life and religion rubbed off on to the Earlham household, and John Scarnell only became a Friend when, after fifteen years' courtship of 'Mrs.' Judd, he married her. All were treated more as part of the family than in more pretentious houses. The children were in and out of the kitchen and the butler's pantry. They watched him supervising the brewing in the back yard, assisted by yard boys and maids borrowed from the dairy; they made 'play loaves' on baking-days in the bake-house next to the brewery; they watched the water being drawn from the well by a horse harnessed to a shaft on a wheel and walking in circles; they took home-made and home-picked presents into the workers' cottages, and accepted their simple hospitality, sitting down to dinner with the cottagers' children when invited. They were an outdoor family. Whenever possible, lessons were held out-of-doors. They ignored the rain, simply 'drying off' in their clothes by an open fire. The girls never wore bonnets when in the grounds. They tore about the garden, hopping down over the ha-ha and making the giant oak into a ship or a prison; racing with their puppies, in scarlet cloaks and hoods made from a bale of cloth imported from Belgium by their father under a drabber-named colour, or so John of Earlham inferred when tackled by his plainer Friends and relations. Kitty continued to take one or two of her children off on their own in her desire to know and treat them as individuals. They would sit on the great white seat together under the trees, or walk round the gravel path that encircled the garden – three times round made a mile, they said.

Catherine, Rachel and Betsy were already, by the time they reached Earlham, 'They Three'. Catherine, energetic, inventive and original; Rachel, eager, entertaining and exceedingly pretty; Betsy, moody, self-absorbed and difficult, only shining and elated when with her parents. Kitty called her 'My dove'. John, by reason of his sex, was a separate entity, anyway. He was the first to be bought a pony and to be taught to ride. It was made much of that he was 'a man', which he was not. The others were little more than babies, but were already lumped together as 'The Girls' or 'The Four', and by themselves 'We Four'. Hannah, lively, gay and impetuous; Louisa, forward in her letters, and anxious to please; Richenda, bustling, cheerful and loving her meals; Priscilla, flaxen-haired and lightly built, a 'midge of a child'.

Within months of moving, the first of three more boys was born in the south room, in whose panelling was set a blue-gowned Bacon ancestress. Sam was easy-tempered and handsome, with his mother's nut-brown hair and a decidedly cheerful countenance, which his nature did nothing to bely.

Grandmother Bett, accompanied by her devoted housekeeper, Mollie Neale, drove at once from Westwick, three miles away, to inspect the new baby. As usual, she brought sugar plums and finger cakes for the children, but this time 'she gave her grand-children a half crown each engraved with their initials and the date October 12th 1786', Rachel remembered. Grandmother was by then 'a stout old woman in a Friend's dress'.

October 12th was a fortnight earlier than Sam's actual birth-day, but perhaps he was expected earlier, or perhaps it was merely part of his grandmother's characteristic vagueness. No-body could help loving this warm-hearted, generous grand-mother who always came to Earlham laden with pleasurable presents, to whom her sons Richard and John had to write from time to time begging her to restrain her extravagances.

Hudson had written a letter to her from Youngsbury, which he headed 'Novus Muncipeum', telling her he had an agreeable companion, name unknown, and the care and attention of his worthy grandfather, who was teaching him and trying to improve his character.

Granny Kett, who still found her rival grandparent too strict a Quaker for her outlook, shook her head, sure, or anyway hopeful, that Hudson's new conscience would not last, and turned to another letter she had received from a young Kett nephew, cheerfully admitting to trying to cure a young apprentice's dishonesty – 'pilfering from the till and using women of ill fame to go on his errands' with a 'hearty hoarse whiping and then I sent him off to town in their carrier wagon. Rather an indirect mode of discharging him.'

Granny Kett now had the consolation of her son, Richard Gurney, and his second wife and his daughter Gatty living mostly at Keswick with their two new baby Gurneys, Dick and Elizabeth. This party, with Hudson, too, in the holidays, often came over to Earlham, as did John of Earlham's other younger brother, Joseph, and his family.

'Grave' Joseph had built a house on the outskirts of Norwich, at Lakenham, and named both it and the holiday house he built on to at Cromer, The Grove. Some confusion over 'grave Joseph' and 'The Grove Joseph' must have arisen at some time in the copying of some letter or journal, which mistake had then persistently multiplied in others. As it turns out, Joseph of The Grove was anything but grave. Although in later life he was a stricter observer of Quaker principles than the others, he was of an exceptionally amiable disposition, always cheerful and full of human sympathy. He was particularly fond of children, as his letters about the little ones show. 'I long for Mary's kiss and Rachel's smile,' he writes, and he thought his little Jane's letter 'ended in dimples'. He loved to see them merry and playful. When he advised his nephews and nieces on religious behaviour, he always did so with affection; they became fonder of him than of his elder, gruffer, less tactful, though bountiful, elder brother, Richard. Although Joseph was initially as keen a sportsman as the others, he later gave up hunting and shooting on religious grounds, but his interest in horses never waned. He continued to ride as a means of getting most quickly from one place to another, particularly when combining banking with Quaker meetings. Neither energy nor courage deserted him after giving up hunting, and he would see how few leaps, on foot, he had to make to descend from the top of the Cromer cliffs to the shore below in competition with the young.

Joseph's wife, one of the daughters of the ship's victualler, was 'refined and proud, particularly of her children's high moral standards', and with good cause, although when the children were little, these standards made them duller companions at Earlham than some of the other cousins.

The favourites were undoubtedly Uncle Bob and Aunt Rachel Barclay's children, with eleven exact opposites, in age and outlook, of all the Gurneys of Earlham (even after four little Barclays had died). The Barclays, too, had left their city home for a country house. Theirs was in Clapham, with a large garden in which Black Bob experimented in growing rare water-lilies, and building an observatory.

At Earlham, a hubbub at the front door sent 'They Three' and 'We Four' helter-skelter down the stairs to see what had caused it. The Barclays' London carriage had drawn up in the three-sided courtyard without any previous warning, and was now disgorging a collection of children who were eager to start playing hide-and-seek without delay. If Hudson had taken a lift with them from London on his way to Keswick, as he sometimes did, John would consent to join in, for Hudson was older than any of them and so could be relied upon not to seem unmanly. Betsy cunningly managed to avoid the actual hiding, for she had a terror of being shut into any of the eighty cupboards.

Lessons continued to follow Kitty's educational plan, made at Bramerton, insofar as it was possible, with the help of a governess. Catherine and Rachel were quick to learn, but always eager to get their lessons over so that they could go out and do something else. Betsy, although she had no interest in learning to read and spell, did all she could to prolong the time with their mother. She loved the closeness of the small ante-room chamber, where she would sit beside her mother, listening to the sound of her voice without making any attempt to understand a word of what she read out loud to the younger ones.

Kitty made her wild-flower beds again, and the children made their own gardens in a walled enclosure that had once been divided by box hedges, for herbs at the end of the kitchen garden.

Attention to the poor also continued as at Bramerton, with nearly always one or two sad characters, who had wandered out from the city or in from the turnpike, at the back door wistfully asking for help for themselves or their hungry families. There was always something ready-to-eat at hand, but Kitty would often go to the kitchen and fill as many baskets as she and such children as had followed her could carry, with food and other comforts for her poor. Often whole dishes that had just been prepared for the next meal would be seized, still hot, off the kitchen table, a performance discouraged by Judd, who took a pride in feeding the family and visitors with as much perfection in the presentation of the dishes as in their quality. Kitty herself would pour the day's soup into jugs which she and the children carried, spilling it as they went. The poorest country people lived in round one-roomed thatched cottages which looked so picturesque from outside but smelt so nauseating inside. Catherine and Rachel went boldly in with their mother, but Betsy was torn between staying close to her mother and standing outside in the pure air where, Rachel said, she did not have to see or hear the scabby babies with no clean places in which to lay them down.

Early in the Gurneys' third August at Earlham, Catherine, aged twelve, was breaking the news to cousin Prissie in Bath that her mother was 'brought to bed with a healthy son and has been as well as she usually is on these occasions, notwithstanding she has the remains of what is supposed to have been the whooping cough'. Catherine described the kind superintendent of the lying-in chamber, but 'my mother, with ourselves, are debarred the pleasure of approaching the infant by the whooping cough,

which is subsiding, after all of us having it favourably except
sister Betsy and brother John. The former is much indisposed
with it. It is not determined whether the child is to be named
Joseph or Jonathan. P.S. Please accept the family's love.'

Joseph John was decided upon. Owing to the whooping cough
he was taken at once to the gardener's cottage in the park by the
bridge to be nursed by the wife of Norman, the gardener. As
soon as the coughs had subsided, 'Nurse Norman' took up her
place with the baby in what Betsy would have felt were the
cleaner conditions of the Earlham nurseries. Betsy was still
'pulled down' by her cough when grandmother Kett died, aged
seventy, in the month following the birth of her twenty-fifth
grandchild. Friends and relations who had come to Keswick for
Bett's last days and funeral included Prissie and Chrissie, who
had been brought up at Great Yarmouth, and they took Betsy,
aged nine, off there afterwards to try to throw off her cough.

Rachel, aged ten, writes to Betsy from Earlham to try to cheer
her up. She makes no mention of Hannah or Sam; so perhaps
they were staying with another of the families.

> Dear sister Betsy with pleasure, and speed,
> I take up my pen to address thee indeed –
> To a nice cutting-out I think thee'd have a liking,
> And so I do send thee one of my own making;
> 'Tis a pretty weeping willow,
> To support its head it has not a pillow.
> I think thee'll be pleased with my ingenuity.
> We have got peaches and nectarines which I call a great rarity:
> Friend Alderson, and Friend Ives, have been here today;
> And I hope with thee soon at Yarmouth, to play
> From what famous shop do you get all your toys,
> Both girls' things and those things belonging to boys?
> Papa, Mama, and Kitty have been taken a ride,
> And dear brother John on a horse by their side
> Dear baby grows bigger and looks very nice
> And I've had the pleasure of nursing him thrice.
> He is a dark little fellow, but no worse for that
> He not only grows bigger but handsome and fat

As for Priscilla she looks very sweet
Knows all her great alphabet,
And works very neat.
Our dear Louisa is in a very sweet mood,
And always inclined to be remarkably good.
Dear little Chenda stole two peaches today
But she was quite sorry, and that turned it away.
John has left off his crying, for many a day,
But roared pretty well when you went away.
I pass over myself, as I think it looks vain,
To talk of myself, and my good actions explained.
My dear sister Kitty is assiduous as ever
And I hope one day hence we shall see her quite clever
My young turtle doves are perfectly well,
And have grown ever since they've been out of the shell.
They all send their love to great, and to small.
I mean the large party of sweet *Earlham Hall*
Farewell my dear Betsy, and farewell to thee,
When *we* meet again what joy it will be!

Rachel Gurney.

Third day.
P.S. Don't think it beneath thee to answer my letter
For I could not have written thee any much better.

Brother John had learned to ride, but he still cried more easily than his sisters. Although only three, Priscilla knew her alphabet and 'worked very neat' through the system, later extended to schools, of the elder children helping to teach the younger ones.

It was hardly surprising that Louisa, who was 'always inclined to be remarkably good' wrote a best-seller when she grew up, entitled *Hints on Early Education*. It was a subject under constant discussion at Earlham when Kitty brought back ideas from Norwich or London, after attending the yearly Meeting in the spring.

Her husband welcomed her intellectual friends, even if not always of his own faith. The children were never sent from the room during adult conversation. If the subject was fit to discuss, their parents agreed, it must be fit for the children's ears – not that the children always paid attention to it or, if they

did, understood such contrary ideas as those of their dear kind
doctor, Amelia's father, who attended radical meetings favour-
ing revolution in France. But the gist of the attitude of the various
and many callers seeped through to them. They were aware of a
certain amount of disapproval over their own dress, speech and
behaviour not being as Quakerly as some more demanding
members of the Society would have them. They remembered
cousin Bartlett's two unmarried sisters coming to Earlham:

> Cousin Henrietta sat in great formality in a very stiff stately dress on
> the huge sofa in the ante-room, [They] used to come in a sort of demi
> Quaker costume always with fans that opened with a spring. They
> were both very plain, particularly Maria. Henrietta was the most
> benevolent but in some degrees comical in person, very fat or rather
> round with a somewhat squeaking voice. It was from her that we
> children learned many of the traditions and stories of the family of
> which she was very proud. She was very active in Norwich charities
> but had a tendency to interfere. 'As charitable people surely *must*
> have,' Rachel added.

Bartlett's unmarried sisters were among those who expressed
surprise at the Church of England, Presbyterian and even Roman
Catholic callers who were made welcome at Earlham, where
there was no curbing of views. Kitty was most emphatic that the
children should be left to judge for themselves which special line
of the Christian path they should follow. They were free to
choose what books they wished to read, and also, at an early age,
what clothes they wished to wear and, later, to order them or
make them themselves, look after them, and pack and unpack
them on journeys. They were not, however, encouraged in any
kind of extravagance and were somewhat surprised by excesses
in other families whom they would have expected to be 'plainer'.

There was a visit from London from the Frys, who had been
neighbours in Cheapside of Kitty's grandfather when they lived
in Bow churchyard over their import business of tea and other
provisions (and only later cocoa). They were expected to be
strict. But their visit to Norfolk in 1789, with their two
daughters, was made most memorable by their being held up by

highwaymen when crossing an open heath in Essex, and handing over five guineas and their watches. Their young daughter had trembled with fear, and no small wonder – for her father had hidden the rest of his money in the *fourteen pockets* he had made in his suit which was 'unusually natty', as were his carriage and horses which were 'neat and perfect'. 'The carriage was a full-bodied coach of a dark claret colour with a black bearskin hammer-cloth which was the highest fashion.' The only concession he made to Quakerism was to forgo the usual silver bear's claws that ornamented the corner of such a travelling rug.

Cousin Bartlett, head of the Gurney family and much the richest, with no children to help to whittle away his fortune, cared little about grandeur in his personal appearance or his possessions. The children remembered him, long after he had left the Society of Friends, wearing the same kind of clothes as their father; a well-cut, well-worn coat with a collar with no *revers*, and no ruffs or frills on his shirt. When hunting or shooting he wore a battered old black hat of, originally, a decidedly Quaker pattern. As he was inclined to combine hunting with banking (visiting branches of the Bank only if the fox ran that way), he was rarely seen in any other hat. He was 'dark-haired and florid with a voice not as nasal as Uncle Richard Gurney's', writes Dan 'but more gorsey [scratchy].' His leaving the Quakers seemed to be not so much a spiritual disaster as an unwise step in business. The impression made on the children was that there was some business he wanted to perform that the Quakers would have disowned him for, anyway, as not complying with their rigid set of business rules; and he preferred to make the first move.

Bartlett's wealth was never very much on view. His hunters had more mettle than looks; his dogs were more highly trained than handsome; his valuable personal possessions were guns, fishing tackle and rare sporting and historical books. His copy of Buffon's *Natural History* had once belonged to Mirabeau, and he owned and used for reference early seventeenth-century editions of some of Dugdale's *Histories*. He had a solid, effective, but by no means ostentatious, equipage, with his coat of arms barely visible. As all the Norfolk Gurneys since Francis had been Quakers, none, since he was found drowned in his own well, had been permitted by their consciences to bear arms. Bartlett, as the first Gurney to leave the Society, now applied to the College of Heralds to trace his descent from Henry Gurney of West Barsham, and was given the arms borne by his family: an inverted gurnet beside a wrestling collar surmounting a cap of maintenance, which was pressing back to the Norman barons rather harder than even Henry's grandson, Ned of West Barsham, would have agreed to.

Less noticeable still was Bartlett's real estate. Besides the Bank house, Foundry Bridge and other property in Norwich, and the Little Barningham estate in north Norfolk, Bartlett owned property in Whitby, Sudbury (Suffolk), and New Jersey. Since his marriage he had been living near Wroxham Broad. With his heart on the north Norfolk coast, where he could combine sea fishing with hunting, he decided, instead of enlarging Little Barningham Hall, to build a new country house at Northrepps, about the same distance from Cromer on the other side. It was typical of Bartlett that, when his friend Humphry Repton produced one of his red books with water-colour sketches of a magnificent Palladian-style mansion on the crest of the hill, befitting Bartlett's financial status, the latter chose instead to have a much smaller, more modest hermitage built in the cleft of the valley below.

Bartlett was not the first of the family to buy land in Northrepps. Already, to the intense delight of the Gurneys of Earlham, Bob Barclay had bought Northrepps Hall as a holiday house for his family and their numerous cousins. In 1790 he built out in most directions, to produce more and airier rooms, with the Earlham carpenter, Dunning, producing window frames and doorways.

With the Joseph Gurneys less than two miles away on the cliffs at The Grove, which is now a Cromer guest-house, the children of the Devoted Four met daily at the shore below, bathing and paddling, fishing and crab-potting. Northrepps Hall was open house for all, and the Earlham and Keswick children stayed there whenever the Bob Barclays came gallivanting 'up' from Clapham. It was the happiest of times for them all.

After the summer holidays, Kitty's search for a true line on which to base her children's education began again in earnest. She read Dr. Darwin, of the Birmingham Lunar Society's *A Plan for the Conduct of the Female Education in Boarding Schools*. She read Rousseau's *Emile*, in which the author bases education on natural development and the power of example, which theory Kitty tried to put into operation. She probably had no idea that the publication of *Emile* was the cause of Rousseau's banishment from France: for her this watchmaker's-son-turned-vagabond might just as well have become a Quaker as a political revolutionary. He held many of the same opinions as George Fox's. Kitty skipped over his violence and his instability in religion and marriage, and expounded upon his imagination and glorification of fine emotions and, above all, his high regard for a closeness to nature. She also read Voltaire and, although his merciless satire and unorthodox ideas were a constant source of irritation to the political and religious authorities of his time, Kitty extracted the best from them, agreeing with much of his enmity to organised religion and to fanaticism, intolerance and superstition. His clever, swiftly-moving historical study appealed to her. She commended his generosity in helping the poor and oppressed, and she admired his personal vigour which persisted in spite of his chronic ill health.

Kitty's own health was by no means good at this time. With her last few babies she had suffered mild attacks of the anciently recognised infection of erysipelas and, although she recovered fully in between bouts, she sometimes found it hard to summon up all her old vigour, with so full a life; moreover she was now, after a respite of three years, pregnant again. John wrote to his old friend and cousin, Joe Bevan, breaking the news but showing more than usual anxiety about her fatigue despite the cooler weather.

Dr. Alderson, on professional calls, reassured her that attending meetings in Norwich could do her no harm. In fact, he took her himself to meetings of the Literary Society Circle led by Dr.

Enfield, who took a few pupils in his house 'over the water' in Norwich, to educate with his own family.

Dr. Enfield conducted the meetings in the Octagon Chapel when it was the Unitarian's turn to use it. Amelia invited Kitty to attend some of these meetings with her. Unitarians were regarded as the most intellectually vigorous sect. As advanced theologians, they were also cultured in the arts of sciences. Although it was generally recognised that Unitarianism had greater political significance than was permitted in the Society of Friends, Kitty found much in common between the two sects. Both their beginnings were rooted in the Reformation, but neither appeared until after the major Protestant sects, such as Presbyterianism, Calvinism and Separatism were established. Belief in the oneness of man with God had long flourished in Holland, but the word Unitarian was not used in England until about a decade after Fox had founded the Society of Friends.

The brilliant statesman and orator, Edmund Burke, voted against the removal of disabilities from Unitarians, and he was highly regarded by Bob Barclay, as supporting Wilberforce in advocating the abolition of the slave trade. Even the smaller children were well enough versed in the anti-slavery cause to forgo sugar in their tea (sometimes) by way of demonstration.

In 1790 social reform, of a kind not far from the aims of the Society of Friends, was being preached by the greatest champion of Unitarianism of the time, Dr. Joseph Priestley. Like George Fox himself, Priestley had been brought up a Calvinist and now, as a Presbyterian minister and brilliant scientist, he was rejecting doctrines that he found unacceptable and replacing them with more rational interpretations of the Scriptures. Dr. Priestley was a Lunar Society friend of Sam Galton, who was married to Kitty's own first cousin, Lucy.

Kitty could see nothing harmful in sending Catherine and Rachel with Amelia Alderson, exuberant and glamorously dressed as always, to lectures at Dr. Enfield's school, which his own son and daughters also attended. This was where the two families first met.

Of the birth, on March 9th, 1791, of Daniel, who was to live to be over ninety, his sister Hannah, then aged 7, remembered, 'We Four were spending the morning at the further end of the kitchen garden, old Nurse with us. Becky, the nurserymaid, came to say a boy was born, and I remember the party of children allowed to go in to see the baby, holding on to each other's frocks in an orderly line.'

Rachel was then thirteen,

a lovely girl, [her sister Catherine later remembered] full of native charm and attraction, very sweet in her person, beautiful dark blue eyes, fair and rosey, and the finest curling flaxen hair. She was all activity and vigour, of a most lively turn, both in her affectionate sympathy and the brightness of her mind. She was gifted with uncommon talent for humour and drollery. She was a fascinating girl, and became the most attractive of any of the sisters. Her voice and singing had a compass and expression of the first order, and she had a strong taste for music, she had no opportunity of cultivating; she warbled on in naked simplicity, and I have often thought I have never heard such touching sounds as her and Betsy singing together, for Betsy also had an exquisite voice, with all the expression that the heart can give. The remembrance of their old songs is one of the pleasantest. Rachel was a most industrious girl, energetic and perse- vering in all she undertook, full of object, and liking to take a part in everything that passed. She was a sweet and lovely creature from beginning to end, and very original in her character.

But it was on Catherine, the eldest, that their mother now leant. Reluctantly she had to relinquish her eldest son, John junior, to go to the Quaker boarding school at Wandsworth, where Bartlett had been educated. Betsy was very shy and retir- ing, and still delighted in her mother's shelter and protection. 'She was sweet and pleasing in her person and countenance, but not so glowing and handsome as Rachel.' Richenda was the leader of The Four, 'all charming, promising children, gifted by nature in various ways with much diversity of character'. Richenda was happy-go-lucky and artistic. 'Hannah had more beauty of feature and complexion with a peculiar charm from a certain naivete and playfulness of character.' Louisa was the most talented and soon the tallest; she had 'a fine understanding, great energy and a turn for excellence'. Priscilla was sweet, pleasing and complete 'and accurate in all she did'. She had 'an exquisite tact and taste'. Sam was essentially manly, with an abundance of brown hair and marked eyebrows, great courage and a laugh that 'seemed to come from right inside him'. He loved to 'help' on the farm and ride home from the fields on the farm horses. With a little stick and an ear-piercing holler he learnt to turn the cattle into the yard. Joseph John, two years younger, preferred to see the cows grazing safely in the park beyond the ha-ha while he stayed with his sisters and nurse, picking flowers. He was 'so innocent and shining in goodness' that his mother called him 'My Morning Star'.

Kitty loved to watch from her window the three older children setting off on their ponies and the little ones dragging their wooden carts along the path to the violet grove, or playing with their carpenter-made hoops and stilts on the lawn. When summer came she liked to sit with them in the long grass, 'their flaxen and auburn heads fragrant as the wild flowers about them, their baby hands like stars'. She would go down to the river with them and laugh at their pranks with sticks and stepping-stones in the shallow pool. The Four were just as keen on building bridges and rafts as the boys were. She set them to make tree houses and showed them how to thatch them with leaves and bracken. She ate the potatoes they baked in the hot ashes of their bonfires and she encored them when they acted plays for her in the glade, with ballets of fat toddlers stumping in and out of the undergrowth. There were visits to Northrepps, and blowy days by the sea with their 'dear opposite family', the Robert Barclays, with whom they all had more in common than with anyone else. At Earlham there were frequent visitors for meals, to stay, or for school outings, as well as cousins to spend the day, with games with her own children in the garden and park.

But gradually recurrent attacks of erysipelas kept Kitty away from her lectures and even, quite often, from first-day meeting. Her delicate skin was too often suffused with the characteristic redness of her infection. Sometimes her whole lovely face was swollen up so that she could hardly see to read the philosophical books she had acquired. More and more she felt too disfigured to receive any but her family or the most tolerant and understanding of her friends, who seemed nearly all to be also Friends in the religious sense. If some of the heroes of the lectures she had attended were turning out to have feet of clay, it is doubtful whether Kitty was now well enough to notice it, though it was now that she came to the conclusion that nothing mattered so much in the education of young women as that they should, she writes, 'be virtuous and good, on the firm basis of Christianity. The opinions of any man or sect should not be inculcated in preference to those rigid but divine truths contained in the New Testament.'

Catherine and Rachel were concerned for their mother, while Betsy became more downcast than ever over the fear that her mother might not recover. If Kitty slept in a chair in the ante-room, Betsy would creep up to make sure that she was still breathing. In the night Betsy would get up and patter along to her mother's room and listen at the door for her sighs. If the worst happened, Betsy hoped, they would all die together, all thirteen of them, preferably by being crushed simultaneously between two walls.

Five years after her mother's death, Louise writes of the last time she saw her.

> It was one evening. Chenda and I were taken into her room very softly. She sat on the side by the closet, my father by her. She begged us to speak but we were so frightened we did not. At last she said only just 'say *chair* that I may hear you speak.' Then Chenda said 'chair' and told her a story that happened that morning about how, as we were walking with nurse a cow lay down in the house they had been making in the wheat field. I then remember kissing her hand because we might not kiss her face for fear of catching her erysipelas. We then went out of the room. The next day we girls were taken to The Grove and though so young I never shall forget the miserable time we spent there.'

Louisa was then just six and Richenda ten. Eighteen months after Dan's birth, Dr. Alderson was holding out little hope for Kitty's recovery. She was in considerable pain and in her last days her mind wandered. Her husband was distraught, and Catherine and Rachel waited beside her for more detailed instructions for carrying on without her than her repetition of her written note – 'Piety is undoubtedly the shortest and securest way towards all moral rectitude.' She did not seem to recognise Rachel, though she mentioned their father, Catherine, her handsome son John, and her little three-year-old 'morning star' Joseph John, as she repeatedly got out of bed and fell on her knees in prayer beside it. Rachel joined Betsy with the younger children in 'numb cloudiness and misery' until their heart-broken father sent for them. Once again they filed in from the garden, across the hall and up the stairs, along the passage to the south room and past their mother, the little ones chuckling and squeaking, expecting to be shown a baby again. But their mother merely stroked their silky fair and red-blonde hair and fondled their ears as they sidled by her, repeating, like a lullaby, 'peace, sweetest peace'. And then, when the little ones had all gone by, she suddenly rallied and with a last burst of strength, she became quite lucid, and commended the flock with proud delight into the hands of Catherine, her eldest, then aged sixteen and a half. Rachel eagerly gave her assent to back Catherine in every way, as her mother lapsed back into her lullaby and died. She was thirty-seven, and John of Earlham just forty-three.

She was buried in the Gildencroft in the Quaker manner, with no headstone, but she was the first Gurney whose obituary was published in *The Times*, which was now in its eighth year.

The Times, November 27th 1792.
On Saturday the 17th inst. died at Earlham Norfolk in the 38th year of her age, Mrs. Gurney, wife of Joe Gurney, Esq., of that place, a woman endowed with every virtue the human mind is capable of possessing. She shone in the respective characters of mother, wife, daughter, sister, Friend and mistress and 'has left' to deplore her irreparable loss a husband and eleven children. She was a friend of the poor, patron of the industries and a warm advocate of youth. She always conducted herself in the most minute trifles with the same desire of doing that which she believed right, as she did in the more

important Duties of Life. She is lamented as she was beloved by all who knew her far and near and has shown by her bright example how easily happiness to herself and all around her is to be attained by religiously and cheerfully walking in the Laws of Divine Wisdom. It is impossible in the limits of a newspaper to do such a character the justice it deserves but it is to be wished that her Example may have an effect on all who had the Happiness to know her and who are, by her Death, deprived of an invaluable Friend.

Chapter Twelve

Rachel and Catherine
1792–1796

For Catherine and Rachel, with no new mourning dresses and bonnets and little winter sunshine to cheer them up, *The Times* obituary at least left the message they had hoped for. Here was an example to try to follow.

Unlike his brother, brother-in-law and cousins, when their wives died, John of Earlham did not marry again, but confirmed his wife's last wishes by placing Catherine at the head of the family. As mistress of the house, she was known as 'Mrs. Catherine' by Judd, the housekeeper, and Sarah Williman, the nurse. She left the room overlooking the courtyard which she had shared with Rachel, and moved to the west end of the house to the little Ante-room Chamber which had its own small staircase from the great communal Ante-room as well as a communicating door into the 'dressing-room'. Catherine's word was hereafter law, based on example and natural development, as interpreted after reading Rousseau's *Emile*.

The little ones continued to till their plots, lisp out their texts, and examine the shells and stones in their mother's cabinet. The Four tried harder for a little while with their lessons, were polite to Governess and hardly complained about going to meeting on Sundays. Betsy was almost grey with grief, which she seemed to feel was almost directly centred on herself. A hint to this effect from one of the others channelled her pity into making every sort of effort to make her father more comfortable. She would set his chair near the fire in the Ante-room, but not so near as to scorch him. She would offer to try to read to him or, more within her compass, sing to him. Catherine busied herself with running the house and superintending lessons. Both she and Rachel continued to help themselves with their mother's books; they discussed them with Amelia, and attended lectures with her. If they had tried to comfort Amelia when her mother died, Amelia certainly did the same in her own flamboyant way when they were in like circumstances.

With the coming of spring, the family slipped back into the more light-hearted occupations that their mother had encouraged them to enjoy. Amelia led them in singing and charades, and Catherine in out-of-door adventures. Their father smiled benevolently on them and wrote to his cousin and old friend, Joe Bevan,

> When I see my children delighting themselves in those pursuits in which my dear led them, and wherein she was chief companion, my feelings are truly mournful. But I feel the necessity of checking an indulgence of emotion, which may become injurious, as I'm always so afraid of throwing a damp on the older children that I endeavour, as well as I can, to keep up the countenance of comfort.

Catherine's attempts to emulate her mother in teaching through example were going well. The younger children really adored her, and soon transferred their love and trust from their late mother to their eldest sister. Louisa writes of her, 'How I do love her! I never saw so generous and noble a disposition. She would give up every pleasure for anothers, even pretending she does not like things in order that others may have them. However I know her arts, when, on mornings she pretends she does not like sitting near the fire, in order that others may take the warm seats. Should she marry, if it was only to be her scullion, I must go to live with her.'

Only Sam's headstrong but cheerful determination was for the moment beyond Catherine. His bright, observant eyes were more often directed out of the window, or, if the children were already doing lessons in the garden, towards the cattle rather than his books, and it was decided that he should join John junior at

Wandsworth School. His sisters took him to the stagecoach and then, finding that Sam, not yet eight years old, was to be the only passenger during the first stage during a violent thunderstorm, all seven scrambled in after him to keep him company to Attleborough. They howled as they left him, but Sam was completely in control and waved them off with a lively flourish as they set off on foot back along the turnpike to be picked up by Peter, driving the slower-moving family carriage that had followed them from Norwich.

Hardly more than a year after their own mother died, the 'opposite family' the dear Bob Barclays, suffered the same loss. Rachel of Keswick, the first of the Devoted Four of Keswick, died aged thirty-nine. Her baby, born at the same time, only survived her by a year. Rachel's name was given to the sixth daughter of Joseph of The Grove, the youngest of the Devoted Four, born a few months after Rachel's death. Black Bob could not bear to return to Northrepps without her. Northrepps Hall, park and fields were bought by Rachel's brother Richard, so that his own children could be joined by his twenty-two motherless nephews and nieces for north Norfolk visits whenever they wished. Richard took over the shooting, which he joined with his cousin Bartlett's shoot which ran down to the sea.

Through their uncle Richard and his wife, the young Gurneys of Earlham met the latter's nephew, James Lloyd, whose brother as well as his father attended the Lunar Society in Birmingham.

From James, when she was just fifteen, Betsy received the first of many proposals made to the seven daughters of Earlham. She refers later to those 'whom in early life were dear to me, particularly James Lloyd, to whom I was once engaged to be married in my young and gay days'. She writes of 'a great deal of serious conversation' with James, producing feelings of which she was put in mind when she became engaged again five years later, this time to her subsequent husband. Later still, she supposed 'the end of my engagement to James must have been temporarily upsetting. I dare say he might be said to have done me hurt in his time.' No other mention is made of this very early engagement, for Betsy was still exceedingly immature and still struggling with her lessons. She writes anxiously, 'There is another little matter which *I do wish* most hartily I could obtain which is to write and speak english better. My want of percevearance is my only objection.'

James Lloyd's brother, Charles, was a Greek scholar. The Lloyds of Bingley Hall, Birmingham, were sincere Quakers with strong literary associations. Could Betsy's spelling have brought the romance to a standstill?

Shortly afterwards, Charles Lamb was writing to Coleridge asking him to tell James's brother that 'I have thought of turning Quaker and have been reading or rather just beginning to read a most capital book – *Good Thoughts, Good Language.*' And also by William Penn he read: *No Cross, No Crown* which he liked immensely.

> Unlikely, tell him, I went to one of his meetings in St. John's Street yesterday and saw a man under all the agitations and working of a fanatic who believed himself under the influence of some inevitable presence. This cured me of Quakerism. I love it in the books of Penn.

And Charles Lamb in his essay on '*A Quaker Meeting*' exhorts his reader to 'love the early Quakers'. He describes the workings of the fanatic but admits that

> Every Quaker is a lily; and when they come up in bands to their Whitsum conferences, whitening the easterly streets of the metropolis, from all parts of the United Kingdom, they show like troops of the Shining Ones.

Keeping a journal was supposed to strengthen the character through self-examination, and perhaps it did, for all the family kept diaries except John junior, of whom his eleven-year-old sister, Louisa, writes that she considers him 'generous, good-tempered and sweet, though I think he has no real character'. The temptation to follow the development of the characters of the others was great, particularly in moments of irritation. 'I was so provoked today by Kitty making me give up something to Chenda because she was the eldest!' And next day, 'I felt angry with Rachel at our lesson with her', again because the slightly older Chenda was treated differently and should have been treated according to merit and not age. As extracts from the journals could be read out, it was a good opportunity to hurl a few restrained insults. 'I quarrelled with Hannah and Chenda this afternoon about their spoiling the candles. Hannah sneered, and Chenda burst into one of her provoking laughs. Her laughs are more than I can bear. I did long to pull her ears, to show that I am not so very contemptible as she seems to think me.' The Four were told to concentrate on their own faults, producing 'a silly little fault which I am constantly doing is a sort of teasing and trying to make others laugh. I do it particularly to Chenda and it does provoke her so.' Absolute truthfulness was demanded.

> In the evening Chenda and I had a quarrel about our shoes. I felt in my heart but I was not certain but I said positively they were mine. I was so very angry with Chenda. We walked but I did not enjoy it in the least. I felt disconcerted with myself and quite uncomfortable however I cheered up at the end of our walk. I *do* promise myself *now* that I *really* and *truly* will take care of my temper. [And then] Rachel laughed at poor Sam at dinner and made him burst out crying. I pitied him very much at first but afterwards I thought that it was so silly I could not help laughing at him too a little.

The required self-examination turned to a mire of grovelling self-accusation, punctuated with accusations of others having brought about the disaster. Louisa gives herself two pages of sharp talking to for losing her temper, with failure again next day:

> Most days that I spend I do not do the least good to anybody . . . I am really a most disagreeable common character, and the reason so many charming people love me is because they wish to make themselves think me sweet and really love me from habit. [And by Friday the 13th,] What a gloom does acting wrong show over the mind! I feel this day as a sheet of paper full of black spots.

Next she lists her sins.

> 1. Selfishness. 2. speaking against people. 3. grumbling at what Kitty tells me. 4. jealousy. 5. not quite open enough with Kitty and

saying often more than I feel. 6. Every now and then behaving very unkindly to Rachel. 7. Giving up my own character to those I love. 8. Roughness of manner. . . . I have more faults that I cannot tell.

Small wonder that Rachel told her at tea that her greatest fault was a continual worry both of body and mind. Later she added 'I tyrannize much too much over the boys . . . I like dressing smart.' Chenda, apparently quite oblivious to Louisa's rages, likes to remind herself at some length of the good meals she had eaten. Louisa decided herself that writing her diary was too much of an indulgence. As the future author of the book on *Education in the Nursery*, that went into twenty-five editions in England and America and remained in print for over thirty-five years, her entry is understandable: 'Farewell *dear* journal, for I quite feel thee as a *friend*. However though I fix not to begin my journal again till next week yet I cannot help writing down a little of what has happened since Tuesday,' which, fortunately, she did. The four journals give close insight into this original family, which brought itself up on definite lines of its own: they reveal that The Four adored Catherine: 'If she was to die . . . we should lose a mother.' They loved Rachel. 'She tells us our faults in such a *sweet* sweet way.' They were often exasperated by Betsy. 'She does little kindnesses even to those who *ignore* her.' They were proud of John junior's good looks and Sam's manliness; they petted the little boys when they were not tyrannising over them (or being teased *by* them) and alternated among their four selves between squabbling and declaring their everlasting devotion. They *did* love their father, but sometimes tired of even his affectionately mild rebukes. They made pincushions for the maids, though they also tested their loyalty to occasional breaking point. Louisa 'went a message' to Judd about not forgetting something she had been told. 'Judd's reply was in the *crossest proudest* way. "Go away child. I never forget anything."' They picked cherries and plums for the poor, and they hated 'their uniformed plain Quaker' governess who sat, unloved and unloving, in the drawing-room, whether they were doing lessons there or not. With even more recurring vigour they loathed 'Goats', their nickname for the meeting-house in Goat Lane. 'I am always so happy to escape the claws of Goats.' 'How often Sundays do seem to come.' 'After breakfast I went to Goats, not *quite* so disagreeable as usual.' 'Kitty and Hannah went to Goats. We Three have been blessed with staying at home lately because of our coughs.' 'I had a truly uncomfortable cloudy sort of meeting. It was real bliss to hear the clock strike 12. I sometimes feel so extremely impatient for meeting to break up that I cannot if you would give me the world, sit still.' And Chenda longed to get a great broom and '*bang* all the old Quakers who do look so triumphant and disagreeable'.

The meeting began in silence, in which 'the clamour of daily life was stilled and they listened.' Sometimes what seemed like hours passed before anyone present felt compelled to pray or burst forth into preaching. Worse still were those who felt compelled to keep going. The children invented various dodges to make the three or even four hours bearable. An interesting line of thought could be followed through or a new arrangement for clothes could be planned. Chenda managed to make the time pass, but 'not very usefully for I only try to entertain and not to improve myself'. They were sure that the meeting did them no good, for when others went to meeting, Chenda walked by herself in the field and came back 'full of reflected thoughts and most comfortable mind', while the others came back 'bordering on disagreeable'. But 'I read half a Quaker book with my father before meeting. I am quite sorry to see him grown so Quakery.' 'Most *dis* Goats', Chenda writes on Christmas Eve. (*Dis* was the family word for anything they disliked.)

John of Earlham was a Quaker with an inherited belief in the sect's wholesome honesty and respectability, rather than a spiritual belief. He owed his success in business to his membership of the Society, for which he would never push his comforts too hard to lose. It was as important that he and his family should be observed at Goat Lane Meeting as it was that he should attend the London yearling meeting at which other matters besides reforms were settled, particularly those concerning the merchants. His 'dear' had only stated her wish that they should be true Christians, and he knew no other way to bring this about other than an occasional flick through the Quaker picture-book he had admired at his mother's knee, and attending meetings.

To him the three-mile walk with his good-looking children, clean, neat and colourful, could be a cheerful and interesting pleasure, as was greeting his brothers and their families and sometimes returning to Keswick or The Grove with some of the children for dinner, or extending the walk home by the river.

Coming home from meeting one afternoon, Betsy was alarmed to see her father jumping into the water at the New Mills (where the Norwich women used to do their laundry) to drag out a poor boy whom she thought drowned. She hoped she would have leapt in after him, if her father had gone under. 'He did it delightfully, with such activity and spirit, it was charming to see him.' She took the wet little boy from him as soon as he was out of the water, but 'it aggitated me extremely.'

For The Four, 'how often Sundays do seem to come!' and 'I went to meeting in the morning and I was sorry to see that place again after a separation from it of a whole fortnight.' For them Sundays seemed to be the same old three-mile walk, talking French the whole way, with a farthing fine if they lapsed into English. After the dread or the even bleaker Gildencroft, hours at Goats, they exchanged a few words (in which the content of the meeting was a topic forbidden by the sect) with various relations, dressed with such dismal simplicity that The Four privately dubbed them by the worst name they could think of 'the Goat Lane girls'.

They did not at that time enjoy going to Keswick unless Hudson was there. Their once-docile aunt had developed a boring habit of bickering with their uncle Richard, something they could never remember their parents doing. The youngest, Anna, later the Anglo-Saxonist who helped to found the Belfry School, had only just been born (and not yet dropped, or caught the polio which crippled her for life). And Gatty, Catherine's nineteen-year-old twin-cousin, had just married her step-uncle Sampson Hanbury, the great brash sporting brewer, brother of her step-mother, on whom their little cousin Dick already modelled himself. Louisa wondered 'that such a charming person as Gatty should marry Sampson Hanbury'. The twin-cousins could not now have been more different in outlook and character. Gatty was sweet, gentle and sensitive, and Catherine, as 'mother and headmistress' of her ten brothers and sisters, determined and already somewhat eccentric. The saving pleasure was Elizabeth, who was said to be 'almost one of the Four', they loved her so much.

The Grove was not then popular with The Four, partly because the eldest daughter was already so 'emphatically a Quaker' and partly because of the long, silent grace, that seemed to hungry Richenda interminable, before the staid dinner. After that came remarks on the colour of their clothes, their laughing too easily, drawing and painting too entertainingly and, worst of all, singing and dancing at all. They felt thoroughly 'goatified' with 'goats casting a gloom over the whole day' till they were safely back at Earlham, where 'Rachel and Betsy sang so sweetly to-gether' and they 'ended up with a romp and a dance'.

How they loved dancing! 'Nothing elates me so much as dancing.' Louisa 'really tasted heaven' when she was dancing. And 'I was in ecstasies after supper dancing.' And 'How delight-ful it is to dance to music!' After any of the eleven had been separated by school or visits, the return was celebrated by a blind fiddler being sent for 'a merry dance' that 'ended with a violent romp'. 'Nothing hardly can be disagreeable with a *dear darling elating fiddle*. I really am fit to jump out of my skin at the sound of it.' There are almost more references to dancing in the journals than to sins committed.

George Fox had not actually forbidden dancing, but he writes. 'It ill befitted a rational creature to dance away a whole evening and to converse only on the most trifling subjects.' John of Earlham, who had himself first enjoyed dancing as a young man in Dublin, not only sent for the blind fiddler but also delighted in watching his graceful children performing the figures of the dances which Amelia had taught them. In fact, when visitors were present, he insisted on Louisa and Chenda performing a Scots minuet for them, which they found 'most *dis*'.

These were the impressions of The Four, but to They Three, now in their teens, dancing meant even more. There were boy cousins; their father's and uncle's apprentices; 'the bank boys'; and there were fellow students at the lectures they attended with Amelia in Norwich. Betsy, who moved with more grace than any of them, observed that dancing made her flirt more.

Chapter Thirteen

Rachel and Henry
1796–1798

'I do long for governess to be gone. I do dislike her so *very much* and that is *so bad* for the heart and besides so wrong,' writes Louisa. When the sisters could bear the unloved and unloving governess no more, the elder ones dismissed her and themselves took over the teaching. Catherine's teaching was erratic but at any rate entertaining. She sometimes encouraged the children to get up early to do lessons before breakfast and get them over, and sometimes chose that they should work in the evening. 'Rather a tug for me,' writes Louisa. 'But I bore it pretty well.' Betsy always lay in if she could, inferring by a reproachful look in her clear blue-grey eyes, borne out by an almost musical murmur, that she had not long to live. She said herself later that her stomach-aches and depressions were due to her nervous nature.

'When They came home from Meeting They brought the news that a cousin [one of Bartlett's six sisters] was dead. I felt very shocked,' writes Louisa. 'I saw her such a little while ago. Nurse was quite angry with me for not appearing to be more sorry'. Their cousin's death reminded her of The Four's concern for Betsy's health, although Rachel had just reassured them that Betsy was well. 'What a blessing it would be if she were to recover! I like to encourage the idea though I think she can't.' However, she continues in triumph that they succeeded in driving the governess away. 'I have disliked her so much I could not bear to hear anything in her praise,' Louisa admits.

They liked Rachel teaching them their lessons, though Catherine's unusual wilder methods were more intriguing. She would suddenly have an idea, that she was sure would be 'improving', to re-enact the defeat of the Armada on the river with lighted logs of wood, or the burning of King Alfred's cakes on a bonfire. Louisa said she hated the common way of treating children. 'People treat them as though they were idiots and never will let them judge for themselves. I do not mean they should judge for themselves entirely because I do not think their reason is advanced enough, but to have an entire strictness over them is what I can't bear.'

The Four hated it when Catherine and Rachel were away. Betsy tried to give them their lessons, but 'when Betsy does it it is quite disagreeable, she is so soon worried.' Catherine was 'like sun on a rainy day' and 'Rachel's singing so touching'. They pitied their brothers going off to school but 'were not entirely sorry for the peace this brought.' Soon they were baking them cakes and sewing them shirts. 'I am making a shirt for Joseph which I like very much,' writes Louisa; 'I mend some of my own clothes of an evening. It is quite fixed that we are *all* to buy and take care of our own things.'

The turnpike had no fears for them. Catherine often took them walking along it. One day, as the London stage coach came up over the crest of the hill, Catherine led them on to the road, all holding hands across it until the horses were reined in. To Catherine this was not so much a madcap prank as an example to be followed.

Perhaps even Catherine's 'donkey cavalcade' was a demonstration of what Rousseau regarded as 'natural education through physical exercise, experience and observation leading to sound judgment and the mastery of difficult tasks.' One October Thursday, when Earlham was milling with Barclay and Hanbury cousins, she sent out for a like number of donkeys. Louisa said she never laughed so much as when she saw 'fifteen capital asses arrive with a variety of saddles.'

During our seven miles ride various changes took place in our cavalcade. Sometimes we went all in a row, so as to form an extremely long string, now and then we went two and two, and then again we were all in a bustle. Three men followed us on foot to pick up those who fell, and indeed we had a bountiful share of falls, which added to the extreme drollery and merriment. We rode up the park with loud Halloos and everything that could show the success of our ride, and the surrounding friends and neighbours were assembled to see us.

This noisy extrovert behaviour would hardly have seemed to suit the timid Betsy, who admitted to disliking riding mounts that were 'too much for her.' And yet, strangely, the challenge brought out not only her greatest courage but also the charm hitherto reserved for her father. Perhaps Rousseau's theory contributed to Betsy's surprising development of character.

There were still numbers of callers, 'hordes of them', Louisa writes. It was a strain having Quakers to stay whom she had never met before. 'I had a most *Dis* breakfast. It was so awkward to sit and know we should say something and yet have nothing to say. I was quite glad when he went away.' And then again 'a great many Friends to tea. I did all I could to please them. How charming it is to feel that we're giving pleasure. I never can say how stupid they were to me. But I did my best.'

But when the favourite cousins came to dine and sleep, particularly Hudson, all formalities were thrown aside. With Hudson they 'had great frolics in the evening. We locked him in the pantry and did a number of tricks.' Hudson sat for a little while, in their room and told Louisa's character, with which she agreed up to a point. 'He said I was bold, impudent and would bear no restraint but I would give up a great deal of pleasure to that of other people and that I was generous, open and I forget what else.'

The Four were becoming more boisterous than ever 'At supper I ate so many brandy cherries that I was half tipsy' so the others took Richenda into their room 'and stuffed some salts of rhubarb down my throat'.

They went out on the turnpike for the express purpose of being as rude as possible to anyone who went by. 'I do so like being rude sometimes,' writes Richenda. Almost every day not only ended, but was punctuated, by 'dancing and a violent romp'.

The Four admitted that they had become really out of hand, 'so disorderly and giving way to just what we felt like at the moment', upon which Catherine gave them one of her talks 'which we almost always have after being in one of these sort of states, and they are almost always successful'.

However, Catherine and Rachel were soon joining in the fun again themselves. 'We acted pantomimes and Rachel was very drole.' Rachel was a relentless mimic. She would dress up as the parson of Earlham or a Quaker minister at Goats, and preach a hilarious sermon. She would pretend to be her aunts or even her uncles. Her excessively high spirits, her good looks and her sense of humour delighted everyone. She dressed up, with the others, as a gypsy, and went round singing and begging on harvest-supper nights when 'the people seemed truly happy.' On a return from a visit to London she arrived disguised as her brother. Catherine had a letter from their father to say they would be home about eight or nine that night.

> After tea, Burton came up just as I had settled down to mend a frock, [writes Louisa], and I heard Danny screaming out they are come they are come. I did not stir thinking it was only a trick but when I heard Danny cry out 'I am right down sure they are come', with such emphasis I flew to the door. The whole household was there too, and almost at the same moment the post-chaise stopped at the door. Rachel was on the box dressed in John's greatcoat and hat . . . 'everybody thought she was John but we were soon undeceived.'

The elder sisters' teaching was backed by extra-mural teachers. Monsieur Lasage taught them French and John Crome Senior was their drawing-master, who walked out from Norwich to sketch with them out-of-doors, often finishing their drawings for them while they went off to play. Richenda, whose work has now come to be set below her master's in the Norwich School, often found him exasperating. She writes: 'Jan. '98. I had a good drawing morning, but in the course of it gave way to passion with both Crome and Betsy – Crome because he would attend to Betsy and not to me, and Betsy because she was so provoking!' John of Earlham liked and admired the young man and included him when possible on family excursions. Later, John Sell Cotman also taught them, and they made a pilgrimage to the 'sweet church' at Felbrigg, where he was married.

A great cause of contention was planning a day that was intended to be a holiday. If *They* could not decide whether to do this or that, the Four took sides and 'at last, after scolding, rowing, bickering and unfixing we all agreed.' On this occasion it was whether or not they should go, in uncertain weather, to visit the Rigbys living at The Mere, 'the large moated farm house at Mannington' (now once again Mannington Hall). Betsy was for going and Catherine, for once, was for staying at home. Eventually two carriages were ordered – the chaise for two, and the other five were to go in the coach. They had not got far when they saw their brother John practising cricket with some young friends. Without waiting for Peter to bring the horses to a standstill, the Four jumped out and tore over the grass to the young men. The drive was abandoned, and they went instead for a chattering, singing frolic and walk, and then back to tea with Pitchford, until their father sent out for them at eight o'clock to come home.

'We had a most charming walk in the afternoon, when we all quarrelled for Pitchford's arm; we are so perfectly free with him. I can't say how I admire him.' John Pitchford 'kept places' for them at lectures. He was the son of a Roman Catholic surgeon living in Tombland, Norwich. His interest in botany first led him to Earlham. 'Pitchford', as they called him, was studying at an 'Elabortory', which, he afterwards said, left him anything up to seventeen hours a day with 'my seven most sweet Earlham sisters' and their cousin Elizabeth of Keswick as well.'

All this was innocent enough love, and it amused their father to hear them sing the ballad which Joe Bevan had written on his own and Kitty's romance, performed with elaborate actions wherever the children happened to be. They sang on their walks, in the woods, by the river, and as they rowed in the flat-bottomed boat.

John loved to see the children of the friends of his own youth enjoying themselves with his own family at Earlham. Thirteen-year-old Mag Barclay-Allardice, who was later to marry Hudson Gurney, came for a long stay during the last fatal illness of her twin sister. Her wealthy mother had married the widowed Great Master of Ury on the understanding that he would use her surname, which he rarely did. After giving him eight children she left him. It was hoped that a spell at Earlham would cheer Mag up. She was, Richenda writes, 'most religious. She is superstitiously fond of the C of E and believes every word of the bible.' But Mag's piety could not always extend to a peaceful understanding in the schoolroom. Richenda's journal still bears the ravages of an early disagreement with Mag, with an angry explanation, written at the time, that Mag had snatched the book from Richenda's hand. 'I entreated her to give it back again but she would not. I then snatched it again and she tore all the pages off. She was in *utmost* rage. I was not much better but I do not at all repent having been in a rage for I had reason so. The 'rattish' Mag was also accused of being afraid of 'sweet harmless cows'. But when she left the Four cried, and Richenda went with her on the first stage of her journey.

Another young visitor who first visited Earlham at this time was Sam Hoare junior, son of John of Earlham's old friend, Sam Hoare. The 'Earlhamites' were told they would have to behave in a Quakerly fashion during a visit from Hampstead from any member of this strictly Plain family. However, the evening ended in as much of a romp as ever, and young Sam was 'dis' enough to kiss the twelve-year-old Louisa. 'I am afraid I shall be a flirt when I grow up. To be sure I am not a flirt yet, but then I think I shall be,' she writes the next day.

When out walking together, Betsy asked Louisa which characters she liked best, Rachel or hers. 'Now I think Rachel's is decidedly the finest character but my answer to Betsy was *equally almost*. I knew I should vex her if I said the contrary for she is amazingly hurt by these sort of things.'

From the children's journals there was clearly always a certain amount of scandalous talk in the schoolroom. Catherine and Rachel were not sure whether Betsy was shocked by it or could not hope to compete. She was untidy and tiresomely obstinate and was averse to learning. She preferred arranging her shells and knick-knacks in their cabinet to playing with her little brothers. Betsy's attractiveness came and went according to her emotions, as did her prettiness and grace. She had a musical ear but would not practice. Her spelling was appalling and when she did a good piece of work Catherine said it was more through cunning than cleverness. Rachel, who admired Betsy for those fleeting moments of calm, gentleness and sympathy that were still rare, always made allowances for her. Sometimes the eighteen months between them seemed nothing, and sometimes Rachel's vivacity, good looks and tremendous industry made her seem much older.

Six of his sisters were summed up later by their brother, Dan, but he makes no mention of Betsy.

Catherine was a tall girl, with straightforward but intellectual face, a decided manner. Rachel largely shared in her sister's cares. Smaller than either Catherine or Betsy, a considerable beauty both of feature and complexion, being fair and bright. She was remarkable for the extraordinary flow of high spirits, accompanied by humorous drollery.

Richenda was light and agile in figure and loved to run and dance about, carolling in her clear voice. She carried her head up in a manner at once simple and lively, in perfect harmony with her bright hazel eyes and energetic mind. She sketched easily and rapidly. Of needlework she knew little and it was doubted whether she even possessed the utensils requisite. Hannah was rather like her, but more of a real beauty, with a mischievous teasing way. Louisa had blue eyes and pink cheeks of a Saxon beauty, a round face and was taller than the others. She was rather boisterous in childhood, but possessed very superior mental powers. Priscilla was gentler and quieter and of the most delicate order and completeness in all, from her dress down to her work-box or her drawings.

The unloved governess was now replaced by the amiable Mrs. Beresford, backed by a niece of Dr. Fothergill, later known as Grandmama Freeman, who came for a fortnight and stayed

234

thirty years. The pert Louisa observed on her arrival, 'I do think she will answer.' Samuel and Joseph John were sent to a weekly-boarding-school in Norwich which was later removed to Hingham, twelve miles from Earlham. It was not a Quaker school, and so a local farmer drove them in his cart to the Meeting House at Wymondham and gave them a good dinner afterwards. John junior was still at Wandsworth Quaker school, but the father of a prospective pupil found the school, by his standards anyway, dangerously lacking in morals, and persuaded John of Earlham to remove his son, too. John junior was sent to Dr. Enfields's school in Norwich to which his sisters were also admitted for certain lectures.

And so began a friendship that grew to such a 'violent attachment' that the two families were inseparable, and 'any day a meeting could not be contrived was considered ill spent.' Maria, Eliza, Henry and little Ellen Enfield were 'delightful, gifted in intellect and good looking'. How everyone adored Henry!

The Enfield children appear again and again in the journals as acting, dressing up, 'playing charades' and 'pantomimes'.

'Maria and Emma came in the afternoon. We Four did something Catherine has forbidden. We jumped in the barn and sat at the top of the high stack. My conscience pinched me all the time but Eliza and I told her all about it. She behaved *most* kind.' After which they wisely confined their activities to playing a game of trap-ball. They cried their way through novels, and laughed their way through endless games of blind man's buff. When the Enfields were there, dancing reached a peak. 'After supper we seven and John went on the gravel walk. We all took hold of hands and danced up and down the gravel walk. We all sang.'

The passionate friendship swept through the family. A sheaf of the Gurney children's letters were so treasured by the Enfield family that even the stains of enclosed fruit and sweets still remain, nearly 200 years later, among the ink blots on these endearing, tiny, torn and much-folded, oft-corrected expressions of adoration. 'How do you all do at Enfield Street? I do so *often* think of you all darlings *three*.' '*Dear* Eliza', 'my darling Eliza', 'my *dearest* Eliza, I cannot say how much I love thee I am sure we shall always love each other though pray don't *force* thyself . . . would thee take a raisin?' – and there is the circular stain of the raisin. '*Dearest* Eliza I am *most* sorry to say that we cannot come for my father fixed this morning that Hannah and I are going to spend the time at Keswick. I am *quite* sorry for it would have been *so* snug, us three alone.' They wrote from the 'Northrepps parlour' and from the 'Earlham Closet'. 'Earlham does look *so* sweet and the park hayfield is dewy. I long for thee to come and stay at Earlham again but when will that be? The boys are crying in concert and one has treated them to four or five long sobbings.' The Three had been away on a most pleasant trip. 'Don't thee long to bathe? It is the first time I bathed I did it most courageous I did not hesitate one moment.' The letters are full of the typical loves and little jealousies of small girls, and even Danny writes a long, almost unintelligible scribble about the box he tried to make but could not, and the cherries and 'Gelly' he is eating (of which some remains on the paper) and of 'romplings' with his brothers and objections to being made to wash by nurse.

Perhaps the most charming is a tiny scrap written all over and addressed 'for all the Enfields'. Inside is 'the eight youngest of us picked these, Rachel hopes the barrens (*sic*) may have some if there is enough, John, Chenda, Hannah, Louisa, Cilla, Sammy, Joseph and Danny send their love to you all.' Rachel sent the message to share the fruit with the Barons, Henry's sister and brother-in-law, and no doubt supervised the note-writing, although Joseph John in a brief scrawl complains that he had nothing to say, but 'Louisa *will* make me write.'

Catherine remembers the stream of *all* their affections 'which became more and more exclusively fixed on our own friends and favourites.' At that time they were all in love with love, far more so than during Betsy's rather cold little engagement to James Lloyd. The little girls loved each other fervently, as little girls will. 'Instead of being *so* jealous of you,' Louisa confides to Eliza Enfield of the latter's affection for Chenda, 'I see the sweetness of your intimacy. I assure you this time I will do all I can to promote your being together and all that foolish jealousy of mine about loving Chenda better than us Three is *most* most silly.' And they

236

loved the boys, too. 'How does thee like Thomas? though I think I don't need to ask thee for I think if thee has a crum (*sic*) of brain thee *must* admire him. I am quite in love with him. I do like him so very much.'

They also loved a man they had heard lecturing at Dr. Enfield's. The lecturer 'spoke so charmingly, I felt so enraptured with him, I felt a sort of admiration and love for him but I know by experience,' writes the eleven-year-old Louisa, 'that that sort of adoration never can last long'. Soon she was 'drudging through a difficult French exercise and bearing it pretty well', and in the evening they were 'all sitting on the bank of the river and singing', well aware of the attention they attracted from passers-by on the turnpike.

There was no restriction on the Earlham reading, and the Gurneys and Enfields read to each other out-of-doors and in, from whatever books they chose to pull down from the ante-room shelves. Even the Four were now burrowing into the revolutionary Rousseau, Voltaire and Payne, exchanging their works with the Enfields for volumes of Cervantes and Montaigne.[1]

These interests were not shared by all their relations. Uncle Richard preferred good healthy hunting-talk, though his son, Hudson, sided with the revolutionaries in France until he went there in style, in his own carriage, and only just missed imprisonment during the Reign of Terror. Uncle Joseph of The Grove was for more playful, athletic interests for recreation, though his wife advised the children of Earlham to read 'four or five large octavo of Travels of Anacharis, as in our library' and 'go on with History of England. I only have to request that something reely (*sic*) important may be at hand for although I acknowledge the

---

[1] In the *Book of Extracts* under the heading of *Books* 'advice' which was first collected in 1697 'take care of inspecting ordering and regulating the press and printing of books', to this was added gradually 'catalogue of books of Friends belonging to any particular Meeting'. 'Parents, Masters and Mistresses of houses to guard against minors and servants reading books injudicious to christian religion.' And in 1764 'under consideration of hurtful tendencies of reading plays, romances, novels and other pernicious books earnestly recommended to suppress same. Acquaint booksellers, entreating them to avoid selling them.'

usefulness of the *pretty*, entertaining and reely instructive books that are poured on the public I think they may be dwelt on too much.' She mentions that her own thirteen-year-old daughter 'much relished the beauties of the Odessey two year ago'. It was only later that their aunt discovered that the 'reely important' books at hand at Earlham were 'cerfused with insurection and atheism'. The children of The Grove learnt French, Italian, Hebrew, Greek, and instead of music and dancing, they were taught deportment by a drill sergeant.

When the Robert Barclays, the 'opposite family' came, 'We Earlhamites still like them all *so* much but fear they are amazingly spoiled by the strictness by which they are governed.' Alas the once debonaire and entertaining Black Bob was now, in Richenda's eyes, 'irritable, unforgiving and impatient', and his youthful sense of fun had shrunk to a 'strict, haughty laugh'. But when Mary Anne Galton came to stay, The Four, as well as They Three, found that she exactly matched their attitude and mood. She was the daughter of Samuel Galton of Birmingham who had married Lucy, the only daughter of the Great Master of Ury's first marriage. Thus, although just older than 'rattish Mag', she was, in fact, Mag's step-niece. Betsy writes that Mary Anne Galton was 'one of the most interesting and bewitching people I ever saw, and I never remember any person attracting me so strongly.' Catherine was her special friend, but they all loved her. Mary Anne taught them how to make history charts, for she was fascinated by the relation between the past and the future. She walked up and down the ante-room at Earlham looking at the Bacon portraits and trying to work out the purpose of their existence. She writes how she loved to assist her grandfather Galton in arranging old letters and papers from friends of his youth or of his ancestors.

> Many of these were so worn with time that they scarcely hung together. I can recall the feeling of awe with which I touched these papers and looked upon the very handwriting and familiar expressions of daily life of those who have so long slept in the grave. I felt they were my relations, my own flesh and blood, they were once

mirthful and cheerful and talked as we talk and now where are they? where we shall soon be. Who will look over our letters as we look over theirs?

Later she wrote religious books, including one on *Spiritual Delights* – but at that time her mind was still as enquiring as any of the intelligent young of the day who had been shaken by the French Revolution into rethinking their faiths and fears, confusing their natural inborn desire for reform with dangerous anarchism, between which there seemed often to be no hard line. It was from Mary Anne Galton that the children learnt, with sympathy, of her father's brilliant friend Dr. Priestley's disaster which had occurred during their mother's last illness. Dr. Priestley had been elected an associate of the French Academy of Sciences and a member of the Imperial Academy of Sciences at St. Petersburg, and so was in close touch with the revolutionary stirrings in Europe. When he announced his intention of being present at the Birmingham Constitutional Society's dinner to commemorate the fall of the Bastille, his house was wrecked and nearly all his books, papers and apparatus were destroyed. Persecution then made his life so unbearable that he was forced to leave for Pennsylvania. His eager young followers read his controversial historical investigation with great sympathy, shaking their heads sadly on his behalf. Betsy even wore a tricolour in her hat when riding through Norwich.

It was from Amelia, daughter of their father's dear friend and doctor, that the Earlhamites learnt that Thomas Hardy, founder of the London Corresponding Society, whose Norwich branch her father and Dr. Enfield attended, had been arrested on a charge of high treason and confined to the Tower. Amelia knew him well, and attended his trial at the new Old Bailey. It was a dramatic trial, made all the more so in Amelia's accounts of it when she returned after Hardy's acquittal.

Most dangerous of all the revolutionaries was Thomas Paine, whose works They Three read with rising excitement. Paine was well known in Norwich as the son of a Quaker corset-maker from Thetford, with, initially, exciting radical ideas for reform.

Dr. Fothergill and David of Youngsbury knew of him as being active on behalf of the colonies during the American Revolution. He was a strong and convincing writer, appealing very much to the young, who could easily confuse his revolutionary ideas with the reform advocated by other radicals. His *Rights of Man* was regarded as 'the manifesto of the party in sympathy with the French Revolution'; for writing it he had fled from one country to another. Paine too was tried for high treason in England for seditious passages in the *Rights of Man*, and though he was acquitted, he was thereafter denounced as a radical, drunkard and atheist.

To the Quakers, revolutionary writers were responsible for all the evil which they saw spreading amongst the young, and when the Gurneys of The Grove realised that these were the authors being so avidly devoured by the young Gurneys of Earlham, Elders were sent to their father, blaming, as always, the dangerous revolutionary influences on such other Nonconformists as Unitarians, Roman Catholics and Jews. He was reminded that the Enfields ('self-confessed' Unitarians), and John Pitchford, a practising Roman Catholic, were frequently to be seen with his children. But evidence must be found that his children were straying from the Quaker faith. This was not difficult to find. They had been identified attending Roman Catholic Mass, the Methodist chapel, Unitarian meetings, and they had even been present at a Jewish wedding, as Louisa's journal testifies. 'The oddest thing I ever saw. There were four old Jews, some with beards holding up a sort of silken canopy upon small poles. The priest or principal Jew then came in and the 12-year-old.' Louisa describes the ceremony in detail, ending

> I think ceremony is almost necessary in such things as marriage. I should think it would have a good effect on some people. It would render marriage more sacred in their eyes and of more importance. But I have a particular dislike to such gross superstitions as was displayed in this marriage, such as people really believing that they would be happier for breaking a wine glass. Nor do I see why the ceremony should be performed in Hebrew. Surely if it be good it had

240

better be open to all people's understanding. I think it a good plan to
have the bride veiled for her own sake.

Associations with the Roman Catholic Church had much the
same effect on Louisa 'I can't express what my feelings are
when he says he believes in the virtues of fasting, confessing
and all these Roman Catholic biggoteries. I feel half angry, half
vexed. I don't know how to bear to see him do these sort of
things. I long to *force* him to eat meat on fridays.'

The accusations made against the children were not enough,
in their father's eyes, to prove more than that they were carrying out their mother's wishes: to compare *all* religions and
choose the Christian sect they believed to be the right one,
regardless of what men said, and it was not until it was more than
hinted that his beloved daughter, Rachel, and Henry Enfield had
been in love with each other for 'ages', unbeknown to him but
encouraged by his other children, that John of Earlham became
anxious. If his other children had really encouraged the attachment, then evidence must come from the children themselves.
He could not bring himself to question them, but they were
asked to read from their own journals, so that he should hear a
little, but not too much, of anything that might make it necessary
for him to take such a stern step as to ban all other denominations
from Earlham. Louisa began, and out came all the pranks with
the Enfields, the loves and the hates, but hardly a word about
politics.

> We seven girls, Mrs. Freeman and Pitchford sat together in the
> ante-room. They asked us to let them read our journals. We refused
> till we could refuse no longer, so I gave them mine. Rachel read
> almost every word – all my feelings and everything. I am truly glad
> now that they have seen it. I would now let them see anything I could
> write or think.

When the truth dawned that an intense affection between
Rachel and Henry Enfield 'was carried on for several years and
concealed from our indulgent father, who had a painful and

confused idea of our going wrong', and yet could not prevent it, 'John, no longer indulgent, demanded the separation, not only of Rachel and Henry, but the whole Enfield family.'

Priscilla, aged ten, made a last attempt to save the family friendship by writing to 'Miss Enfield', describing how very differently they behaved from the way everybody evidently suggested. No doubt the letter was available for all to see before it was sent, and perhaps Catherine and Rachel gave a little help with the spelling.

> We are always dressed by 6 and get as many lessons done before breakfast as we can and how hard at lessons they are – they come in and write their journals till supper, Kitty and Rachel and all . . . This is how we spend our day unless company or going out inter- rupts us which it seldom does. We are now reading Livey's Roman History which is very interesting and I fully advise thee to read it. [She writes how much they love each other and how wonderful their elder sisters are.] Everything we know, and all the little good we can boast of we owe almost entirely to Kitty, Betsy and Rachel too I love more than I can say.

The letter was sent, and treasured by the Enfields, but it was too late.

August 20th, 1796 was the day to which Rachel looked back when she was to write, seven years later, 'I have thought of the 20th of August this day 7 years. Surely I shall never forget the misery of it' and 'our parting scene under the old wall.'

The parting scene, and the scene with her father, can only be imagined, for Catherine and Betsy destroyed their journals and later replaced them with memoirs written anything up to seventy years later. Rachel also burnt hers, but still a few home-made notebooks survived. Two of Rachel's still bear scorch-marks from when she made a fire of hers. Some prying, loving little sister must have raked them out of the ashes and treasured them.

With the journals destroyed, it is only passing allusions in much later journals to 'the remembrance of scenes that sink into my very soul' that tell of the youthful romance.

Louisa only wrote, on the 20th August, 1796, of feeling 'very angry with Rachel', but no doubt she wrote this early in the morning, and by the next day Rachel had gone off with Kitty to Northrepps Hall to recover. By then all at Earlham were repentant. Louisa writes, on Sunday August 21st,

> I *do* [underlined four times] love my father with my whole heart. I feel as though I could give up my own happiness to his. I am *determined* I will do all I can to make him happy. Dearest Rachel has been most sweet. What a courage virtue gives and strength to go through anything. We read in the afternoon. I almost enjoyed it, with the idea that I was pleasing my father. We Four had a charming talk with Rachel and Kitty in the evening. The Others write that day: 'I was in fidgets' 'I felt perfectly stupified by dinner bustles.' 'What a family we are for the hurries.' 'All I can say is *For Shame*'.

They were now determined to reform. They performed curious little acts of attempted charity, such as going out on the turnpike and begging to be allowed to carry a 'clean woman's pattens as she had walked such a long way and was so tired.'

Louisa does 'now determine not to give way to the family failing of greediness' and [on rising late] 'I did not scold myself because I so seldom indulge in the bed way.' In spite of not being 'in the bed way', she went to read on Betsy's sofa, and, feeling sleepy, instead of checking it, she 'fell fast asleep' and 'everybody was rather displeased with me that I had been asleep and I was most displeased with myself.' But she writes,

> I had a pleasant Goats. I fell into thinking and forgot what surrounded me, no I did not forget them neither, for when I first got to Goats I as usual turned my eyes on most of the Goat leaders with contempt and disgust. These feelings were particularly directed to the Goat Lane girls. I exclaimed to myself how disgusting when it instantly struck me how truly uncharitable and wrong this was and I began to reason with myself about it.

Reluctantly the Four accepted 'the relinquishing of their greatest pleasure', the company of the Enfields, and turned, for a while, back on themselves. The handsome John junior began to take an almost fashionable interest in his appearance. Betsy took to 'mumping' more than ever, and Catherine devoted herself to comforting Rachel. Rachel herself grew pale and thin and cried often. Her distress was more than her father could bear and at last, indulgent again, he promised that she and Henry should be allowed to meet again if they continued in the same mind after a separation of two years. This would be on her twenty-first birthday. It was now November 1777.

With permission to exchange letters and portions of their journals, Rachel cheered up. Louisa writes:

> Rachel said the other day what an amazing deal of animal spirits she had that buoyed her up and made her appear most happy and contented when really her mind was in rather a melancholy state. I think it is a blessing to possess animal spirits. It makes other people happy and merry without their finding out our sorry.

So buoyed up was Rachel by her animal spirits that she was able to go out to dances and enjoy the company of other young men, including Pitchford who, although he knew about Henry and was even allowed to hear some of his journal read out to the others, now loved Rachel more than any of them. When he read from his journal he hoped that she had not noticed the special references to her charms.

Christmas was becoming more and more 'celebrated' at Earlham in the manner of other 'worldly' people. Richenda writes of the pleasure in eating turkey and plum pudding. Greenery was trailed in from the garden and park and festooned about the house, and there was a round of post-Christmas dances and parties.

By the end of February, Louisa was writing that Uncle Joseph of The Grove, and two of his daughters had been to Earlham 'and uncle Joseph spoke to Rachel about going out to dances. He took her into the study and when he was gone she burst out crying. I did pity her so much. I am afraid she must give it up. All our hope is now laid upon her having a pianoforte at home. They are trying this grand point with my father: May they succeed, but I much doubt it.'

But succeed they did, and all learnt to play, and 'the instrument was rarely silent,' although later Louisa had to admit that 'music has been a real source of pain to me.' Later still, 'When I hear any of them playing well on the piano or tambourin I am ready to wish that none of us might learn music that it may not be expected of me who don't choose to do it.'

Their father had no wish to prevent their dancing at home, but he did now make an effort to change their friends. He took to inviting the younger members of the country families, with whom he had shot as a boy, to shoot at Earlham and stay on afterwards for dancing and supper. The Earlham game was preserved with care, and so, when he caught a poacher red-handed and found he was a young officer stationed in Norwich, he asked him how his father would treat a like case. The reply was that, as a good Christian, he would ask him to dine. John of Earlham therefore did the same.

At about this time the great-grandson of the late Prime Minister Walpole, whose brother had complained of the Gurneys of Little Barningham poaching his pheasants half a century before, was first invited to dine at Earlham. He too was stationed at Norwich. Prince William Frederick of Gloucester, with three brother officers, arrived for five o'clock dinner. Among the company at Earlham that evening were Dr. Anderson, Amelia and Alderman Ives. The dinner was most elegant, and afterwards the children went up to the top of the table where Catherine sat beside the prince and 'They' sang. When the ladies rose it was half-past eight ('How late for us!'). In the drawing-room all was new for the younger ones, and new too, no doubt, for 'his princeship', as the eleven all stood round him singing, to his delight and amazement, a chapter from the Book of Kings.

On the Prince's next visit, when their father was away, they all repaired to Rachel and Betsy's room, where Rachel dressed up as a Quaker minister and preached one of her 'capital sermons'. The fun turned into dancing and from dancing on to serious talk. A young Unitarian now making himself felt in London was

William Hazlitt, the art student who 'had not yet begun to write but had already learnt to talk and dream'. He had lectured on the evils of legitimacy, which was of particular interest to the prince, since he said he was proud to be the illegitimate great-grandson of the first Prime Minister. (The first Prime Minister's second son, Sir Edward Walpole, had never married, but left three illegitimate daughters, one of whom, Maria, married, as her second husband, Prince William Henry, Duke of Gloucester, they became the parents of Prince William Frederick).

When 'other officers and gentlemen' came in, Louisa found them 'most dis and flirtatious', and again, 'I think satire carried too far is disgusting, but I like a bit of it. I am naturally satirical but it must be checked or it will grow too much on me.' Richenda writes, 'Betsy had an offer from one of the officers. Colonel Heley who is about sixty is the man. He did it in the drollest way and was most loving to her. He continued his addresses and Betsy carried on most drolly. He kissed 'Cilla so much that her cheeks were quite sore.'

Catherine writes that 'the people we were now frequently with went far beyond our dear friends the Enfields, who were never infidels.'

Chapter Fourteen

Rachel and Betsy
1798–1799

'Rachel is the alcohol and Betsy is the cream of human nature.' In his leather-bound journal John Pitchford was casting an anxious glance at his friendship with 'my seven most sweet Earlham sisters, which I trust will last forever', and last forever it did, for there was no complete severing, as with the Enfields, after John of Earlham was again reproved for allowing his 'children's friendship with those of other dominations'. There were still 'many hours of rapture, many of calm, tranquil happiness, many of lively animated hilarity passed in their delightful society'. The sisters said afterwards that Pitchford and a Baptist minister were the only Christian influences that really affected any of them at that time. They discussed it all quite cheerfully with Pitchford and decided that cutting his visits down to once a week would be reasonable. Finally they settled for once a fortnight.

Frivolous entertainment at Earlham was also under observation. The earlier warning that John of Earlham had been given, however hurtful to his children and their friends, did not appear to the Elders of Goat Lane to be taking effect. 'The Prince is coming again next Sunday to meet the [Grove] Gurneys, who have made a great scolding about it,' writes Louisa. Since Christmas, the drawing-room at Earlham had been done up for entertaining, and the schoolroom had been moved downstairs to the little parlour. Prince William, the King's nephew had been visiting constantly with a great deal of company.

I never saw the prince so sociable and agreeable as this time [writes Richenda]. He does so admire Rachel. After dinner we began to sing.

247

Rachel sang delightfully. I don't know when I have heard her sing so well. All joined in, single and married, old and young, little and great. I had no idea that gay company could be as pleasant as it was. Rachel did look beautiful and talked so cleverly all the time, and she enjoyed it as much as any of us which I am very glad of, as she seldom enjoys these sort of things now. It was droll to have a dance on Wednesday night and Thursday and Friday and on Saturday we went to Dr. Anderson's and had a most pleasant evening indeed. We danced from 7 till 12.

Friends were still expected to adopt plainness of speech, behaviour and apparel. 'Plain' Quakers conformed to these expectations. 'Gay' Quakers modified them, but were still accepted, though if they became too outrageous they were disciplined by the elders. The Gurneys of Earlham were certainly 'Gay', in the Quakerly meaning of the word, and were frequently disciplined for overstepping the mark.

Uncle Joseph of The Grove, 'summoning' it was said, 'all his humility, benevolence and moderation', spoke to Betsy about her rare appearances at meeting. She promised to try to do better, and began by adding to her list of faults in her journal and warning herself against them.

I must beware of being a flirt, it is an abominable character. Pride and vanity . . . I have done little today, I am so very idle; instead of improving I fear I go back, my inclinations lead me to be an idle, flirting, worldly girl . . . I had very much set my mind on going to the oratorio, the Prince is to be there, and by all accounts it will be quite a grand sight, and there will be the finest music; but if my father does not like me to go, much as I wish it, I will give it up with pleasure, if it be in my power, without a murmur. [And, with a change of ink] I went to the oratorio, I enjoyed it but spoke sadly at random; what a bad habit! . . . greatly dissipated by hearing the band . . . there is much distance between obstinate and steady; I'm obstinate when I contradict for the sake of contradiction; I'm steady when I keep to what I really think right. If I am *bid* to do a thing, my spirit revolts; if I am *asked* to do a thing, I am willing. I am now 17,

248

and if some kind and great circumstance does not happen to me I shall have my talents devoured by moth and rust.

There are many various versions of the 'great circumstance' that did happen to her at Goats on February 4th, 1798. Richenda's oft-quoted account was, in fact, given years later from memory.

The seven sisters sat in the front row of the gallery. Betsy had on a pair of new purple boots laced with scarlet. They were a perfect delight to her, and she intended to console herself with them for the dullness she expected. However, the American Friend, Savery, rose to speak. His manner was arresting, and Betsy's attention became fixed. She began to weep. After meeting she went at once to my father and asked if she might dine at Keswick that afternoon, where Mr. Savery was staying. She did, and came home crying. Next morning William Savery came to breakfast at Earlham and preached to us afterwards, prophesying a high and important calling into which our sister Betsy would be led.

The shrewd Louisa observes:

Friend Savery has been here, who seems a charming man and a most liberal minded Quaker. Betsy, who spent all yesterday with him, not only admires, but quite loves him. He appears to me a truly good man, and a most upright Christian, and such men are always loved. To me he is quite different from the common run of disagreeable Quaker preachers. In every society and sect there is always something good and worthy to be found.

Savery himself thought it 'the gayest meeting of Friends I have ever sat in, and was grieved at it . . . the mark of wealth and grandeur are too obvious in several families of Friends in this place.' Betsy's own impression, written the day the events occurred, was

This morning I went to Meeting, though but poorly, because I wished to hear an American Friend named William Savery. Much passed there of a very interesting nature. I have had a feint light spread over my mind, at least I believe it is something of that kind,

249

owing to having been much with and heard much excellence from, one who appears to me, a true Christian. It has caused me to feel a little religion. My imagination has been worked upon, and I fear all that I felt will go off.

And how right she was, for two days later she had 'a very serious ride to Norwich', but a meeting with some gay people 'brought on vanity' and she came home 'as full of the world as I went to town full of heaven'. And the following Sunday was 'very different to this day week . . . today I have felt all my old irreligious feelings.' However, only a few days later she admitted that they went to hear the band, for which she was sorry because she had not the courage to tell her father: 'I wish I had not gone; I will not go again without his knowing it beforehand.'

She asked her father if she might go to London and he, no doubt feeling that a round of dances with the cousins would frisk her out of her religious dumps, agreed, but 'my thoughts,' she wrote, 'are far more risen at the thought of seeing him (Savery) than all the playhouses and gaiety in the world.'

John of Earlham took his daughter, in his own carriage, with her maid, to stay with Lindoe relations in London. Betsy's chaperone was Mrs. Sampson Hanbury: Catherine's cousin-twin, Gatty. They arrived on Saturday. On Monday Betsy was extremely disappointed by Drury Lane. 'To be sure, the house is grand and dazzling, but I had no feeling whilst there but that of wishing it over.' On Tuesday 'after Covent Garden' she 'continued not to like plays'. On Wednesday she 'felt proud, vain and silly and in the evening went to a dance'. On Thursday she had her hair dressed 'and felt like a monkey', saw Hamlet and Bluebeard and was glad when they were over'. On Friday she said uncharitable things and gave way to inclination, 'for I own I love a scandal'. On Saturday she had a dancing lesson and on Sunday 'Savery's sermon, from Revelation, hit the state I have been in; I trust I may not remain in it.'

The following week she stayed more quietly with the Sam Hoares, who had moved from the city to a country house on the heights of Hampstead Heath. Sam Hoare's wife had died not long after her fourth child was born and he was now happily remarried to their devoted stepmother, Hannah Sterry, who, young as she was, regretfully never had any family herself. Savery describes staying at the Heath the week before, and walking in the grounds and gardens 'which are in high style much beyond the simplicity of a Friend. The sons and daughters, although they are quite in high life and gay in their appearance were as loving and kind as possible.' Sam Hoare kept open house for Friends and for writers and artists of all denominations.

'The Heath' still stands at the top of Spaniards Road in a rambling country garden, though long ago Sam Hoare's descendants handed over their part of the Heath for public recreation.

Altogether, Betsy was away six weeks, entering various scenes of gaiety and attending balls and other places of amusement. But best of all was 'the high advantage of attending several most interesting meetings of William Savery and having at times his company, and that of a few other Friends'.

She had hardly come down to earth at Earlham when the children brought her a reply from a letter she had written to Savery. It was 'a long and useful sermon in which he pointed out that blessed confidence cannot be enjoyed by the gay, the giddy, proud or wanton votaries of this world.' His letter ends,

> My dear child, my heart is full towards thee, I have written a great deal more than I expected; but I feign would take thee by the hand, if I were qualified so to do, and ascend, as our Heavenly Father may enable us together, step by step, up that ladder which reaches from earth to Heaven; but alas! my weakness is such, I can only recommend both myself and thee to that good hand, that is able to do more abundantly for us than we can either ask or think; and bid thee, for the present, in much Christian affection, farewell. Willliam Savery.

Betsy's journal and her whole attitude to life were now filled with desire for a change. As hoped for by her 'dear dear William Savery,' who, she could not help observing that summer, 'is, I think, only five miles off me this night. Perhaps we never again shall be so near each other, but I firmly believe we shall. I long to know how he liked my pocket book I gave him this morning.'

Not unnaturally Rachel suggested that Betsy was in love with William Savery. 'I answered I did not think I was but I own I felt not clear in my mind respecting him.'

Richenda looked back on her extreme discomfort about Betsy's increasing Quakerism. 'She no longer joined in our pleasant dances and singing she seemed to give up; she dressed as plain as she could, and spoke still more so. We all feel about it alike and are truly sorry that one of us seven should separate herself in principles, actions and appearances from the rest.'

Richenda felt, however, that in many respects Betsy's character was much improved since she had adopted her new principles. 'She is industrious, charitable to the poor and kind and attentive to all of us.' She had, indeed started to teach some of the village children to read, and had been to visit old Nurse Norman's husband on his deathbed, telling him how happy he should be in expectation of immortality and everlasting bliss.

She went to Bedlam lunatic asylum with Amelia to study, through bars, the unfortunate inmates. Amelia was strangely attracted by the weird and terrible and perhaps found the sensitive Betsy, who recoiled from both so easily, a satisfying companion. Amelia liked to pry into and retell ghost stories associated with Earlham. There was supposed to be a lady in blue (indeed she was sometimes the lady whose portrait was let into the panelling in the late Kitty's bedroom), who alternated between stepping out of her frame and gliding out of the cupboard in the blue room, which was the very room that Betsy shared with Rachel.

Without much difficulty Amelia could send Betsy into near paroxysms of terror, and then laugh at her in the most cheerful and natural way at the whole idea of ghosts existing at all.

Betsy was determined to overcome her fears, and writes in her journal:

A plan, at least a duty that I have felt for some time, I will now mention. I have been trying to overcome fear; my method has been to stay in the dark and at night to go into those rooms not generally inhabited; there is a strange propensity in the human mind of fear in the dark, a sort of dread of something supernatural; I try to overcome that by considering that, as far as I believed in ghosts, so far I must believe in a state after death, and it must confirm my belief in the spirit of God; therefore if I try to act right I have no need to fear the directions of infinite wisdom. But my most predominate fear is that of thieves; and I find that still more difficult to overcome, but faith would cure that also, God can equally protect us from man as from evil.

My father not appearing to like all my present doings, has been rather a cloud over my mind this day.

Betsy was absolutely sure that pleasures of the world – music, dancing, art and cheerful company – must be renounced for ever. She refused even to look at a picture John Opie was painting of her father; this not unnaturally hurt his feelings.

It was at Earlham that Amelia Alderson frequently, if not for the first time, met her London-based husband the Cornish painter, John Opie, who was brought to Norfolk by John Crome. Opie was divorced, and had a deliberately oafish manner, observing of Norwich hospitality that, 'I have occasionally some agreeable conversation with some not unclever people.' Amelia now moved in wide circles through her plays, which were acted in Norwich and read in London, but of all the men she met, Opie was the one she chose to marry. John of Earlham secured him commissions to paint some of the Norfolk county notables. At the same time Opie painted a conversation piece of Richenda, Chenda, John and an old gipsy woman, and another of a child sitting in a favourite position of his, which is said to be Betsy with a greyhound licking her forearm.

Betsy was now eighteen and had taken to wearing occasionally 'fully Quaker costume'. But not entirely; her love of dress was too strong. She loved designing and cutting out original clothes, though she admits she was very slow at making them. The day on which her future husband first noticed her on a walk down Bluebell Lane, she was wearing a brown silk scarf and a black veil wound round her head like a turban, the ends hanging at one side of her face against her flaxen hair. Joseph Fry, son of the Frys who had been attacked by highwaymen, had come to Norfolk to study farming before going into his family provisioning firm. 'The motherless condition of the seven, their singular charm, both in person and mind, their joy of freedom and general circumstances' charmed 'young fry' as they called him (because he was too big and awkward to call 'small fry'.) Betsy ignored Young Fry's advances, and concentrated on her soul. 'This evening I have got myself rather into a scrape; I have been helping them to beg my father for us to go to the Guild-dinner and I don't know whether it was quite what I approve of or think good for myself.'

Catherine remembered Betsy sitting on the window-seat in the blue room with her feet up, in deep meditation, her fine flaxen hair combed simply behind and parted in front, her white gown fitting her figure, which was becomingly in proportion. 'When she told me that she could not dance any more, which at that time was my greatest delight, I argued with her, persecuted her, but it was all in vain. I never shook her on one single point which she felt to be her future.' Throughout all this, she remained amiable, patient, forebearing and humble. The change from a grumpy, lazy, unwilling, self-confessedly cowardly schoolgirl was miraculous.

Pitchford had a long tête-a-tête with Betsy

during which she communicated to me a great deal. A great change has taken place in her sentiments concerning religion. From being sceptical she has become a believer in the great truth of Christianity. During the whole of our walk she displayed a great sweetness, much good sense and a charming confidence in me. I did all in my power to confirm her present state of mind.

This was not what her father had in mind. The Roman Catholic Pitchford, far from weaning Betsy off her desire to 'go plain', seemed only to be encouraging her.

Pitchford writes of spending the afternoon at Earlham where

he 'enjoyed a most sweet tranquil happy time. I'm never so happy as when with them – they're so artless, so affectionate and so kind that they make my heart quite expand towards them. Sweet delightful girls, may you be forever happy!' But John of Earlham was beginning to feel that even fortnightly visits could be too frequent, particularly after he had heard extracts from Pitchford's journal discussed with some 'enthusiasm' by his family. Pitchford nearly always brought his journal with him and, given the opportunity, he would read extracts from it by way of introducing a topic. He now refers to a letter received from Mr. Trafford, requesting him to meet him and some other gentlemen at the Maid's Head, to consider the propriety of arming themselves for the present crisis. 'I feel quite undecided what part to take. I abhor the present conduct of the French and earnestly wish they may not invade this country, but I do not feel at all inclined to take up arms.'

Maybe Pitchford did not feel at all inclined to take up arms, but John junior, now a tall and handsome eighteen-year-old, was quite elated at the idea. He liked the uniform and the general fashionable air he had admired among the Prince's friends. His father reminded him that to enlist in the army would lose him his membership of the Society of Friends and this could not even be considered until he came of age in three years time. John of Earlham's determination to try not to give way to his natural indulgence towards his children was further strained by the deepening of Rachel's longing to see her Henry again, which now neither animal spirits nor innate glee could conceal.

There were still two whole summers left of the long separation from Henry which they all knew would end for Rachel when she came of age in November 1799. Their father had promised that Henry could renew his suit, and Rachel had kept up her spirits with the joy of knowing that he loved her. Even if his letters were not shared with her sisters and closest friends, the extracts from his journals, which he sent regularly in exchange for hers, were read out within the innermost circle of the family.

A few years later Rachel was writing in her diary of how she had been talking to Pitchford 'about my past attachment which strongly awakened past recollections. This subject I always feel to be more affecting than any other that does not relate to our religious concerns. This reminds me of what Henry Enfield said in one of his letters that his affection for me could easily be equal or excelled by the superior affection of love to his Creator.'

Whereas, usually, Rachel's 'natural animal spirits and glee' concealed her longing, there were times when they could not help flagging. She was born in the same year as William Hazlitt and, like hers, his spirit was awakened by a desperate love affair in the year 1798 of which he wrote 'the figures that compose that date are to me like "the dreaded name of Demogorgon".'

The hot, sultry July weather, even just outside the dustbowl of Norwich, was trying to them all. Even 'Mrs.' Judd and Scarnell were 'lowering and touchy' with everyone, as well as each other. Scarnell would not, for all Betsy's pleadings, bring himself to join the Society of Friends for Judd's sake. And Judd had no intention of giving up her membership for him.

John of Earlham felt it was time to take them all away for a change of air on a tour through England and Wales. He planned to leave Betsy for a short stay on the way with his dear, charming, upright little first cousins Chrissy and Prissy Gurney, of the long-ago Wroxham Broad drama. Prissy had long renounced the world and its fascinations for a splendid life of goodness and help as a Quaker minister. Prissy Gurney knew enough about the more solid side of Quakerism to show Betsy that it was not all composed of forcing yourself to stand in dark rooms or being a wet blanket among everybody else.

The attention of all of them would be drawn away from their various worries and indecisions by the new experiences, not to mention risks and discomforts found on the road.

The family left on 'one of the very bustling mornings to which Earlham is subject'. Their usual cortege for such a journey was 'three chariots and a whisky'. In one of these was Judd, Scarnell and the luggage.

While they were away Pitchford kept his promise to Catherine to have Sammy, Joseph John and Danny to tea. He took them for a long walk in Norwich and enjoyed their company 'as they put me in mind of their sweet sisters'.

Meanwhile on the journey to the west, Betsy, for one, was soon 'tired, quite fagged, body and mind'. At Weymouth they went to sea, where Betsy always felt 'doubtful of ever seeing land again', and feared 'that if the least accident was to happen I should be drowned.' On board a ferry boat at Plymouth she felt no less afraid. She expressed his disapproval of a naval review, and on the same religious grounds refused to listen to a very famous band of the Marines. She accompanied Judd and the men servants on board a man of war, which she referred to as a fine but melancholy sight.

As for the visit to Prissy and Chrissy, after much talk and many 'opportunities', as Friends call those moments when it is easy to unburden the heart, and many more still longer silences with Prissy and others whom she met with her, Betsy left absolutely convinced that she was to be a light to the blind, speech to the dumb, and feet to the lame.

She hoped it would not hurt 'them'. 'I know it hurts Rachel and John the most. Rachel has the seeds of Quakerism in her heart, that if cultivated, would grow indeed, I have no doubt. I should never be surprised to see us all Quakers,' she added wistfully.

Even on the way back Betsy practised her new role and found that 'any alteration of speech is very difficult to make.' In New-market she saw 'H –' and was so worried as to whether she would be able to address him as 'thee' that she took to her heels and ran away. But she collected herself and, without much difficulty, 'I did it.' If 'H –' was Henry Enfield, the worry may well have been whether or not she should have spoken to him at all.

Next morning Rachel sent the milk-boy from Earlham with a parcel for Pitchford, containing a note saying that they had arrived home last night and hoped to see him at Earlham. In the parcel was a splendid knife which she had bought for him in Birmingham. 'The little boys from Earlham accompanied by Mrs. Freeman, took him two pictures Richenda had drawn for him.' Rachel then followed in person and asked him to come to a dance a week later and to bring a friend, as the Bob Barclays were coming from Clapham. It was, Pitchford writes, 'a very agreeable dance and altogether a delightful afternoon and evening', but Betsy refused to dance 'because of the danger of dancing throwing me off my centre'. Catherine gave her a talking to and said she was too young and inexperienced to take up one party's opinions. Betsy said she would give up the company of Friends if Catherine requested it but she firmly believed she could never be happy unless she was a Quaker.

Scarnell also, after the journey, agreed that he could never be happy unless he became at any rate enough of a Quaker to marry 'Mrs.' Judd. After fifteen years' courtship, John Scarnell and Hannah Judd were married at Thursday meeting, Goat Lane, on 13th October, 1798. All the Gurneys of Earlham were there, most of the Keswick and Grove Gurneys, and a large party of Bob Barclay's and Pitchford's.

Betsy started an early version of wolf cubs and brownies, first up in the eleven-sided garret, and then, when the 'Imps', as the others called them, increased in numbers, in the laundry when it was not in use for the quantity of linen washed in a household that often rose to fifty people. The children found Betsy irresistible, and more and more joined in until there were over eighty. The family took to going to the laundry door to look through the open top half at the proceedings, and to watch the attentive reactions of the children. Sometimes Betsy's father joined them and gradually it became a sight and sound to which he treated visitors. The 'Imps', as much for Betsy's sake as for that of the other folk, did their best with her help to be seen in a clean and presentable state, and Betsy became accustomed to an audience.

And so began her training for her appearances in Newgate prison twenty years later, which no self-respecting visitor to London wished to miss. Betsy's voice was so musical that she seemed almost to be singing her instructions. But 'plain' Friends did not sing. George Fox himself said that music was almost as dangerous as gunpowder, and Tom Paine, the Norwich corset-maker's son, had blasphemously written that if a Quaker had been consulted at the Creation 'not a bird would have been permitted to sing'. It was a great 'worriation', in the vernacular of the Earlhamites.

Betsy writes of singing. 'I believe singing to be so natural that I may try it a little longer: but I do think dancing may be given up. What particularly led me to this state, was our having company, and I thought I must sing; I sang a little, but did not stay with them during the play.'

The next day she decided that 'my best method of conduct will be to tell Rachel how I am situated in mind and then ask her what she would advise; and be very kind and tell her the true state of the case. Is it worth while to continue in so small a pleasure for so much pain? The pleasure is nothing to me, but it is a grand step to take in life.'

The writing is re-started.

I have been and spoken to Rachel, saying I think I must give up singing. It is astonishing the total change that has taken place; from misery I am now come to joy; I felt ill before, and I now feel well – thankful, should I be for being directed, and pray to keep always to that direction. After having spoken to my darling Rachel, where I fear I said too much, I rode to Norwich after some poor people. I went to see many, and added my mite to their comfort. Nothing I think could exceed the kindness of my dear Rachel. Though I have no one here to encourage me in Quakerism, I believe I must be one before I am content.

The rest of the family were far from content. They were all, technically Quakers, but Betsy was to set herself in an entirely different category.

In December 1798 Betsy writes

This day finished with a dance. If I could make a rule never to give way to vanity, excitement or flirting, I do not think I should object to dancing; but it always leads me into some one of these faults; indeed, I never remember dancing without feeling one if not a little of all the three and sometimes a great deal. But as my giving it up would hurt many it should be one of those things I part with most carefully.

259

And on 1 March 1799

There is going to be a dance. What am I to do? As far as I can see, I believe, if I find it very necessary to their pleasure, I may do it, but not for my own gratification. Remember, don't be vain, if it be possible, dance little. [Here there is a change of ink]. I began to dance in a state next to pain of mind; when I had danced four dances, I was trying to pluck up courage to tell Rachel I wished to give it up for the evening; it seemed as if she looked into my mind, for she came up to me at that minute in the most tender manner, and begged me to leave off, saying she would contrive without me; I suppose she saw in my countenance the state of my mind. I am not half kind enough to her, I often make sharp remarks to her, and in reality there are none of my sisters to whom I owe so much; I must think of her as my nurse; she would suffer much to comfort me; may she oh God, be blessed; would'st thou, oh would'st thou let her see her right path, whatever that may be, and wil't thou enable her to keep up to her duty, in whatever line it may lead. Let this evening be a lesson to me, not to be unkind to her any more. I think I should feel more satisfaction in not dancing; but such things must be left very much to the time.

Once again it seemed the moment for the family to be packed into two vehicles, with two or three attendants, to be taken by their father on another journey. This time they headed for the north. They spent three days visiting the Quaker school which nearly thirty years before John of Earlham had heard being planned in Cheapside. Now the plans had come to fruition and they dined with a very large party of boys in the Ackworth school dining-room, and were taken all over the school and grounds. Next day They Three were asked to take classes. Betsy rose at six to hear spelling, but admitted that she had only a slight knowledge of grammar when invited to attend the grammar school. To her relief she was only expected to admire writing, cyphering, sewing, mending, spinning, and knitting.

They moved on to York where they all sighed over the beauty of the minster. But Betsy sighed over 'how much people spend about a pious building! Would they spend as much time and trouble about their own soul?' They trotted, lumbered, and occasionally cantered on through beautiful scenery which was particularly so on entering Durham. They arrived in Newcastle in thunder and lightning but, despite heavy showers of summer rain, they walked happily about through the bustle of Newcastle, seeing different sights. Next day they arrived at their father's sporting estate of Sheepwash on the beautiful banks of Wansbeck, where they stayed for a few days to ride round it while their father shot, an activity which Betsy still distrusted. Moreover, she had to summon up all her courage to manage the unruly horse she had been allotted. They reached and admired Edinburgh, and then turned for home. They were back at Earlham by the end of August, with less than three months before Rachel came of age on 21st November.

Two varying accounts exist of the meeting between Rachel and Henry. Ninety-six years later, Augusut Hare, the Victorian travel writer and biographer wrote:

The Enfield family, who had formerly been the dearest friends of all the Earlham sisters, were still under sentence of exile. The separation lasted three years. All the sisters had felt it, but to Rachel it had been a bitter trial. During the interval, however, – partly through the influence of young Mr. Pitchford, but more perhaps as an effect of the trial itself – Rachel's mind had undergone a great change on religious subjects, and though her knowledge of them was obscure she had begun to seek consolation in a form which she would have joined Henry in ridiculing a few years before. It had been promised that she was to see him again when she should be 21 in *November 1799*, and with a most intense anxiety she looked forward to the interview which would decide her lot in life. As the time approached, she wrote to beg him to give her full notice before their meeting. But he did not do this, and on the very day his probation was ended he unexpectedly appeared at Earlham. Rachel and Henry Enfield were shut up together for a long time. She scarcely spoke afterwards of what had passed between them, but when he came out, he went away without seeing any other member of the family. The unsympathetic pride with which he had scorned the change in her feelings had pained Rachel bitterly. Henry Enfield had parted with her coldly; nothing was said as to the future.

Rachel was left in a state of extreme disappointment and stress, and as day after day passed and she heard nothing, Mr. Gurney's tender heart was moved, till at last he began to wish to bring about the union with Henry Enfield which he had opposed so long. But then a strange report came to Earlham that he was engaged to someone else. Mr. Gurney sent his faithful servant Scarnell to Nottingham where the Enfields lived to gather information, and find out if the report was true; if not, to tell young Enfield all his opposition was withdrawn. But the report was perfectly true; Henry Enfield was not only engaged but was already married to another. From that day Rachel's spirits were broken and her beauty faded.

Long after the event Rachel's sister, Catherine, writes:

Rachel's grief was most bitter, and she was long in a state of great depression, but by degrees her fine vigorous nature, aided by the increasing sense of the power of religion, prevailed over her senses, and her mind and affections were turned to other objects. She did indeed work her way through many clouds of sorrow and much darkness, with few outward helps, but the diligence of her mind being once directed to attaining a resting place in religion, she gradually became established in the habit of daily reading in the scriptures and a measure of religious retirement. Her diligence and duty however, her remarkable cultivation in the gift of serving others that was in her, was apparently one of the principle means of leading her into higher light. [Hare adds]: John Pitchford, who had been long so devotedly attached to her, had proposed to Rachel after he knew that her engagement to Henry Enfield was at an end, but entirely without success.

Betsy's eldest daughter, Katie Fry, wrote of her aunt in her family scrapbook years later:

Rachel, the second daughter, largely shared in her sister's cares. She was smaller in person than Catherine or Elizabeth but she had considerable beauty both of feature and complexion being fair and bright. As a child she was remarkable for the extraordinary flow of her animal spirits, accompanied by humorous drollery. But these traits had been sobered in her 20th year by a bitter disappointment in love.

Between one Henry Enfield of Norwich and Rachel a strong

attachment sprang up, which existed for two or three years before her father was made aware of it. Lovely, joyous and warmly affectionate, Rachel had entered early on the career of life unprotected by a mother's care. She became entangled in this wrong and unfortunate affair which cast a shade over the whole of her future life. The religious faith of Mr. Enfield was decidedly unsound, while his pecuniary means were quite inadequate to maintain a wife as Rachel had been accustomed to live..

Mr. Gurney, on discovering the state of their feelings insisted on total suspension of intercourse during a whole year, as a test of their solidity, promising that if at the end of the year it was still found that a union was essential to their happiness he then would no longer oppose their wishes. Well it was that he took this precaution!

Mr. Enfield was established in the office of an attorney at Nottingham. Time rolled on and the year expired. Rachel knew no change in her affection, and believed Mr. Enfield's also incapable of diminution. She watched first confidently, then anxiously, for some overture on his part. None came. Then the rumour breathed that he was false, and had transferred his love to another. It was but the old story!

The suspense became intolerable to Rachel, so Mr. Gurney secretly sent Peter Witton, his coachman, an old and confidential servant, to Nottingham privately to ascertain the real state of the case. Peter discovered and brought back proofs to his master that Henry Enfield was paying his address to a young lady of that place, and was soon to marry her.

This struck at the real root of Rachel's happiness.

There are certainly discrepancies between these versions. In one, Scarnell brings back the bad news, and in another, Peter Witten. In one, Rachel was twenty-one and in another, nineteen. There are many other adaptations evidently taken from these accounts, with embellishments such as that of Rachel and Henry being shut up for a long time in the ante-room, with her six sisters waiting anxiously outside: of stolen kisses and secret exchanges of letters, and of Rachel found constantly sitting and crying over her little Bible.

Rachel herself, in her later diaries, refers to the whole, but never to that one particular day, November 21st, 1799.

She writes in 1804:

That such a love as *ours* was should come to so melancholy a conclusion has at times appeared to me to be a mystery not to be unravelled and at times hardly to be borne. I have at times been inclined to murmur at this dispensation of Providence and ask *why* so *pure* and so great a blessing was taken from me. Alas, it is known only to the searcher of hearts what mine has past through in its separation from its once most beautiful object; but this separation is at last effected and though the bent of my affectionate tastes remain the same, so that no other earthly object has excited them at all in the way that they were once excited, they are now, I hope, sanctified by a degree of faith in our Heavenly Father that perhaps I might never have known had I not travelled to it by the thorny road that I have trodden.

In 1806 Rachel writes in a letter to Fowell, 'If I had married when I wished to do so, I should hardly have known the girls in their present state. Thus there is generally a mixture of good and evil in all things.' And in a letter written to him and Hannah immediately after their marriage on 22 May 1807, 'I dare say, dearest Fowell and Hannah, you do not wonder that, in certain moods the past should rise up mournfully before me. The sight of you all happily married brings some sad regrets, but happily their acuteness is very much gone, and in the awful and blessed moments when I am enabled to wait at the footstool of my great lord and master my murmurings are hushed, and the storm becomes a calm.'

What really happened?

Recently a direct descendant of Hannah Gurney and Sir Thomas Fowell Buxton, Erica Wathen, learnt just before her own marriage to Jonathan Strange, that her bridegroom was a direct descendant of another of the eleven Gurneys of Earlham. Jonathan's great-great-great-grandmother, Rebecca Read, neé Gurney, was, she was told, the daughter of Rachel Gurney of Earlham and Henry Enfield, born in 1800 in the London house of Elizabeth Fry.

To almost any known descendant or adherent of the Gurneys of Earlham, such a suggestion could only be as much of a shock as if it concerned one's own sister. The lovable Rachel, with her glee and charm and understanding of children, would, of course, have made a delightful mother. The illegitimacy would have been no harder to overcome than that of the daughter of Rachel's own first cousin, Dick Gurney of Keswick. His Mary Jary was not only happily accepted at Earlham but also its then master, Rachel's pious brother, Joseph John, allowed her to marry his son, Jacky, (whom Mary Jary later left in favour of Jacky's groom). No, the hurt stems from the blow of having even possibly been deceived by the hitherto trustworthy Rachel. A resentment burns, akin to Louisa's, of 'They Three' keeping a secret to themselves. Certainly Catherine and Betsy must have known whatever the truth was. Perhaps they all knew. But what disillusionment if they were all allowed to run on in their re-freshing and convincingly innocent journals, read by all round the fireside or in the garden, already knowing that a child of their home was to be born unwanted and to be given away! Had the Society of Friends found out, Rachel would have been disowned. As she remained a member of the Society until 1820 and ap-parently a deeply religious woman throughout, the Society would have been deceived, too.

It would be impossible to prove for certain that Rachel never had a child. But, so far, insufficient official records have been found to prove for certain that Rebecca was her child. Rebecca's death certificate shows that she died at Shoreham in 1893, her age given as ninety-four, which takes her birth back to 1799 or 1800. Her marriage certificate records that Rebecca Gurney married John Read of 15 Bury Street, Piccadilly (now Quaglino's Res-taurant) on 27th February, 1826 at St. George's church, Hanover Square.

Rebecca's great-granddaughter, Phyllis David, still living and born within five years of Rebecca's death, was told that Rebecca often talked of her Gurney grandmother and the Gurneys of Earlham from whom she was descended. She referred to Elizabeth Fry as her aunt and Samuel Gurney as her uncle. The latter, she was told, often visited them. Her great-grand-daughter, Phyllis David, has a miniature of Samuel and a photo-graph of Rebecca, showing a formidable old lady wearing beaded and braided widow's weeds and a fur-lined cloak. Her hair is parted in the middle, with side ringlets, and she has the unmistakable strong jowl of a Gurney. Phyllis David also has a photograph of Rebecca's great-grandson who died of a fever in Mesopotamia in 1916. The boy has the curly hair and humorous eyes of many of the Gurney cousins.

The romance of Rachel Gurney and Henry Enfield was handed down by word of mouth by Rebecca's descendants, with the details that she was born in Betsy's house (which pushes the date on to some time after August 1800), and was adopted by a well-to-do lady who brought her up in Queen Anne's Mansions, which have now been demolished.

The only known Rebecca Gurney related to Elizabeth Fry and her brother, Samuel Gurney, who could otherwise have been the bride at St. George's, Hanover Square, on 27th February 1827, was born in Bristol thirty-one years before. She was the great-granddaughter of the Benjamin Gurney who died in debt for two wigs and a pair of fustian breeches. His son had married one of the more Plain Quakerly Dutch-dealing half Hopes of Amsterdam. Their son, Joseph Gurney, was the father of this Rebecca, and his address in Bridge Street, Bristol, is among John of Earlham's papers. By now this branch was more than well enough off in the watchmaking business to be married in the smart, relatively new church of St. George's, Hanover Square. They could have had a town house in the area to qualify Rebecca for being 'of the parish'. The marriage certificate was witnessed by Charles Gurney and E. Gurney. There was only one of each in this generation: Rebecca's only brother, Charles Gurney, and her uncle, Edmund Gurney. There is only one snag. This Rebecca Gurney is recorded at the Bristol Quaker meeting as having died unmarried aged sixty-three.

Another red herring occurs in the same set of John of Earlham's accounts that included the fustian breeches, when the then Johnny-for-short was paying for schooling and firing for his ward B. Read (J. Read being Rebecca's bridegroom). Later, John of Earlham's permission was sought for a proposal of marriage to B. Read's daughter. Why B. Read was ever John of Earlham's ward is not known. To have been old enough to need schooling, B. Read could hardly have been his child. Could he have inherited a ward from any of his all-too-holy forebears? Or from his cousin Benjamin of the fustian breeches? Could some semiconcealed confusion over the identity of B. Read account for the unmistakable Gurney jowl to be seen in the photograph of Mrs. Rebecca Read, who died in Shoreham in 1893? And yet her descendants have always been convinced that she was the illegitimate daughter of Rachel Gurney of Earlham and Henry Enfield.

Did Elizabeth Fry's eldest daughter, Kate, know the whole truth? Her brisk reference in her version to 'the old story', suggesting the well-known infidelity of all men, does not tally with her aunt Catherine's own memories of her girlhood days.

Kate Fry and her sister, Rachel Cresswell, who edited their famous mother's journals after her death, put their own interpretation of high moral tone into their comments, and cut accordingly. Other family journals and letters have been copied and edited on the same lines; sometimes the latest copy has almost completely departed from the original, as in the game of Russian Scandal.

A recently unearthed account, playfully written by another descendant of the Gurneys of Earlham, Helen Wilson, in January 1894, reveals that 'on the occasion of Mr. Augustus Hare's visit to Colne House, Cromer' with the object of writing a book about the Earlham Gurneys, the family literally *sat* on papers they did not wish this author to see.

There is a touch of *Watership Down* about Helen Wilson's allegory: leaving Augustus as a hare, she turns the family into rabbits by way of a bit of whimsy, explaining how the forefathers had chosen a bank (Northrepps Hall) and burrowed into it, and all succeeding descendants had burrowed further and enlarged its bounds. 'Only a family of rabbits? yes, but such a family so respectable and well doing and pious and dated back as far as rabbits went', and like rabbits it married and inter-married, started new burrows and kept its family relics in the main burrow. She made playful suggestions of what these relics were – little white tufts tied with straw, and bundles of leaves tied neatly together and dated; several piles of rat-skins stolen from the gamekeeper's fence and written inside as diaries. The rabbits would sit round listening to their journals, and laugh till their sides ached. She referred to a young rabbit with a fair-sized moustache saying, 'When I was at Sandborough and that was where the rising generation went to college, I met a Mr. Hare who might write up the family, he was a clever sort of a fellow and he would do anything for a good supper and a little money, he is rather grand in his way but I dare say he would do it.' The hare accepted the invitation and arrived with his valet, a most respectable hedgehog. His first appearance was at supper, and clearly, even for a hare, he was overdressed –

> an immaculate white shirt front with one large stud made out of a jackdaw's eye. He had elegantly greased moustaches which he constantly twirled while speaking and when he spoke he drawled; he looked superior to his surroundings which of course he was. He moved in a higher circle altogether, he hardly ever associated with rabbits below him in social standing. Every token of honour was shown to him, the best things were put on the table, old things belonging to the original rabbits.

She suggests bits of dog bone stamped with the family crest, namely four sharp teeth-marks (it smelt rather, but that only added to its value) and an old coconut shell stolen from the tits. Anyway, Mr. Hare much admired these dainties and the evening passed successfully. Next morning, 'a burrow was prepared and all the young rabbits assisted to carry the family manuscripts.' They piled them higher and higher and then the hare was shut in with much ceremony. Ah, Mrs. Rabbit gave a sob as she turned the key upon him and scratched her ear with her paw. At last it had come! her family was to be immortalised. 'There sat Mr. Hare, the august Mr. Hare, writing. He looked half asleep and there was a suspicious nest in the heaps of letters.' In fact Mr. Hare was a relentless researcher and his hostess found it more and more difficult to place before Mr. Hare only the things that were to be recorded, for he was not to know if the family had failed for one moment in this pious respectable life. There was one picture drawn on a large dock-leaf which caused a great deal of excitement as Mr. Hare was not to see it, it was too frivolous by far, though only a drawing of Mr. Rabbit kissing Mrs. Rabbit under a fern, but Mr. Hare must not even know that the family did kiss, fancy having that recorded, it would never do! However as the young rabbits passed it round among themselves the hare grew curious, he would stand on his hind legs and look over their shoulders and the rabbit who was holding it would promptly sit on it.

After he had gone 'they each returned to their nooks to write about the event in their diaries.' 'The book,' you say: 'Well, it has not yet been published, and when it is we shall see what we shall see!'

The Gurneys of Earlham came out in two volumes the following year, and was an instant success. Augustus Hare picked the excerpts carefully from such journals as he was permitted to see, highlighting the entertaining and cutting down the pious entries, and bridging gaps with his own enthusiastic inventions. Elizabeth Fry was by then as famous a woman as our top film stars and television personalities. Her family circle had already been introduced in her own biographies, but only as examples of virtue triumphing over evil: Augustus Hare showed them through their own dialogue as lively, independent characters. But he was essentially an entertainer and as such was liable to let his own descriptions fall short of accuracy, when compared with the original letters and journals, in favour of keeping the tale going. Nor was he averse to adding a few romantic turns to any theme that attracted him. He rounds Rachel's romance off with a death-bed scene not at all in keeping with her entry into the hereafter as reported in detail by those present. By none of these is there mention of the letter to which Augustus Hare gives such dramatic importance. But perhaps there was a reason for this letter being removed from the memories of those present on this holy occasion, which occurred in the year following Rebecca

Gurney's marriage to John Read at St. George's, Hanover Square. Augustus Hare writes:

> On the last day of Rachel's life a letter arrived from her long lost lover Henry Enfield. He touchingly bade her farewell and assured her that he had never – in all the 28 years they had been parted – passed a single day without thinking of her. Her sisters hesitated whether they should tell her of this letter, but at length they decided to do so. It was read to her. She listened with glistening eyes and intensive thankfulness. She desired that the letter might be given to her to hold in her hand as long as she lived and she died holding it.

Augustus Hare dismisses Rachel with this apparently early death. In fact, she lived to be forty-nine, with more than half her life to live after separation from Henry. Much of this life was involved with that of the much better-known Betsy, to whom their youngest brother Dan writes, 'Rachel was united by almost as strong a tie as could exist.'

Returning to their girlhood, when Rachel was twenty-one and Betsy not quite twenty, this tie was already strong.

Chapter Fifteen

Rachel
1800–1827

In April 1800 Betsy wrote from the 'opposite family' at Clapham to her 'dearest cousin', Joe Bevan, 'whom I love as my kind friend', telling him that some time ago 'young Fry' paid them a visit at Earlham and made her an offer of marriage. Since her stay near London he had renewed his addresses. 'I have had many doubts, many rises and fallings about the affair. My most anxious wish is that I may not hinder my spiritual welfare, which I have so much feared, to make me often doubt if marriage were a desirable thing for me at this time, or even the thoughts of it.' She ends, excusing her hasty scrawl, 'believe me, my dear cousin, thy very affectionate, E. Gurney'.

Betsy's journal shows that Joe Fry called almost every day at Clapham and, when she went on to the Sam Hoares at Hampstead, his continued calling 'produced various changes of emotion'. A sudden decision to marry him for Rachel's sake could surely not have arisen. Or could it? At first she 'longed to have the matter ended'; then 'he had bed and breakfasted with us and I really enjoyed his company very much. I had thought I should not be surprised if I was to be his before long.' And next day, 'after we had been together some hours I seemed to feel I could in a manner accept him.'

According to Augustus Hare, once Betsy had written to Joe Fry on these lines, he had turned up at once at Earlham, and the whole family weighed in as to whether or not Betsy should marry him. Catherine 'ached for her sister', but thought the marriage would 'wean her from the exaggerations' into which

271

she perceived her to be drifting. And 'the gentle Rachel wept constantly because she thought, against her natural inclinations, the proposal should be accepted. Richenda, Louisa and Priscilla expended reams of closely-covered paper in written prayers that Betsy might be helped through her difficulties and be guided to do what was best for her eternal welfare (though they had great doubts whether this was the best).' Hannah tells in her journal how 'she cried all night because she thought that the marriage must be.' None of them found Joe particularly attractive; his appearance was greatly against him and his manners were 'most uncaptivating'.

If Betsy had already told Rachel that she intended to marry Joe as the only way to find a home for her sister in a predicament, Rachel may well have 'wept constantly' because she thought, against her natural inclinations, that the proposal should be accepted, even if there were a secret to hide. Even if nobody but Betsy and Rachel knew it, there would anyway have been much family emotion about the offer.

The story, passed down by the sisters, of Joe Fry forcing a decision with his gold watch is confirmed in Betsy's journal next day; in this she writes that she was 'much fluttered by Joe's determination', and that she put off the hour of the decision, 'but Joseph showed me his watch last night with the understanding that if I gave it back in the garden by nine o'clock this morning, he never more would renew the affair. If I kept it after that hour he would receive it back.'

Augustus Hare confuses the tale by concealing the six sisters six laurel bushes and causing Joe Fry to lay a specially-bought watch on the white seat in the garden.

Later tall graceful Betsy, her flaxen hair hidden under a Quaker cap, shyly emerged upon the gravel path. She reached the seat and there in the sunshine lay the glittering watch but she could not take it and she fled swiftly back into the house, [Urged back by her father, she makes another dab at it] 'faltering as she walked, but slowly trembling, she took up the watch and the decision was made. She never again regretted her action.

Meanwhile, she wrote several increasingly warm letters to Joe, mostly discussing the practicalities of their marriage. Three weeks before the appointed day she writes, 'Thy letter led me to think more of the plan for our being alone the first few days of our marriage and the more I think of it the better I like it.' She thinks it would be pleasant to accept her Uncle Richard's invitation to spend their honeymoon at Hempstead Mill, adjoining their cousin Bartlett's Little Barningham shoot, 'for we are within three miles of the sea and sweet country surrounding us, quite retired and, as well, we should live free of expense'.

Joe Fry replies a week later from the Frys' business house in St. Mildred's Court, London, that he would meet Rachel and Joseph John when they arrived by coach next day. Rachel, he says, had already written of her determination to go to the Bob Barclays' 'instead of staying with us, but that I do not wonder at considering old acquaintance and similarity about ideas and things which the plainer part of our family differ from her in. She is, however, coming to dine on sixth day.'

So Rachel was visiting relations and making no attempt to conceal her person only just before Betsy's wedding.

Betsy was married to Joe Fry at 'Goats' in Norwich on 19th August, 1800. She and Joe spent less than a fortnight in Hempstead Mill, which still stands serenely at the end of the two quiet ponds in which the Gurneys still love to fish. Rachel went with them, on what she playfully called a 'treaclemoon'. It was not unusual for a sister to accompany a bride on her honeymoon.

On 31st August Betsy writes of arriving at Plashet House, Essex, the Frys' country house. A month later she writes, 'After breakfast, my husband and I set off from Plashet in my father's coach with Nurse Barnes for Mildreds Court. I felt rather low at the prospect before me, and more so when I saw the state of the house: confusion at every part. I had a bedroom turned into a sitting-room, put in order and then went to put myself in order for dinner.'

St. Mildred's Court was the Fry version of 108 Cheapside, which was within sight of it. Like Bob Barclay, a generation before, Joe Fry, as a junior partner, was expected to live in the house of business. Betsy's fourteen-year-old brother, Sam, was so inattentive at school that his father removed him and he, too, settled into St. Mildred's Court, as an apprentice in the book-keeping department of the Frys' tea-importing firm. The first recorded guests to stay at St. Mildred's Court were Betsy's eldest and youngest sisters, Catherine and Priscilla, who came within three weeks of her move in. Amelia Opey paid her first visit three weeks later. A travelling Friend from Philadelphia came on 7th November for six weeks. There was also often Joe's brother, William Fry, and sister Eliza, not to mention the in-laws. Betsy writes during these months, 'I do not think since we were married we have had one-fourth of our meals alone.'

Could Rachel have stayed on, perhaps with the faithful ex-nurserymaid, Becky, discreetly looking after her, at Hempstead Mill until Betsy had prepared a sitting-room for her with Nurse Barnes at St. Mildred's Court? She has no obviously recorded alibi during this period, but the birth of a baby even in so large a house would have been a difficult secret to keep, and, without keeping it, in so essentially a 'plain' Quaker establishment, Rachel would have suffered inevitable disownment. But there could have been further deception. If Rachel kept out of the way, and she is not mentioned as being at St. Mildred's Court, then the confinement could have been palmed off onto Becky, and the baby, Rebecca, named after her.

A suggestion has been made that Betsy's acceptance of Joe Fry in marriage *at all* was initiated as an act of supreme self-sacrifice in order to protect her dearly-loved Rachel's membership of the Society, in the same almost fanatical way as she had forced herself to endure standing in the dark at Earlham in rarely-used rooms. There is no doubt that Betsy loved and admired her slightly elder sister and, as she herself admits, Rachel was so beautiful, lively, warm-hearted and attractive 'as even to excite in some of us, who were less so, feelings of jealousy'.

Betsy certainly writes in her journals of her early distaste for Joe Fry and his addresses and, with her fairly confused and often obsessive attitude to religion, she might have gone so far as to marry him making this inverted sacrifice in order to provide a haven for her now undoubtedly unhappy, insulted and deprived, if not wholly betrayed, sister. Betsy herself admitted to being desperately homesick till long after her marriage, and constantly refers in her journals to those 'at home' at Earlham. Over a year after her marriage she writes in her journal, 'I accepted my Joseph more from duty than anything else, and how much I love him now!'

If, as Rachel's sisters insist, the last time Rachel and Henry ever met was on her twenty-first birthday, on 21st November, 1799, then if Rebecca Read, as she was to become after her marriage, was Rachel's child, born in Betsy's home, it would not have been in her London home but at Hempstead Mill, during her sister's honeymoon. Could Rachel have concealed her condition under the folds of a Quaker gown before and during the wedding?

Almost exactly a year later, Rachel was present at Mildred's Court during Betsy's 'fearful confinement' with her first child, Katharine, to be known as Kate. Betsy had loved gossiping with Mrs. Scarnell after the one-time Judd's lyings-in and Betsy believed she knew it all. She was in for a rude awakening.

Hannah, not yet seventeen, listened outside the door and must, her innocent young sisters suggested, have heard only 'the sweet cries of the child. Thee (Rachel) must feel so satisfied in having been with Betsy through it all.'

Betsy was to bear eleven children, one of whom died young. Her daughters were named almost in the same order as her sisters. Rachel attended every one of Betsy's confinements. If she had had a child herself, it was an extremely well-kept secret and Rachel can have seen nothing more of her since her birth. Nearly all the Gurneys of Earlham kept outspoken private diaries, and there is no indication that Rebecca Read, as she was to become, was of any interest to any of them.

Seventeen closely-written volumes of Rachel's journals chiefly religious, remain, written between 1802 and 1827. 'Those written before 1802 were either sent to Henry Enfield or filled with too many melancholy thoughts of him to preserve,' writes Hannah. From 1802 onwards, Rachel's joy in her brothers and sisters is touchingly expressed in her voluminous journals. Although her youngest brother, Daniel, suggests that her mind was turned by her tragedy, Rachel's approach to religion, as seen in her journals, seems exceedingly sane. She desperately seeks an understanding of the truth with an apparently alert and enquiring mind. At the time her journals were written and long afterwards, they were a comfort to many pious readers. The Rev. Charles Simeon, oft-heard Anglican divine of the time, writes of them as 'nearly transporting me to heaven and making me almost thankful for the lumbago that has confined me to the house and enabled me to read them'.

From time to time references to Henry Enfield occur in them, but there is far more about the present and the future, particularly of her family and their spiritual welfare. Such brief references as she makes to the past suggest that it was not only in Norfolk but also during visits to the dear Bob Barclay's family in south London that they enjoyed some of their memorable moments. Was Betsy's careful explanation to Joe Fry, just before the wedding, of Rachel's determination to stay with the Bob Barclays' instead of at Mildred's Court with her, in any way associated with Henry?

In 1803 Rachel writes of talking over, with Catherine and Mary Anne Galton 'Camberwell, Greenwich and our parting scene under the old wall. The remembrance of such scene still sinks into my very soul; indeed it seems but a little while since they had complete possession of it; now I hope to seek the perseverance and more unfailing source of joy and peace. How imcompatible *flighty romance* is with good sense!' and, in the same entry, 'heard of poor Bartlett's illness and death. Prayed for help, and comfort though some clouds still hang over me. Have been shocked by his death and have hardly been able to look upon it in the right light. Oh that I may die the death of the righteous than that my end may be like his'. '(How beautifully was this prayer answered!)' her sister Richenda pencils in years later.

Soon after Bartlett's death, their father took over his partnership in the Norwich bank and their uncle Richard, of Keswick, bought Bartlett's estates at Northrepps and North Barningham. Rachel, at Earlham nursing Betsy in her second lying-in, and writes, 'Talked to Betsy of Henry Enfield which took up all my thoughts and I felt grieved to find that I hardly so much as lifted up the eye of my mind to God before I fell asleep.' And she ends with an endeavour 'to be cheerfully resigned in that affair'. But later in the evening when they all sat on the study green, [the small, sheltered lawn outside the study], 'making verses', she thought of the 20th August 'this day seven years. Surely I shall never forget the misery of it?' In the evening she was walking and talking with Kitty of dear Joseph John going to Oxford to study with a tutor, and the fear of his being led astray. 'It is a great trial to us both.' A greater trial still was their elder brother, John, who had been studying at Cambridge, joining the volunteers and so being disowned by the Society of Friends. There was still a chance of re-entry, but only if John would abandon the army, which he refused to do with his country on the brink of war and his home, father, sisters, and little brothers threatened by invasion from Napoleon.

Rachel writes to Betsy that 'the volunteering business continues to be a *corroding* care on my father's mind. Kitty and I think he will make one more grand effort to disengage John from this occupation, for by joining he will be no longer accepted by the Friends.' It was typical of their father that, although he failed in his grand effort, he continued to give John a monthly allowance.

It was on 28 December, 1804, hidden among her queries and biblical quotations, Rachel confided in her journal that she had been discussing the subject with Anna Buxton and Pitchford that she always felt to be more affecting than any other that does not relate to their religious concern.

> Alas it is known only to the searcher of hearts what mine has passed through in its separation from its once most beautiful object; but this separation is at last effected and though the bent of my affectionate tastes remain the same, so that no other earthly object has excited them at all in the way that they were once excited, they are now, I hope sanctified by a degree of faith in our Heavenly Father that perhaps I might never have known had I not travelled to it by the thorny road that I have now trodden.

277

Had she been a Roman Catholic she might have entered a convent. Brought up as a Quaker, the responsibility was directly between herself and God. She lived her life entirely in the heart of the family and absolutely gave up any idea of making a new relationship with a possible husband, despite other offers besides Pitchford's. She had been spiritually as good as married to Henry for two or three impressionable years. She loved him. He loved her. They shared their innermost thoughts, their journals and letters and, like many an actual widow, she was unable to detach her loyalty and love for him for several years after they parted. She writes of 'mental palsy which benumbs my right disposition' and of how she was 'thrown off my centre'; but one thing is clear. She never blamed her father for bringing about disappointment.

During a huge family holiday at Cromer, when brothers and sisters, cousins and uncles and aunts were all staying in different houses and lodgings, Rachel mentions the 'heartfelt favourites in the whole party', Fowell Buxton and his sister, whose long-widowed mother had been threatened with expulsion from the Friends 'by marrying a person not of their Society'. The Buxtons were staying with their aunt, Mrs. Richard Gurney, at North-repps. Rachel writes, 'They are so like brothers and sisters that I have sometimes been tempted to wish we were more nearly connected, but must own the folly of castle building.' When he was only twelve years old, Fowell told his mother he never would marry anyone but Hannah Gurney. This was when Sam Hoare junior was giving Louisa her first kiss. Sam was now paying too much attention to the enchanting young Elizabeth of Keswick and Northrepps. Richenda writes to Betsy, who was not at Cromer, 'Rachel is on the whole in good spirits. I have not seen her so since her unhappy affair. She has felt Sam's neglect of Louisa more than any of us, having been through the same herself.'

Rachel was taking no chances of allowing the beloved-by-all Fowell to slip through Hannah's fingers. She and Catherine shut them up together in a room for an hour and a half until they emerged, engaged. Sam Hoare and Louisa received like treatment in a one-horse whisky on a family tour in Scotland, with the same result. At Inverness, John of Earlham recognised the writing of his boyhood friend, Sam Hoare senior, on a letter approving the match. He was sure his son was 'so ardent a lover that it will be difficult to restrain his impatience'. It put him in mind of their own youthful days 'but I hope Louisa will take compassion upon him soon after your return', and can be persuaded to commit young Sam to ask for his certificate at the first meeting possible.

Now that Louisa was being asked to name the date, she was not likely to put any obstacles in the way. In a month's time she would be twenty-two.

'On the Scotch tour John and Elizabeth tasted almost perfect enjoyment together,' writes Rachel, always loving and never resenting lovers, despite her own past sorrow.

Richenda writes how she was struck with the cheering and happy effect of this journey on dear Rachel:

> Our affections are so deeply interested for Fowell and Hannah, John and Elizabeth and Sam and Louisa that appears to supply to her own warm and affectionate feelings an object which to some degrees fills the painful void that her own bitter disappointment has occasioned. What an inexpressible blessing it was that the deep affections of her heart were, we may joyfully believe, set upon things above and from this source alone did she obtain true peace and rest of mind!

For the marriage of Sam Hoare junior, and Louisa, all the eleven, their father and their one brother-in-law, Joe Fry, and his four children assembled at Earlham, and on Christmas Eve they drove the seven miles to Tasburgh Meeting House for the wedding. It was testimony upon testimony and blessing upon blessing. The marriage certificate measures sixty by sixty centimetres, with sixty-eight signed witnesses, including John Pitchford, John Crome and John Crome junior, and all the surviving uncles and aunts and first cousins. 'Rachel Gurney – Elizabeth Fry' are in one line, but there is not an Enfield among them.

The bridegroom's sister writes that no event gave her father more pleasure than the marriage of his son to the daughter of his old friend. 'He was pleased with her being, like my mother, a

Norfolk woman, and he talked of procuring for them Heatt House at Hampstead (London) to be near him.' She describes the large dining-room at Earlham, which was dressed like a church, with Christmas holly for the entertainment of the guests, who feasted on swans.

The bride's debonair brother, John junior was in high spirits. His sisters' prayers that he too might find a pearl of great price had been answered and, only twelve days later, he was married in Northrepps church to the same lovely Elizabeth of Keswick with whom Sam Hoare had been philandering on Cromer sands four years before. This time the two fathers, Richard and John Gurney could not entirely show their pleasure, owing to the couple being first cousins. To make his point, Elizabeth's father, Richard, walked ostentatiously through the village away from the church so as to avoid all chance of being said to witness or even to countenance the marriage.

Five months later, after a necessarily long engagement while Fowell took and passed his examinations, he and Hannah rose early on a mild May morning on their wedding day.

> We led our sweet bride to the stairs, [writes Rachel] where our men joined us, and we had all a pleasant drive to Tasborough. Our dear couple spoke with much feeling, and Fowell with his usual dignity. Preparing for dinner took up the rest of the morning and nothing could be prettier than the train of bridesmaids dressed alike in white, with small nosegays, except the bride, who looked lovely, who was still more white, and was distinguished by one beautiful rose. [Rachel adds finally,] Our dearest Fowell was most affectionate and sweet to us all; I think there was scarcely ever such a brother admitted to a family.

In due course Rachel's 'three dear pairs', as she called them, were all inviting her to attend first confinements. Louisa's son was born first, at Hampstead, and then Hannah's daughter at Earlham. Elizabeth was expecting her baby in the summer.

Rachel's journal continues in its partly descriptive, partly reflective manner and then, perhaps because she was so busy nursing her sisters and their babies or because she could not bear to write, it ceased between March and the end of Decmber 1808 except for one entry. 'Dear Elizabeth's death took place at 12 o'clock on Thursday night May 12, 1808. I was kneeling by her side at the awful close.'

The 'awful close' is described by the Rev. Edward Edwards of Lynn, where John and Elizabeth lived. While he was having supper with friends after a clerical meeting, 'Mrs. Catherine Gurney' called to ask him to visit her brother, 'who was under great affliction with himself, very ill and his wife not likely to outlive the night. The calmness that the message, so distressing to herself, was delivered was remarkable, and only one example on this occasion of the equanamity of the Quakers' trying circumstance, instilled in their earliest education and cultivated throughout their lives.' Mr. Edwards had been ill for several days with bronchitis, but could not refuse to go. He felt his insufficiency. He was taken up by some back stairs and entered Mr. John Gurney's apartment. 'He seemed almost distracted with grief, crying like a child, a few of his sisters weeping around him, but though drowned in tears, not a cry, nor scarcely a sigh was heard. All was silent.' Mr. Edwards hardly knew how to interrupt the secret silence of their grief, and he tried to administer consolation with the truth of Christianity. With difficulty he gathered from John's broken answers that they had had his confidence. Miss Gurney, sitting next to him, whispered the desire that he should go and look at Mrs. Gurney, who was in one of the parlours on the ground floor. 'The room was nearly dark. I was directed by the sound of her breathing and a feeble cry of pain to the sofa on which she was lying.' He thought her unconscious and so speech useless. He tried fervently to pray. He returned to Mr. Gurney who anxiously asked after her, and when no reasonable hope could be given, his sorrow broke out again.

Later Mr. Edwards learnt that during the night Miss Rachel Gurney, with much composure, had gone to John with the news that his wife had died soon after midnight, but when she came into the room her brother said. 'You need not speak. I know your errand.' They sat some time in silence and then, when he became very agitated, he was prevailed on to go to bed, where he immediately fell asleep.

Later in the summer Mr. Edwards spent a week at Earlham. When John wept, he said, 'My dear Sir, God who has inflicted this wound can alone heal it.' This was when the first seeds were sown in Rachel of the idea of joining the Church of England, to which she became increasingly drawn. The Rev. Mr. Edwards was to come frequently to Earlham and, with his friend the Rev. Charles Simeon, to become an intimate friend of all the Gurneys. He even wrote a letter of proposal to Catherine which, as she was busy with others things when it arrived, she stuffed into her pocket and forgot to read. The next time he called, she remembered it, and was about to read it when he snatched it from her, thankful for the divine intervention, since he had already felt her conversion to the Anglican Church, or his to Quakerism, would be beyond either of them at that time.

The next proposal in the family was made by young Samuel Gurney to Elizabeth Sheppard, of Ham House, Upton, one-time home of Dr. Fothergill, which Samuel Gurney later acquired. Elizabeth's mother was one of Bartlett Gurney's six sisters.

Samuel Gurney had left the Frys' counting-house to join a business so humble that the rest of the family would not allow the name of Gurney to appear in its title. However, it was not long before Samuel was showing a skill with figures, unbelievable by his past school masters, which raised the firm, re-named Overend, Gurney & Co., to the position of the foremost bill-brokers in Europe. As a committed Friend he became known as 'the Quakers' Rothschild', combining his great generosity with his huge success in business. He was a devoted family man and his interest in farm animals never flagged. One day in the City of London, when he met with bullocks being mismanaged, his well-known voice like a trumpet was heard shouting, 'That's not the way to turn a bullock', and he took off his hat and gently turned the creature's head in the right direction.

In October 1809, not long before his sixtieth birthday, John of Earlham submitted to an operation which was 'too much for his nervous system'. He lived for eighteen days, during which his

282

mind was 'distressingly mazed', Rachel writes. 'On the last day of his life he fell asleep, and awoke saying that he had been to heaven in a beautiful dream, and that he had seen all his children there with him.' Despite Joseph John having scarlet fever, Betsy and Richenda hurried from London, hearing at the different stages on the road that their father was still living, as he was when they arrived at about midnight. The next morning he died. The whole family collected at Earlham for the funeral and many friends and relations travelled from London by post-chaise, Amelia Opey taking laudanum to get her through the trying journey.

It was at her father's funeral that Betsy preached for the first time. Amelia describes how the sound of her voice was 'so sweet, and so moving as never heard I before. It was not *speaking* prayer but *chaunting* it and sort of recitative music, decided *music*, and to those tones she married words of strong and luminous meaning and sentiments glowing with Christian and universal bene-volence. I could have listened to her for hours.'

John junior was now master of Earlham, but a sorry master indeed, limping on a stick, owing, he said, to straining his back when carrying the dying Elizabeth. Gradually it seemed rather his mind that was strained, for he became more childishly de-pendent on his sisters. Catherine was still mistress of the house, Joseph and the youngest sister Priscilla were steadily becoming plainer in dress, speech and heart, while Catherine, Rachel and Richenda were turning, with John, towards the Established Church.

Their cousin Hudson had already left the Society of Friends, to the intense disappointment of his grandfather, David of Youngs-bury. He later married the one-time 'rattish' Mag. Hudson's father, Richard Gurney, died two years after his brother, John of Earlham. Richard's widow lived on at Keswick, with holidays at Northrepps Hall. Later, her 'sparkling' but disabled daughter, Anna, and Sarah Buxton, Fowell's younger sister, lived at Northrepps Cottage and together founded the Belfry School, Overstrand, which primary school still uses their original building.

Dan took over his ailing brother John's job in Lynn, and

Rachel went to look after him in the house in which their sister-in-law, Elizabeth, had died.

In 1812, Joe Fry, through general extravagance and some rash speculation, for which he blamed his brother, was on the brink of bankruptcy. The family helped him out, some with their own small savings, as was expected of Friends. Bankruptcy would have led, as it eventually did in Joe Fry's case, to disownment. It was the Quaker policy to try to prevent this and 'give and lend' until the unfortunate Friend was on his feet again. Betsy's boys were sent to Earlham to be cared for by Catherine, and her two elder girls to Rachel at Lynn.

Betsy, their country house abandoned, their carriage and horses sold and their children dispersed, found herself with enough time on her hands to accompany Anna Buxton, Fowell's elder sister, to Newgate prison with blankets for the prisoners. From then on her interest in the misery of prisoners grew to be the chief object on which she lavished her soothing but compelling voice and healing hands. Whether she was chairing a committee for prison work, nursing the sick, comforting the dying, or being seen and heard by eager witnesses, teaching the women prisoners to read in Newgate prison (just as her father's friends had been taken to see her teaching her Imps at Earlham), she was, and still is, an inspiration to thousands. To her sisters, however, she was much the same as she had been in the schoolroom – moody, unpredictable, complaining about her own health, and now, however calm and dignified she was in public, she seemed totally unable to control her lively and undisciplined children, yet it was Betsy for whom they sent when they were ill.

Dan moved a few miles out of Lynn and enlarged and glorified a modest country home into the full grandeur of North Runcton Hall, which has only lately been demolished because of its unwieldy size and number of towering chimneys. During some of the bouts of reconstruction, Rachel took the children to Earlham where, Kate Fry remembers, 'dinner at 4 or 5 for which everyone dressed. After dinner there was drawing, sewing or reading aloud. In summer there was drawing lessons with Mr. Crome or Aunt Richenda.'

Kate writes of having to end a letter through hearing 'the rattle of the tea tray coming across the hall'. Tea was a substantial meal, the table spread with white and brown bread, varieties of cake and biscuits, with Mrs. Freeman still making the tea. 'In those summer evenings it generally took place in the dining room which was still called by its old name of the great parlour.' She writes of the windows open and the setting sun gleaming across the study green, 'then the noble lawn itself, and how everybody use to walk upon it, or sit in groups under the surrounding trees. Life at Earlham was a very out-of-door life.' Among the summer-houses and arbours was a pair of straw shelters with seats mounted on revolving circular floors so that they could be turned to catch the sun, or, as the children said, so that the occupants might sit face to face or back to back as they were disposed. This idea gave rise to their pet name of 'the sulkies.'

Earlham was becoming more and more oecumenical. Vast bible-meetings were held in the great parlour, and there were now as many parsons as Quakers staying at Earlham. Indeed, before long Richenda, aged thirty-four, married one of the former. The Fry children attended her marriage to the Rev. Francis Cunningham at Earlham church. All kinds of philanthropists and politicians 'dined and slept'. William Wilberforce, without any warning, stayed with his wife, children, servants and horses for a week, and then came back for more. He was intrigued to find how early the pianoforte had been installed in this Quaker household, and liked to think of the young all singing round it. 'Whatever you did, you did, I do not doubt, to please God. But why so much about music in the New Testament, for *any* to banish it? What we need is friendly freedom,' he writes to Rachel.

As more Fry children were born, so they were kept in circulation among their aunts and uncles, and only returned to their parents during the latters' periods of prosperity.

Rachel writes to Betsy of 'the privilege' of also having their increasingly ailing brother, John, thrown upon her, but Rachel was 'sensible to *all* the peculiar blessings and privileges which we

285

enjoy at home'. Privileges for Rachel took many forms, not the least of which was the chance to choose between Quakerism in its various forms and the Anglican Church. Betsy was well aware of Rachel's leanings towards the Church and frequently begged her not to give up her membership of the Friends. She was also emphatic that, while she could hardly bear the agony of being parted from her children, the thought of their spirits being contaminated (presumably by the Church) was totally unacceptable. Catherine and Rachel were careful to keep the children under much stricter Quaker discipline than they themselves had had. Rachel writes, 'but indeed my dearest Betsy, I think this thee cannot understand.' It was true that Mr. Edwards had introduced family prayers to Earlham, but this informal praying and bible-reading over the breakfast table had more the form of a Quaker meeting than a ceremony. Much later on, Betsy inevitably blamed her elder sisters for the fact that her own children left the Society of Friends for the Church.

Among the more obvious 'peculiar blessings and privileges' which the Gurneys of Earlham enjoyed was travel. As Quaker ministers, Betsy, Joseph John and Priscilla travelled widely on the Continent and in Ireland, and Joseph John in America. To a lesser degree, Rachel travelled, too. She went with Dan to Switzerland, to Weymouth with Fowell and Anna, and on to the Isle of Wight. She paid visits to Chrissie and Prissie in Bath and to the Bob Barclays now in their new home, Bury Hill, near Dorking. In a last hope for his recovery, she stayed with John, at Clifton near Bristol, but to no avail. He returned to Earlham to die in September 1814 in the little ante-room chamber, after insisting that it was the happiest day he had ever spent.

In a letter there is a glimpse of Rachel and Catherine coming up the hill to Hampstead in a post-chaise, whose horse would have to be watered and fed before being returned to the last posting-stage by Sam and Louisa's groom. A note to Rachel encloses 'a little paper of sweet meats to accompany you on your journey'.

Even travelling by stage coach was still comparatively expensive. Back in that mysterious year of 1800 it had cost Rachel's father £4. 16s. 9d to send her to London, but Joseph John only cost £2. 16s, as he could travel by ordinary stage-wagon, and liked to walk part of the way. In May 1800 a journey to Clare, Suffolk, for Rachel and Richenda, and to London and back for the four other girls, cost him £12. 5s. od. The family trait of paper-saving reveals these secrets. Rachel made a Sunday book for the Earlham grandchildren by sticking prints into an account book of her father's that had begun in 1785. The first part of the book of Genesis is illustrated with the text in five languages in rhyme beneath each picture. Peeping out from old Nicodemus are intriguing snippets of life in those wonderful if hazy years – an account paid for a new gate – matching the mood in Rachel's journal when 'we went round by Bramerton, rousing powerfully a train of recollections so remote as to be almost like a picture rather than reality, recalling our dear mother, whose memory I have lately felt peculiarly tender.' When she was quite alone she read her mother's old letters and felt they would never really be separated, and that 'everlasting union exists'.

Betsy writes that Rachel was 'cheerful, hopeful but *very sensitive.* Her sound mind, good understanding and clear judgement were very conspicuous. Her patience and long suffering, united with natural sympathy for others, very marked.' Amongst her minor virtues, order, regularity and punctuality were high. 'She has a peculiar power over children,' Betsy adds wistfully, 'and possesses, in no small degree, the gift of training and educating them.' She admits that she was strict, 'though most kind to them; she particularly cultivated habits of industry, and having whatever was done, well done.' Betsy mentions 'the strong attachment Rachel formed when quite young under very painful circumstances. This produced a wonderful change in her, destroyed her naturally fine spirits, brought her into deep distress, but I believe also led her to seek better consolation.'

Rachel may have lost her looks and earlier outgoing abandon; she may have given up singing and dancing and acting, for, at first a more Quakerly and then a more evangelical approach to life, but she was still remarkably good company. Her visits to the Frys did not only hang upon Betsy's confinements: particularly at the time of the Yearly Meeting, she attended Betsy when all around them were clamouring to catch even a glimpse of her famous sister. At a royal ceremony at the Mansion House, Rachel and two of the 'small fry', as she called them, were summoned up on to the platform where Betsy was presented, without a curtsy, to Queen Charlotte before joining the bench of bishops for a theological discussion. The children were greatly impressed, and even Rachel had to admit that 'dearest Betsy looked very tall, particularly when the Queen, who is so short anyway curtsied to her'. In the old days, the scene would have been re-enacted in a charade, bishops and all.

Kate explained 'my mother has three great gifts – stately presence, exquisite voice and unruffled sweetness of expression.'

Visiting Newgate prison to witness Betsy's performance, author Maria Edgeworth reports Rachel's reply to her own surprise at the ingenuity of the women prisoners' needlework: 'We have to do Ma'am, not with fools but with rogues.' At Hampstead, with Louisa, Rachel re-met some of the poets and authors she had first encountered on journeys with her father: the Wordsworths, the Coleridges, and George Crabbe. With Hannah, it was politicians. Fowell Buxton, Hudson Gurney and later Dick Gurney of Keswick were all Members of Parliament. Sam Hoare, Sam Gurney and Joseph John all backed them in their reforms, though, as Quakers, they could not be M.Ps. themselves as until 1833 an oath was still required.

At the much enlarged North Runcton Hall, Rachel taught history to Katherine Fry, as she had taught Dan before. Both Dan and Katherine had more of a taste for historical delvings than Rachel had ever had. Now, in between her lessons and writing prison reform letters for her mother, who was in London, the industrious Katherine helped Dan edit his mammoth history *The House of Gournay*.

Dan, whose ideas of grandeur had increased with that of his house, was courting Lady Millicent Acheson, and was anxious to prove that his family was as ancient as hers.

Priscilla writes anxiously about this to Betsy while staying at North Runcton. She and Rachel were 'under much discouragement with respect to Dan's object. We were a great deal with our ladies last week and had the most familiar kind of intercourse. Dan had frequent opportunities of being with Lady M – alone and yet it is almost impossible to understand her real feelings and we cannot discover anything like heartfelt interest in her towards him or any of us though much kindness is so.' Rachel was so distressed that she did not feel strong enough to 'encourage Dan to come forward'.

> Priscilla thought 'their views and habits in many different respects *very different* to ours. Lady M – though truly amiable and possessing excellent principles is far more trained to a wordly life. She has also, we have no doubt, been much sought after and is made very much of. Were the thing attainable I have, and so has Rachel, most serious doubts whether it would lead to happiness.

Dan, however, was 'not much cast down' and 'never lessening his dignity'.

Maybe Lady Millicent detected some of the fanciful inaccuracies that caused Hudson Gurney to call the 1096-paged tome 'the Apocryphal Book of Dan'. Anyway, Dan's offer, when he made it, was refused by Lady Millicent, but later accepted by Lady Harriet Jemima Hay, daughter of the 15th Earl of Errol, whose great-great-great-grandmother had visited Dan's and enjoyed Quaker fair at Ury.

One of Dan Gurney's orphaned grandchildren who lived with him, Laura Troubridge, describes North Runcton Hall years later when Dan was eighty-seven:

> It is a very pretty house, large but not too much so. 43 rooms – it was a cottage when grandpapa first came here, about 60 years ago when he built on to it. The garden is *very* pretty, not *very* large but so nice – I like it better than any other I have ever seen. The schoolroom which we have made much the prettiest room in the house is on the same floor as our bedrooms. The boys sleep upstairs, close to the nurseries. That is enough about the house. I will now write about the servants.

And delightfully she does, all eighteen of them, at a time when Dan had lost all his money in the bank crash five years before.

From North Runcton Rachel went to stay with Hannah when some of her babies were born in 'the rooms over the brewery' where the beloved Fowell worked. 'I was up this morning at 4, and do not expect to finish my day's work before 12 tonight,' he writes to his mother in July 1808. The Brewery is very much still there, with the old buildings surrounding the brewers' yard at 91–95 Brick Lane, lately preserved partly by the huge glass roof. The name Trueman Hanbury Buxton & Co. Ltd. Licensed Common Brewers is still above the gate. The cobbles that caused the heavy dray wheels to wake Hannah's guests so early are still there and the charming bow-windowed partners', brewers' and apprentices' domestic quarters remain, now as offices, built over and into the more factory-like brewing premises.

Rachel continued to keep up the warm association, begun in childhood, with the 'opposite family', the Bob Barclays, after they moved in 1805 to the Earl of Verulam's beautiful Bury Hill near Dorking, Surrey. In 1812 Robert Barclay bought it. A genus of water lily which he cultivated in his 'botanical lake' was named 'Barclaya' after him. Bob was Master of the Worshipful Company of Brewers in 1813, but handed the active share of his business over to his son in favour of his anti-slavery and horti-cultural interests. Rachel stayed at Bury Hill, particularly when Maria and Lucy, who both married members of the Cornish Quaker Fox family (no relation to the founder, George Fox) were there. This was not very often, for the journey from Cornwall, before the railway came, was long and tedious par-ticularly when Maria brought her two children, Barclay and Caroline, both of whose lively intelligent journals have been published. Some of Rachel's Gurney and Buxton pupils joined with the Fox children in inter-family essay competitions, in which, Quaker fashion, there were no winners. Epic poems and dramatic scenes, actable and otherwise, are included in the col-lection.

Rachel encouraged all her pupils to memorise facts by writing them in their own rhyming couplets. At Earlham one nine-year-old nephew composed a family history back to 'Willie the Conc' who 'o'er seas did row.' He refers to Henry Gurney of Great Ellingham as a 'peaceful squire', on whom he 'love'd, on the stag to pour his ire'.

Hudson later relented over his criticism of the history and admitted that the heraldry, excellent illustrations and painstaking research were valuable leads to original sources. It was merely Kate's and Dan's interpretations of their finds that sometimes seemed suspect. 150 copies were eventually printed, and, half a century later, Dan writes to Kate, after her mother had become nationally famous, 'My dearest Kate, I often sincerely regret that I did not entitle our book by Daniel Gurney and Katharine Fry, it would have been only just and would have added to its popularity. I am afraid however it is too late to alter. What say you?' Dan, who himself lived to be ninety, said he often picked up clues to lead him to churchyards and records and pedigrees through talking to old people about their memories of even older ones. In this way, a century and a half or more of otherwise dark ages could be covered.

When he was twenty-eight, Joseph John, after feeling low and depressed all the winter, sought out the daughter of one of Bartlett's six sisters, whom he described as 'one of those hardier souls on which weakness is prone to lean but her feelings were nevertheless warm and acute'. Jane Birkbeck married the optimistic Joseph John Gurney of Earlham (whose mother had called him her Morning Star), at the Friends' Meeting House at Wells-next-the-sea in September 1817. For his honeymoon, Joseph John chose to take his brother Samuel, his sisters, Hannah and Richenda and their husbands, as well as the bride, into a dense autumnal fog in which they drifted about for two days and nights before reaching Calais in order to examine systems of prison discipline adopted in Antwerp and Ghent. This venture lasted a month, and he cannot have been the only one to feel 'what a blessing is there in such an arrival at home.' Here the young but forceful Jane was to take over Earlham from Catherine who, while still under forty, was to retire.

Joseph John writes in his journal 'my wife and I spend our evenings alone together. I do not think our dear sisters will be the least interruption to us.'

Hardly surprisingly, Priscilla went on a long ministering journey in Ireland, from the effects of which she never recovered. Rachel, while staying with Louisa and Sam at Hampstead, took the final decision to leave the Society of Friends and was baptised in Harrow church. Hannah and Fowell, now living nearby in Hampstead, had just endured the almost unbearable tragedy of four of their particularly endearing children dying within the space of five weeks, aged ten, four, three and eighteen months. Hannah and Fowell were, by Rachel's standards, the most loving, playful and Godly parents imaginable, and that they should receive this blow was as heartrending as the deaths themselves. They moved away to Cromer with their three remaining children and here, at Cromer Hall (which has since been rebuilt) they courageously received the fading Priscilla, with Rachel to nurse her with the gentle yet practical text Priscilla loved to hear; 'Peace, be still.' 'At the last Betsy came,' Rachel writes, 'wonderfully strengthened in faith and empowered by the spirit and addressed the dying one in a strain of confidence and assured encouragement.'

Meanwhile at Earlham, Catherine's early retirement was anything but lasting. Jane's first still-born daughter was followed a year later by the arrival of Jacky, and in the following year, by Anna. Except when she was needed, Catherine kept quietly in the background, dealing with her 'poor' and the family's 'ragged school'. She had a special garment made that was neither worldly nor a Quaker habit, but which had something about it easily recognisable, at any rate for the next century, on lady workers for worthy causes.

Jane's diary for 1821 mentions that 'the Cromer hall party are, I expect, today all breaking up', and, a week later, 'the Cromer party could not get off last week and so are now on the icy seas. The weather is not so favourable and will, I fear, cause both tension and sickness. We *wish* all had not gone together.' The Fowell Buxtons, the Sam Hoares and a sprinkling of Gurneys were all going to London by boat on this occasion, owing to one of the Buxton daughters being 'on an unwieldy stretcher with a dislocated hip'.

'No measles yet!' writes Jane. 'The week has been a mixture of calm and enjoyment but my dearest being overburdened by his many cares.' Perhaps measles did break out, for here her diary peters out. The rest of the little book of hand-cut pages is empty. Her husband writes, however, 'It is probable that the north wind, which blew upon us, was made the cause of her illness. She asked me to take her a drive in the pony chair. The evening was bright and pleasant and our minds were calm and united.'

When Rachel and Richenda went into Jane's room, a few days later, they found her asleep. She woke and said, 'I look upon this as an awful and sudden call out of the world and from all things that are in it.' She added, 'Give my regards to the servants and tell them how much I have desired that they might be brought under the influence of vital religion,' upon which she died.

Catherine and Rachel returned to their posts, with their brother's little children 'increasingly the object of their tenderest solicitude'.

The Fry children returned to the Earlham schoolroom and, when Joseph John's Jacky and Anna were still very small, they joined them. Rachel taught Jacky an equal delight in natural history and its Creator by encouraging him to underline the names of the birds and beasts in the Bible.

When Kate Fry's sister left the Society of Friends and was married in a church, Betsy could not, of course, be present. This time the guests feasted on peacocks. A year later, on 1st November, 1822, Betsy gave birth to her eleventh child, who, like Betsy's mother's youngest child, was named Daniel. In the afternoon of the same day, her first grandchild was born in Blackheath.

In 1825 Joe Fry was again near to bankruptcy, 'and further reductions in expenses was thought desirable'. Now it was the riding horses that were parted with.

Rachel stayed with the Frys that summer at Dagenham and Kate writes:

the solitude of the two small cottages with their imperfect ac-
commodation, which more resembled a primitive Highland inn, but
little inconveniences were to our large party a joke. There was
fishing, boating, driving and riding inland by day and when night
closed in over the wild marsh scenery the cries of water birds, the
rustlings of the great beds of reeds, the strange sounds from the
shipping on the river, gave the place an indescribable charm.

It was here that the hapless Joe Fry, always so accident-prone,
tried to destroy a hornets' nest with gunpowder and almost blew
his hand off. What turned out to be more worrying was Rachel's
cough and her 'anxiety to keep out of invalid habits'. 'The
doctors,' Kate writes, 'thought it very serious and very threatening.' At Earlham, Rachel was too engrossed in the development
of the children to pay much attention to her cough. She often felt
tired, but reminded herself that very young children can be
tiring, particularly bright, enquiring ones.

The failing health of Dr. Alderson, who had been present at
nearly all the family's births, now claimed the attention of them
all. Hudson, by today's standards a multi-millionaire, took Dr.
Alderson to stay at his house in St. James's Square where the now
anything but rattish Mag dispensed charitable benefactions while
dressed in the height of fashion. To her sorrow, she had no
children. In Dr. Alderson's last weeks in Norwich, Hudson went
every day to sit with him and cheer him up. Amelia nursed him
and begged Joseph John to reform the self-confessed old atheist
'in time'. After frequent sermons from Joseph John, Dr.
Alderson said with a sigh, 'I do assure you I have not one sceptical
feeling left.' After his death, Amelia herself became a Quaker,
but somewhat after her own fashion, with silken gown and
elaborate printed writing paper, illustrated with silhouettes
rather than the engravings she had used before. She claimed that
religion was never presented to her in any serious form 'until she
saw it in the *drab*'.

Hudson records all this in his 'secret' journal, which can easily
be decoded with the help of the Greek alphabet, which he uses to
disguise ordinary English words. In fact there is little to conceal

more dashing than the first entry in one journal: 'Confound that fellow! I wanted a pocket book and he has made me a volume as if I were on an expedition to explore the uppermost parts of the earth instead of a six weeks trip to Paris.' And even his dissertation on seasickness and Paris itself is entirely innocent.

In the year 1826, there is no indication in Hudson's or any other available journal or letters that any of the family, including Rachel, was aware of the marriage at St. George's church, Hanover Square, on the 27th February between John Read and Rebecca Gurney. Not even Betsy, who was alive to all London's social events, makes any possible enigmatical comment in her surviving letters and journals. Surely if the bride were Rachel's daughter, some sign or hint could be detected?

There was one forthcoming marriage which did interest the family deeply that spring, because of the effect it would have upon Earlham. Joseph John visited Elm Grove, near Melksham, in Wiltshire, to become engaged to Mary Fowler, a cousin of his late wife. However, 'feeble health' and fear of handling Joseph John's children caused the event to be postponed for a year. Meanwhile, Louisa writes from Earlham in September 1826:

> We are very happy in this dear place which seems to me as lovely and engaging and interesting in its age as in its youth. Uncle Joseph John, Aunt Catherine and Aunt Rachel, [she tells her son] are specimens of what single life and the love of brothers and sisters may be. Aunt Rachel is on the whole in a favourable state, though her cough continues. The dear little ones are in full enjoyment of the garden, the apples, the acorns, the company of each other – all are delightful. Now they are all at play in the great parlour, where I am writing this for the sake of the fire.

The following summer, Joseph John returned to Melksham to marry Mary Fowler. The same day, 18th July, 1827, he writes to Rachel and Betsy, neither of whom was well enough to attend. With the usual eye to paper-saving, the sisters shared both sides of a page to greet the honeymoon couple at Ilfracombe in Devonshire. Rachel and Betsy were staying at 10 Marine Parade, Brighton. Rachel begins:

My beloved brother and sister,

Dear Joseph's letter, kindly written on your wedding day, has been highly welcome to dear Betsy and myself this morning; it breathes a very comfortable and happy spirit and brings a good report of your pleasant party – I trust that you will by this time be settled in your retreat which I imagine to be rather a profound one.

In these very interesting and important junctures in life, a pause from our common concerns is a good thing for us and we do affectionately desire for you that the present one may be blessed to you in every way and prove a comfortable preparation to our dear Mary to enter upon her new career with peace and confidence. I have myself been under a considerable cloud from a severe bilious attack, in which dearest Betsy found me, when she arrived on Wednesday evening (Louisa had left me only in the morning) so that for my sake it seemed a providential thing that she could come here, and I am thankful indeed to tell you that it seems to have the best affect on her own ailments. If not, they were kept at bay! I am now coming round to my old state and we intend being at Plashet (if so it may be) by the end of next week in the hope of my reaching home punctually as fixed. During this little trial I have hardly known how to bear to dwell on anything interesting, or you would have had a better share of my thoughts, being most nearly and tenderly interested in your happiness. Betsy will add. Farewell dearest Joseph and Mary, your truly affectionate R.G.

Betsy then takes over with some confusion of syntax.

My beloved Joseph and Mary, I hope in future to be less anxious and more full of trust when events turn out differently to what we wish or expected this fresh proof of our reason for doing so, I hope, may produce a lesson *not only to myself*. I got low on my journey here and fanciful about not being with you but as soon as I arrived I could not but be truly thankful that even though suffering my feet had been turned this way and that I was enabled to help one who I *owed so much to* and was so inexpressibly beloved by me. I have thought much of thee dear Mary I feel for thee in thy new allotment and thy leaving home. I found it meant so much to me but I fully believe thou will much enjoy this time of repose it will prepare thee for what is yet before thee. I long for a further account of thee and hope that some lady writer will give us an exact history of the proceedings of the day. I am your loving and affectionately interested sister Eliz. Fry.

Rachel adds a P.S. Dear Betsy very much coming round to her usual state. Pray write us a full account of yourself.

It was only now that the sorrowful conviction was driven home to Betsy that, whereas she herself was suffering temporary indisposition, Rachel's case was becoming truly alarming. She was coughing blood, the only certain sign of incurable consumption. Memories of their childhood together, when 'one cabinet, one little set of tea things, one small little closet,' had been shared between them, welled up. Their love had flowed on, deepening and strengthening with life and its vicissitudes. The depth and fidelity of Rachel's attachment to her sister had in truth been wonderful. Self-sacrificing, considerate and protecting – most sensitively alive to Betsy's interests, her cares and her joys. But there were distresses approaching, from which this devoted friend and sister could not shield Betsy. Throwing off her own malaise, she set to nursing Rachel with her own confident but soothing hands.

In a few days the sisters were able to set off to Plashet, to which the Frys had now returned. Kate Fry writes that 'our Aunt Rachel paid us a visit, and we found her greatly changed, her hair perfectly white, and her figure greatly emaciated. It was obvious that she was returning to Earlham but to die.'

Very peaceful was Rachel's return to the home of her childhood. 'The quiet travelling has been only a luxury,' she writes. 'Both morning and evening have been delightful to me, as to weather and scenery. I have felt soothed and comforted.' She was deeply sensible of the blessing of Betsy 'putting her in the right way of taking, bearing and feeling my present allotment.' She lodged in the ante-room chamber and was wheeled into the dressing-room on to a couch. The view of the Keswick woods from her window was a constant pleasure.

Thou wouldest be pleased with the beauty of my luxurious apartment; the window, to the south being opened, is a beautiful improvement; In short it is something of a paradise here below, that Joseph John brings his bride to take possession of. How differently we are led, and allotted, in this world. Some seem to be taught by trial and bereavement, and others by having all things richly to enjoy. [And then again she writes to Betsy] It is almost beyond my power to describe to you the relief to my feelings, in being put into these two rooms of profound quiet, and wheeled from one to another without an effort; looking from my bed, where I am only for some hours of the day, on the peaceful lawn, and green trees, surely, He maketh me to lie down in green pastures. He leadeth me beside the still waters.'

She writes to Betsy of the homecoming of the bridal couple; though she was ill the day before and could only just bear the preparations,

but we were all in high order. Catherine alone went down to the door to meet them. The children behaved beautifully and there was much sweetness in her manner towards them. She has great gentleness and humility and is evidently pleased with everything here; so all is cheering before us and it was delightful to see Joseph John again so happy. After tea the children and Aunt Catherine went with papa and mama round the garden . . . though I have been a most passive observer the new state of things here has cheered my saddest hours. The real sweetness of mind and principle that evidently prevails in our new sister's character shed a happy influence over us. We seem to have everything to hope in her so she will have much to learn from her experience of this new world.

Louisa writes to her son, 'Your new aunt is more and more liked and seems to fall in with all the family ways admirably well. Indeed in the midst of sorrow we have remarkable causes for thankfulness.'

Rachel faded slowly. Catherine was constantly with her and Richenda, who sent daily letters to her husband to describe her sister's spiritual peace 'but at times she breaks forth in a tremulous voice but firm spirit in supplication for us, her most beloved sisters.' When little Anna came in, Rachel said 'Thee sees, dear, how very ill I am, but God makes me happy and will take me to his own kingdom.'

298

Betsy was sent for and found

Our much-loved invalid was certainly sunk, since we were last together, and in many things gone some steps lower; but there appeared to me so strong a vital principle remaining, that I think weeks rather than days are likely to be her portion here below. Her mind is in a most favoured state, she appears to feel it wonderful how easy her circumstances are made to her, all fear of death seems to be removed from her, she talks of it with ease, almost pleasure.

On Rachel's last Sunday, Betsy decided to stay away from Goats and hold a little meeting at home with her 'beloved suffering sister', but when Rachel was dressed and moved into the dressing-room on to her couch and Betsy began to preach, Rachel was so overcome with sleepiness that she could not keep awake. Only Betsy's thanksgiving appeared to revive her. Then Rachel herself prayed 'beautifully and powerfully for them all'. She also sent a particular message to some of the absent – her 'dear love, and that they should be told, what a rich blessing she had found there was in seeking the Kingdom of God and His righteousness'.

Later in the evening, a week later, she fell asleep. 'They came to let me know about 12 o'clock, how she was going on,' writes Betsy on 17th November, 1826, 'but, at first, I felt unequal to go to her, and she did not want me; but, gradually, I found my tribulated, tossed spirit, calmed, animated and strengthened, so that I joined the company round her bed.'

Rachel never woke from her last sleep. Although no longer a Quaker, she was buried in the walled garden of Gildencroft, whose avenue of tall trees shelters the path leading to the Gurney burial ground. When gravestones were permitted by the Friends, Rachel's grave and her parents', grandparents', and most of her brothers', sisters', cousins', uncles' and aunts', were marked with simple matching headstones giving their names, ages they lived to and years of their deaths. The Gildencroft is a comforting place to be alone in.

After Rachel's funeral, there was a pause among the remaining eight of Earlham and their husbands and wives; there was a stillness, stirred only by the awe of the children, most of whom Rachel had taught and all of whom she had loved. Then life went on.

APPENDIX

From a Manuscript written by Henry Enfield's niece,[1]
daughter of his sister Anna.

A Visit to Earlham in 1817

It was in the Spring of 1817 that Harriet and I went first to
Norwich. Harriet was 18 and I was just turned 17. We had,
previously to our leaving home, been much interested by hearing
my mother read parts of her correspondence relative to the
Earlham friendship and separation and by knowing all that had
passed between my mother and her friends there in the previous
summer of 1816 when the meeting took place which renewed
their friendly intercourse with many tears. I can well remember
the first time we saw Catherine Gurney. It was in the street – she
was a tall gaunt looking woman and as she had an utter contempt
for a bonnet and never wore one but when going into Norwich
and propriety required it, she generally had on very shabby ones,
which *looked* as if they had been despised by her. The one of this
day was a leghorn which seemed as if it had been *sat* upon, so flat
was it to the sides of her face that it was almost impossible to see
her face, but we heard the soft mild accents of her *peculiar* voice
speaking to us as she squeezed our hands long and with anxious
interest. Yet I think our first feelings were *amusement* rather than
respect on knowing our mother's old friend. The next time we
saw her was at tea at Aunt Barron's. In a letter written at the time
I find I said 'Catherine and Joseph Gurney drank tea with Uncle
and Aunt Barron. How Miss Gurney stared at us! Just as my
mother told us she would. I could hardly help laughing. Mr.

[1] Anna Enfield became Mrs. Fletcher and this daughter later became Mrs. Roscoe.

301

Joseph John Gurney has a charming benevolent countenance. At
length a time was fixed for our going to Earlham and Miss G.
called for us in the carriage just before dinner. Two other young
ladies were in the carriage but she did not introduce them. On
arriving at the old stately house, she took us up a broad staircase,
up which the coach might have driven, to the top of the house
where our bedroom was prepared. It was an immense westy
room with a small love of a dressing room out of it looking upon
the trees with an open casement. 'I have brought you here, my
dear girls', said Catherine 'because it is the yellow garret where
your mother slept for the first time when she was not more than
your age, and I thought you would like to sleep in the yellow
garret.' Then she welcomed us very affectionately to Earlham
and went away. This remains of young romance, her singular
appearance, and tender voice and manner so peculiar and so full
of deep still feeling, the westy yellow garret, the green trees and
birds close to our little boudoir, all tended to impress us at the
first go off with a *particular sensation* of *sentiment*. We were now
ready for dinner, so down we went and with timid joyfulness
glided down the wide passages and stairs to the hall, but as we did
not know into what room we should go, we wandered into the
garden, then brilliant with summer beauties and bounded on
either side by large shadowy trees and walks winding about
under them. The old butler soon came out to us and said that
dinner was ready. He led the way up one flight of stairs through
an immense ante drawing room, hung round with pictures, into
a large and long room, commonly called the drawing room, but
in which was a sideboard and here we found the dinner laid out
and 5 persons assembled, besides the men servants. Miss Gurney
we looked in vain for, and none of those in the room did we
know. One beautiful placid lady came forward and in the sweet
musical voice of the family, welcomed us and asked us to sit
down to dinner. This we immediately guessed was the only other
sister then at home, Richenda. Presently Catherine came and
seated herself at the top of the table and after a silent grace we
commenced the meal. But we were not introduced to any of the
guests and I could only by degrees discover who they were as the

Gurneys addressed them each by their Christian name. The droll little young man at the bottom of the table called 'Sowell' we found out to be a Cantab who had left Cambridge on account of the fever there and was staying with his brother, Mr. Brereton, the clergyman at Earlham. The ladies came from Norwich all 3 Evangelical Church. After a dinner of rarities Harriet and I went out into the garden with Catherine Gurney. She took one of us under each arm. She was wrapped up in a large red shawl, but had nothing on her head, and such large shoes on her feet that she was obliged to lean her body back and slide her feet along as if she were skating so that altogether she presented a most peculiar appearance. She held our arms tight in hers, the intensity of her interest for Anna Enfield's children exhibiting itself in this and every respect. She entered with the kindest interest into a conversation with us – asked a hundred questions about us all, our mode of thinking and education. And in the anxiety of her feeling she briskened her pace and whisked us round the walks under the trees with great celerity. There was something about her that interested me warmly. I felt grateful to her for talking to us so kindly. At last she said 'Do you ever read the Bible?' I answered 'Oh yes!' there was a degree of pride and indignation in my answer, but that question was doomed to produce a very lasting and wide effect and I gratefully think of Catherine Gurney's asking me under the trees 'Do you read the Bible?' whenever I dwell on the blessing which I found in the Bible. 'That's well,' she added. 'How do you read it? I always begin at the beginning and read regularly through and I should decidedly recommend it to every young person.' After some conversation in which no cant was mingled but merely an affectionate anxiety to see if we were brought up Christians – (one of the Gurneys asked my father when he married my mother, Do you believe the Bible?) we went into the house driven in by a heavy thundershower. We went into the same room – we found the party employed in various ways. We established ourselves in the bow window at a small table to look over Priscilla's and Richenda's large collection of drawings (they drew masterly). The comical merry Sowell Brereton was so very obliging as to assist us in advising them.

303

Catherine kindly explained the scenes they represented and related the history of their delightful Highland journey. But my attention was continually diverted from the drawings to the fair artist, whose appearance I never can forget. She had fetched in a small white deal table or desk from her schoolroom. I believe she sat in the middle of the room designing some little Scripture subjects for prizes for her scholars. Quite inattentive to all that was going on, she sat like an angel in calm benignity. I never beheld anything like her. She was about 30. Dressed in a pure white gown and muslin handkerchief, fastened in front with a pearl brooch – her neck and hands were almost as white. Her face too had very little colour but was quite illumined with *mind*. Her hair which was auburn had a natural wavy curl in it, was cut short on her forehead and carelessly fastened up behind in a small twist of velvet, the same colour was wound round it. The light was shining full upon her and her motions and postures were so elegant and her face such a sublime expression, as I never shall forget and cannot describe. After a short time twelve of her schoolgirls came in to take a lesson in singing. A grand pianoforte stood across the bow window. She opened it and the children formed a circle round her and commenced their lesson in 'Solfa.' This sounded so discordantly that it was irresistible; Sowell Brereton and ourselves and at last Richenda herself laughed immoderately. Then she said, 'This really will not do. I must banish you the room.' So Catherine, Harriet and I and Mr. Brereton set out to take a stroll as the rain was over. Catherine led us all to the favorite spots that she and my mother had loved in their youth. And she introduced us into one or two cottages where old servants were settled to whom Anna Enfield had once been well known. There was a great melancholy pleasure to Catherine thus to recall one after another all her young associations and she trailed along in the dripping wet grass apparently unconscious how she was getting herself and us wet. When we returned to the trees under the drawing-room windows, which were open, the sweet full sounds of the sacred hymn came over our heads, the birds were singing in the branches above and the beautiful distant prospect extended itself beyond the trunks of

the wood. Miss Gurney gave way to her romantic sensations.
She rolled her shawl tight round her tall figure and leaned herself
in silent meditation against the trunk of a tree. Sowell Brereton
kept pulling the grass and plucking the flowers and we, with half
a smile, watched them both. At last we went in the big ante
room. The children were singing the 100th Psalm. Miss Gurney
placed herself on the window seat by the open window, put her
feet up, folded her arms and sat contemplating with the tears
streaming down her cheeks. Dear Lady! Many most affectionate
good wishes for us mingled doubtless then with the tender
thoughts and recollections. Harriet and I and S. Brereton occupied meanwhile 3 immense, old fashioned red stuffed arm chairs,
that were half a foot higher in back than our heads. We had placed
them by the fire, a large blazing one and sat drying our wet feet
and keeping silence as well as we could, but he looking quite as
full of fun as we *felt*. The room was very lofty and surrounded by
old-fashioned portraits and furniture, but it had peculiarly an air
of comfort, which the open window and with the trees almost
coming into them and the blazing fire and the great red armchairs
assisted to produce. I do not know whether I ever felt so happy in
my life as I did at that moment. When the children and Mr.
Brereton went, we got our work and formed a happy female
group round the fire and table and candles, working, whilst
Catherine read with great effect, in her slow deep measured voice
'The Minstrel.' She was however continually interrupted by
large flies and 'harry long legs' sweeping into the candle. And she
kept explaining 'I cannot help wondering where these things
come from. How strange, how extraordinary.' She never remembered that the windows were wide open and the trees close
by, though the nightingales who sang all evening made it sufficiently evident to Harriet and myself. At 10 she read – then
Richenda – a chapter or two from the Testament then we kissed
one another affectionately, Catherine taking us upstairs left us in
our 'yellow garret'. Next morning we had a hymn, a silent
prayer and a chapter read by Chenda before breakfast. After
breakfast Richenda and the 3 other ladies went up to Richenda's
school, which she held in a room at the top of the house. We

regretted very much indeed *we* did not go up, but we were not invited and didn't like to ask them to take us. It would have been a beautiful sight to have seen the gentle Chenda among her little country girls. As Catherine was housekeeper she said she should be engaged, so we went into the park to sketch. It was a fine summer day and the old house, covered over with vines and surrounded with trees looked very respectable and interesting. After luncheon we all took a walk and visited several places in the neighbourhood where my mother was accustomed to enjoy herself. We then left the others and Miss G. and ourselves approached the brook upon which we discovered Sowell Brereton paddling in an old crazy and very little boat. The brook is a broad and rapid stream, very deep in some places and overhung with large trees and branching willows and no path along its banks. As soon as Miss G. descried Sowell Brereton, fishing quietly under the trees she cried out 'Oh, there's Sowell – let us go and speak to him' and she ran into an old rotten bathing house, through the chinks of which she espied her young friend and cried out 'Oh how charming! how delightful! Can we get in Sowell?' running out of the bath house to the edge of the stream. This said boat was quite out of condition, full of water, without oar or rudder and *very* little. Mr. S. B. was poking it along stern foremost with the crooked branch of a tree. 'Is there room for me Sowell?' 'Yes, I dare say,' said he laughing at the very idea of it. 'Well bring it to the edge' and with much difficulty he brought it to the edge and Miss Gurney stepped in, but the boat was so unsteady she could hardly keep her balance and she caught hold of Sowell, begging to be let out, but he, in a *roar of laughter* refused to let her out – pushed off and began paddling about in the middle of the stream whilst Miss Gurney's tall figure swayed backwards and forwards and we thought the boat would overset every minute. But she contrived to seat herself at the bow of the boat, taking hold of either side with her hands, with her knees level with her chin and with her hair streaming in the wind. Her weight lowered that end of the boat to a level with the water and as the boat twisted round and round, she sat with her lips stuck out in an attitude of sulking endurance, but sometimes joining us

306

and the boatman in our long and hearty peals of laughter and then again entreating for mercy to be released. At length he let her out and she taking us one under each arm, set out home saying 'Now wasn't it droll! how droll! I do think there is nothing so pleasant as a good laugh! – It was *so* wet and *so* bad.'

And a good laugh was one of the pleasures that few of the family denied themselves, particularly when wet or things were bad.

Index

314